Transforming Workplace Relations in New Zealand 1976–2016

Transforming Workplace Relations in New Zealand 1976–2016

edited by Gordon Anderson, with Alan Geare,
Erling Rasmussen and Margaret Wilson

Victoria University Press

VICTORIA UNIVERSITY PRESS
Victoria University of Wellington
PO Box 600 Wellington
vup.victoria.ac.nz

Copyright © the editors and contributors

First published 2017

ISBN 9781776561735

This book is copyright. Apart from
any fair dealing for the purpose of private study,
research, criticism or review, as permitted under the
Copyright Act, no part may be reproduced by any
process without the permission of
the publishers.

A catalogue record for this book is available from the
National Library of New Zealand.

Printed by Ligare, Auckland

Contents

Preface *The Editors*	7
List of Authors	9
Introduction: Four Decades of Documenting Transformation *The Editors*	13

Driving Transformation

The Changing Landscape Of Workplace Relations *Ian McAndrew, Alan Geare and Fiona Edgar*	23
The Politics of Workplace Reform: 40 Years of Change *Margaret Wilson*	44
Administering Workplace Relationships: From IR To HR *Jane Bryson*	60

Measuring Transformation

A Brief History Of Labour's Share Of Income in New Zealand 1939–2016 *Bill Rosenberg*	79
Collective Bargaining Across Four Decades: Lessons from CLEW's Collective Agreement Database *Stephen Blumenfeld and Noelle Donnelly*	107

Areas of Transformation

Reforming Workplace Health and Safety Regulation: Second Time Lucky? *Viktoriya Pashorina-Nichols, Felicity Lamm and Gordon Anderson*	129
Women in the Workforce: Still Unequal after all these Years? *Amanda Reilly and Annick Masselot*	149
Waves of Interest in Employee Participation in New Zealand *Erling Rasmussen and Ronny Tedestedt*	169

Legal Transformation

Competing Visions and the Transformation of New Zealand Labour Law *Gordon Anderson*	191

The Influence of the Legal Profession on Dispute Resolution
   after 1990   210
Susan Robson

ACC and Workers' Health: Compensation, Compromises
   and Consequences   230
Dawn Duncan

Conclusion: Industrial Relations in Forty Years   247
The Editors

Preface

In 1976 the first issue of a new academic journal, the *New Zealand Journal of Industrial Relations*, appeared. The *Journal*'s inauguration was well timed. In 1973 New Zealand's labour law, in response to a rapidly changing industrial relations system, had undergone the most extensive reform since 1894 and for the next three decades the pace of change was to accelerate. Four decades later the industrial relations certainties of 1976 had largely disappeared into the mists of time. Industrial relations has not only been totally transformed, but even the term 'industrial relations' has largely vanished from academic discourse – 'employment relations' has become the buzzword. This change was reflected in the *Journal* being renamed the *New Zealand Journal of Employment Relations* in 2004.

The Journal is now 40 years old and over that time it has been the primary source for the publication of academic research and commentary on the changing environment of New Zealand's labour relations. Throughout that period the *Journal* has sought to publish material from across the broad range of disciplines that contribute to our knowledge of relations in the workplace – not only the views of academics, but also those of practitioners and politicians.

The *Journal*'s 40th anniversary provides an opportunity to look back and reflect on the massive changes that have taken place over the last 40 years and to look to the future of employment relations in a period where both the character of employment and the nature of work are rapidly changing.

While the *Journal* has been published by various entities, it has been edited by teams at five universities:

1976–1980 Auckland University. Editorial team: John Deeks and Margaret Wilson.

1980–1989 Victoria University of Wellington. Editorial team: Gordon Anderson, Peter Brosnan, David Smith and Pat Walsh.

1990–2003 University of Otago. Editorial team: Alan Geare and Ian McAndrew.

2004–present Auckland University of Technology. Editorial team: Felicity Lamm, Erling Rasmussen and Rupert Tipples (Lincoln University).

The editors of this collection represent the various eras of the *Journal*'s editorship. They and their editorial colleagues over the years would like to thank not only the enormous number of contributors that made the *Journal* feasible but also the number of largely invisible people who have provided the support needed for any journal – the referees, the support staff at the universities who hosted the *Journal*, and the various printers, many in the days before camera-ready copy, who made the *Journal* possible. The *Journal* is, of course, now published on-line. We would, however, also like to acknowledge the work of the digital services team at the Victoria University Library, who digitalised the earlier issues of the *Journal* so that the *Journal* as a whole is now readily available to current and future researchers.

Finally we would thank the people behind this book: Nadia Cooper who did the initial proofreading, reference checking and formatting and the like, and the publisher and editorial team at Victoria University Press.

The editors wish to dedicate this collection to the memory of
Professor John Deeks (1940–2015).

John was one of the founding editors of the Journal. In the Introduction to the first issue of the *Journal* he wrote:

> ... we wish to recognise that industrial relations issues and practices impinge upon, and are in turn modified by, a wide range of influences that make up New Zealand culture. Whilst this modest journal aims, therefore to increase understanding and to raise the level of public debate on industrial relations matters, and to provide a forum for discussion of ideas, the development of theories, and the dissemination of research results of interest to industrial relations practitioners, it does so in the hope that such activities will inevitably lead to some broader reflection on the nature of our diverse culture.

We would hope that John would have agreed that the *Journal* has fulfilled this mission.

The Editors
July 2017

List of Authors

Gordon Anderson is Professor of Law at Victoria University of Wellington, New Zealand. He is an author of *Mazengarb's Employment Law* (looseleaf, LexisNexis) and has published an account of the legal nature of labour reforms over the last four decades: *Reconstructing Labour Law: Consensus or Divergence?* (VUP 2011). His most recent book, *The Common Law of Employment*, written with Douglas Brodie and Joellen Riley, will be published by Edward Elgar later this year.

Stephen Blumenfeld is Director of the Centre for Labour, Employment and Work (CLEW) (formerly Industrial Relations Centre) at Victoria University of Wellington in New Zealand, a position he has held for the past eight years. In that capacity, he has presented its annual series of Employment Agreement seminars on wages and conditions contained in the Centre's collective agreements database to employment relations practitioners. He has also researched and published widely on numerous aspects of employment relations, both within New Zealand and internationally, for more than two decades.

Jane Bryson is an Associate Professor in Human Resource Management and Industrial Relations at the Victoria Business School, Victoria University of Wellington, and a member of CLEW. She researches the range of factors (institutional, organisational and individual) which influence human capability at work. Most recently she has examined the impact of employment regulation on workplace management practices, and is currently engaged in a study of schools as workplaces. Before moving into an academic career in 1999, she worked for 15 years as an organisational psychologist, management consultant and HR manager.

Noelle Donnelly is a Senior Lecturer in Human Resource Management and Industrial Relations at the Victoria Business School, Victoria University of Wellington, and a lead researcher for CLEW. She is co-editor of *Labour & Industry* and an associate editor of *The International Journal of Human Resource Management*. She holds a PhD from the University of Warwick and previously held positions at the Michael Smurfit School of Business, University College Dublin, Ireland.

Dawn Duncan is a teaching fellow and doctoral candidate in the Law Faculty at Victoria University of Wellington. She has practised as an employment lawyer in New Zealand and Australia, and has taught commercial and employment law. Dawn's research interests focus particularly on work health and safety and workers' compensation.

Fiona Edgar is a Senior Lecturer in the Department of Management at the University of Otago, Dunedin, New Zealand, where she teaches and researches in human resource management. She is widely published, with contributions in *Personnel Review, International Journal of Human Resource Management, International Journal of Manpower and Economic and Industrial Democracy*.

Alan Geare is a Professor in the Department of Management at the University of Otago, Dunedin, New Zealand. He was Head of Department 1986–1998 and again 2008–2013. He teaches, and has published widely in the fields of Employment Relations and HRM, with over sixty journal articles and over a dozen books. Journals include *Academy of Management Review, Journal of Industrial Relations, Personnel Review, International Labor Review, International Journal of Human Resource Management and Economic* and *Industrial Democracy*. He has worked as a consultant to organisations and unions, and as a government appointed mediator and arbitrator.

Felicity Lamm is an Associate Professor and Co-Director of the Centre for Occupational Health and Safety Research at the Auckland University Technology (AUT), New Zealand. Dr Lamm has been teaching and researching in the area of employment relations, occupational health and safety (OHS), and management for over 25 years and has been involved in a number of governmental inquiries into OHS and employment relations. She is also co-editor of the *New Zealand Journal of Employment Relations* and is on a number of editorial boards.

Annick Masselot is Associate Professor at the School of Law of University of Canterbury, New Zealand. Her research interests focuses on gender equality and equal treatment, social and employment law, reconciliation between work and family life, and pregnancy and maternity rights in a comparative context. Annick is the author of *Reconciling Work and Family Life in EU Law and Policy* (Palgrave Macmillan 2010) with E. Caracciolo di Torella.

Ian McAndrew is an Associate Professor in the Department of Management at the University of Otago. He has written extensively on negotiation, mediation, facilitation, arbitration and employment relations. He practised in the labour relations field in the USA for 15 years, including eight years as the chief negotiator for the major California police federation. He was a member of the Employment Tribunal from 1993 to 2002, and served two years as Chief of the Tribunal. He remains an active employment mediator and tribunal adjudicator.

List of Authors

Viktoriya Pashorina-Nichols is a Solicitor and Barrister of the High Court of New Zealand. She holds a LLB(Hons)/BCom from Victoria University of Wellington and is currently working for Simpson Grierson in Auckland.

Bill Rosenberg was appointed Economist and Director of Policy at the Council of Trade Unions in May 2009. He holds a BCom in Economics, a BSc Hons in Mathematics and a PhD in Mathematical Psychology. Bill was previously Deputy Director, of the University Centre for Teaching and Learning at the University of Canterbury and has published on labour and social issues, the economy, globalisation and trade. He has been an active trade unionist for 35 years, including the Tramways Union and Association of University Staff where he was National President for several years.

Erling Rasmussen is the Professor of Work and Employment at Auckland University of Technology, New Zealand. He has worked in employment relations in academia, and the public and private sectors since the 1970s and has had extensive experience of public policy formation and evaluation. He is an editor of the *New Zealand Journal of Employment Relations* and has co-authored New Zealand's leading textbooks on employment relations.

Amanda Reilly is a Senior Lecturer in the School of Accounting and Commercial Law at Victoria University of Wellington. Her primary research and teaching interest is labour and employment law, with a particular focus on gender and work family issues. She is also an associate of CLEW at Victoria University of Wellington and an associate editor of *Labour and Industry*, a journal of the social and economic relations of work.

Susan Robson was an originating member of the Employment Relations Authority. She subsequently practised as a lawyer in employment jurisdiction, as a commentator and critic of the Court decisions of that jurisdiction and as the author of an online text on employment law (LexisNexis Practical Guidance series) and a Laws of New Zealand text about gambling and lawyers.

Ronny Tedestedt, a Swedish national, has recently completed a Masters of Business at Auckland University of Technology in New Zealand. His thesis, titled "What Did You Say? Worker Participation in Cooperatives", looked specifically at opportunities for employees in cooperatives to have input into decision-making processes. He is currently working at the Swedish Confederation of Professional Employees after having taught and researched in the areas of employment relations and occupational health and safety at Auckland University of Technology.

Margaret Wilson (DCNZM) is Professor of Law and Public Policy at the University of Waikato, Hamilton, New Zealand. Margaret was a former Member of Parliament 1999–2008 and held several Ministerial appointments including Attorney-General, Minister of Labour, Minister of Commerce, Associate Minister of Justice and Minister Responsible for Treaty of Waitangi Negotiations, and former Speaker of the New Zealand Parliament 2005–2008.

Introduction: Four Decades of Documenting Transformation

The Editors

Introduction

In 1974, a group of people drawn from management, government, trade unions, the legal profession and the universities met to form the Industrial Relations Society of New Zealand Inc. The primary aims of the Society were to organise and foster discussion, research, education and publications within the field of industrial relations, and to bring together industrial relations practitioners to exchange ideas, share experiences and develop greater understanding of industrial relations matters.[1] The most enduring result of that meeting was the publication, in 1976, of the first issue of the *New Zealand Journal of Industrial Relations* (NZJIR) edited by John Deeks and Margaret Wilson.

The launch of the *Journal* coincided with the most turbulent period of employment relations in New Zealand's history. It was a period of rapid change. For much of the period, wages were regulated, there were historically high levels of sustained industrial unrest and industrial relations legislation was constantly amended. That period ended with the short-lived Labour Relations Act.

During the decade of the Employment Contracts Act the overt signals of ferment, industrial conflict and legislative change may have largely abated, but the pace of change in industrial relations, slowly becoming employment relations, continued unabated as union density plummeted and employers increasingly used their new-found, and largely unconstrained, powers to reshape employment relations in their own interests. The pace of change has slowed considerably since 2000 but has not reversed. Employers still dominate in setting the conditions under which work is performed, workers have little voice industrially and are only slowly regaining an element of effective political voice.

---

1 New Zealand Journal of Industrial Relations (1976) 1(3) Back page.

The 1970s also witnessed major social changes, particularly the increasing entry of women into the paid workforce. This development had a significant impact on workplace practices: anti-discrimination laws were introduced in 1971 (Race Relations Act) and extended in 1977 (Human Rights Commission Act), equal pay legislation had already appeared in 1960 (Government Service Equal Pay Act) and was generalised in 1972 (Equal Pay Act). Social changes brought with them a plethora of other issues: problems of sexual harassment became more visible and were slowly addressed, and child care and parental leave became increasingly important issues. And, of course, the ethnic make-up of New Zealand has changed massively over 40 years and brought with it other problems that needed to be addressed, such as the problems of migrant labour and racial discrimination.

For 40 years the *Journal* has provided a consistent vehicle for analysis and commentary on the shifting nature of work and workplaces from a variety of perspectives – industrial relations academics and practitioners, the emerging generation of HRM academics and practitioners that appeared over the period, sociologists, economists, legal academics and practitioners, psychologists, political scientists and occasionally a member of the judiciary.

The Journal is now in its 42nd year of publication as the *New Zealand Journal of Employment Relations* (being renamed in 2004). It continues to provide a vehicle for commentary on traditional and emerging issues: equal pay has again moved to the centre of workplace debates and new modes of employment and new technologies have opened up new areas for analysis: the gig economy and increased levels of inequality and precarious employment.

This book is published to mark the 40th anniversary of the *Journal*'s publication. It contains chapters by editors from throughout the *Journal*'s existence as well as chapters by a number of other academics, those in mid-career and early-career – a blend of the past, the present and the future.

Transforming Workplace Relations

The theme of this book is transforming workplace relations, a theme we have attempted to present from a variety of different disciplinary perspectives from across the New Zealand academic community with an interest in the dynamics of the workplace and the drivers of change in the workplace.

Analysing Transformation

The collection begins with three chapters that look back over the last 40 years and discuss the changes that have taken place over that period.

Ian McAndrew, Alan Geare and Fiona Edgar approach this task by discussing workplace change in the context of overall societal change using a modified version of Dunlop's model of industrial relations. This model postulates that industrial relations requires an understanding of the interrelation among and between three major parties: managers, employers and their organisations; the state, courts and agencies concerned with the workplace; and employees and their organisations – and how each seeks to obtain, regulate and modify the rules that govern the work environment for the purpose of enabling their own particular industrial relations objectives. They conclude that "the actor with the power to really influence industrial relations is the State", but they are pessimistic that this will have benefits for workers and especially those at the lower end of the labour market who, having seen collective bargaining systemically eroded, have no power to accrue substantive outcomes They conclude that the "political landscape, such that it is, makes it difficult to envisage any radical changes to the current framework in the near future."

The political dynamics of the period are explored by Margaret Wilson. Margaret draws attention to the role of the *Journal* as a venue for political debate, referring to articles by Max Bradford, a future Minister of Labour (and of course Margaret herself contributed to the *Journal* both before and after her period in politics), as well as those commenting on future political change. Margaret's chapter traces the changing political ideologies and policies that have driven change, concluding that, while the evolution of our statutory framework has resulted in the government still having a substantial role in the employment relationship, the nature of that relationship has changed. She speculates that what "we may be witnessing is the reinvention of the role of the state in the regulation of employment relations", but a role exercised in a very different environment than in the past. She argues that, with pressures such as globalisation and the increasing use of technology and artificial intelligence, the time has come for a fundamental rethinking of the values and principles that need to underlie a new regulatory framework. She concludes that a return to the idea of a public interest as opposed to a sector interest in such a regulatory framework may be worth consideration.

The final chapter in this group is by Jane Bryson. Jane suggests that two major drivers have underpinned change in the administration of workplace relationships: the neo-liberal agenda and the revolutionary growth in the capabilities of information and communication technologies. She argues that the neo-liberal policies drove a shift from administering awards to managing employer risk and organisational image. She identifies a core element of this change as being the reinvention of personnel management and industrial relations as human resource management. The chapter discusses some key features of the transformation, including the role of legislation in the changing role of IR to HR; the professionalisation and feminisation of HR; and the changing scope of HRM in managing risk and organisational image. She argues that the result has been that management behaviour has become increasingly unitarist, driven by a combination of factors including perceptions of what successful businesses do, the advice of management and other consultants, and the institutional signals expressed through international corporate HRM practices. Jane concludes that "HR is unlikely to re-establish the social contract with workers until there is institutional pressure to do so" and that "legislation is an unequivocal signal of what a society values in the workplace relationship".

Measuring Transformation

The second group of chapters provide a quantitative account of the changes to working conditions over the past few decades.

Bill Rosenberg's chapter traces the history of the labour and capital shares of New Zealand's national income since 1939. Bill's analysis shows that labour income share for wages and salaries rose steadily throughout 1947 to 1974, in part because of a reducing income share of the self-employed. This share plateaued at a new level between 1976 and 1981 when it plummeted until 1984. After a brief respite in 1988, following intensive industrial activity, it began a long fall to 2002. A partial recovery to 2009 under the 2000 legislation is now being reversed. Bill also describes the path the labour income share would have traced if the real product wage had followed labour productivity and shows that it follows the rising actual share until the early 1970s, then levels out until the early 2000s. It then continues to rise. He shows that by 2016 the gap between the theoretical and actual labour income shares was worth approximately $6,000 or 11 per cent on top of the annual income of the average wage and salary earner.

Steve Blumenfeld and Noelle Donnelly look at trends in collective bargaining, utilising the data in Victoria University's Centre for Labour Employment and Work (CLEW) collective bargaining data base. The then Industrial Relations Centre first began gathering data on collective agreements shortly after enactment of the Employment Contracts Act. Steve and Noelle's chapter traces the decline in collective bargaining and the impact of the shift from occupational/industry bargaining to enterprise bargaining, a change that occurred effectively overnight in the early 1990s. The authors identify trends in bargaining coverage as well as in the content of collective agreements. Their chapter suggests that, after the massive changes of the 1990s, bargaining has now entered a new pattern of relative stability but with some areas of growth where unions have had some success in extending bargaining, for example the retail sector. However, Steve and Noelle make the point that the majority of workers on CEAs are employed in the public sector with more than half of all employees on CEAs working in three sectors: education and training, health and social services, and government administration and security services. The chapter suggests that the content of agreements has remained stable in the main, but does identify developments such as more flexible working hours and an increased concern with issues impacting on work-life balance.

Areas of Transformation

The next three chapters consider specific areas where transformation might be expected over four decades: health and safety, women in the workforce and worker participation.

Viktoriya Pashorina-Nichols, Felicity Lamm and Gordon Anderson examine the development of health and safety legislation, focusing particularly on the reforms of 1992, 2002 and 2015, and worker participation in health and safety. The authors address the question of whether the Health and Safety at Work Act 2015 will address the systemic regulatory failures identified in both the Pike River Royal Commission Report and the Report of the Independent Taskforce. The Taskforce described New Zealand's health and safety culture as having inadequate leadership in the workplace; poor and ineffective worker engagement; a risk-tolerant culture, making workplaces liable to develop, accept and defend low standards and dangerous practices; and a weak regulator. While the authors conclude that the new Act and the creation of WorkSafe New Zealand may ameliorate, even if not eliminate those problems, they make the point that the most obvious long-term failing of health and safety regulation, the absence of clear and effective worker voice, has not been fully remedied by the new Act and that many workers in New Zealand are still left without adequate representation and voice on their own health and safety.

Amanda Reilly and Annick Masselot, drawing on articles published over 40 years in the *Journal*, address the changing role of women in the workplace. They point out that, in spite of increased labour market participation by women, female labour force participation is still lower than their male counterparts, that the number of women in senior positions is declining and that the gender pay gap is increasing. While workforce transformation has been dramatic for New Zealand women, there is still some way to go to reach gender equality here. Amanda and Annick argue that, while women have come a long way since the 1970s, women are still unequal in the workplace and that further transformation is required if parity is to be achieved. They identify some key areas where change is required, that is, an effective pay equity system, effective mechanisms to prevent discrimination and to address gender bias (both conscious and unconscious), and suitable mechanisms to ensure that work and family can be managed and the unpaid work evenly distributed, including improved access to child care. They conclude with Judy McGregor's comment that "women's progress in closing the gender pay gap in New Zealand at a governmental level is marked by the ebbs and flows of political will", and comment that, while governments vary in their enthusiasm for pursuing measures to further women's equality, all are nervous of any major interventions in the market.

The final paper in this group is by Erling Rasmussen and Ronny Tedestedt, who review the debate around worker participation, a subject of strong international interest in 1976 when the *Journal* first appeared, and which attracted some interest in New Zealand to the extent of a Private Members' Bill introduced to Parliament in 1974. Since then, however, there have been considerable changes in employment relations, which have affected the debates and implementation of participation schemes in New Zealand. The authors argue that workplace 'voice' has long been contested terrain, but that it is only on the union side that mindsets appear to have changed over time. Mainstream employers have continued to advocate 'softer', more direct forms of employee participation, though this has taken on a more unitarist tone which entols the virtue of managerial prerogatives. Given the lack of progress on legislatively backed participation structures, the authors focus on the only legislatively stipulated participation structures, health and safety committees, which appear to be an area where there are some common employer-union-employee interests.

Legal Transformation

The final three chapters consider the ways in which the law has changed over four decades.

First, Gordon Anderson suggests that the values of pluralism and worker voice, which were at the heart of the IC&A Act 1894, were a product of the particular settler society that rejected the coercive master and servant laws that regarded workers, both in practice and in law, as subordinate to the traditional aristocracy and the emerging capitalist class. Through the arbitration system New Zealand labour law maintained this pluralist vision for almost a century. However, in 1991 the Employment Contracts Act, using neoliberalist ideology and the master and servant values inherent in the common law, introduced a unitary model of labour law intended to destroy the pluralist vision and to deny workers effective voice in their employment. Since 2000, there has been some movement away from the neoliberalist model, but this has been slow and erratic. The article suggests that fundamental changes are needed to again incorporate a pluralistic vision in labour law for the 21st century.

Susan Robson's chapter shows how the replacement of a collectivist by an individualist advocacy culture contributed to changes to the significance of the personal grievance claim in labour relations, the means by which grievances were resolved and imposed additional cost on the public purse. Susan describes how the 1991 reforms, which were not reversed in 2000, led to the substitution of stakeholder representatives in resolution roles by mediators and adjudicators; dominance by lawyers of the resolution system; and exclusive reliance on employment contracts. Legal capture of the dispute resolution process, Susan argues, was an important tool for the imposition of flexible labour markets via the replacement of a pluralist with a unitarist approach to labour relations. The common law and legal method were vital elements of this power transition by their focus on the recurring problems of individual dismissals as the means of ignoring the collective detriments of a dominant non-union sector. This sector was based on the principle of cost-minimisation; it experienced higher levels of turn-over and injury rates, and made greater use of casualised labour and compulsory redundancy. Its dismissal rate was twice that of the unionised sector. The result was higher proportions of employees who could be dismissed, effectively at will. The promise of money as the means of exchange, she argues, was crucial to widespread employee acceptance of this particular bargain.

The final chapter by Dawn Duncan deals with some of the consequences of the compromises made when the ACC scheme was introduced and in particular those flowing from the boundary line for cover drawn around 'accident'. Her chapter outlines the key compromise of the ACC scheme and the consequences for working people in the following decades. Dawn argues that key areas of reform are needed to ensure the ACC scheme can meet the needs of New Zealand working people in future. In particular she focuses on the failure of the scheme to properly address non-accidental work-related health problems, a failure that left a significant gap in the cover of, and data on, chronic work-related health problems with the consequence that worker health became "the poor cousin" to accidental physical injury. Dawn argues that, while the need to address these failures is being recognised by WorkSafe, the goals of improving worker health in New Zealand will not be achieved without reforms to the work-related cover provisions of the ACC scheme. She further argues that reconceiving of the ACC scheme as a distinguished social insurance scheme could allow for both the universal care advocated by Woodhouse and the specific needs of workplace health and safety to be met, contributing to the future health of New Zealand working people at work and outside of it.

Conclusion

Together the chapters in this book provide an overview of some of the central influences that have driven workplace changes over four decades. The authors analyse and describe the impact on change and particularly its impact on working life of the 2,000,000 or so employed New Zealanders. While the book shows that the effect of 40 years of change has varied in its impact, it also demonstrates that for most workers there have been significant negative effects. Some workers, of course, obtained significant benefits from the neoliberal reforms, but this is certainly not true for the majority.

When the *Journal* was first published in 1976 the great majority of workers were, sometimes unwillingly, members of trade unions and had legitimate expectations that their union would not only seek to obtain acceptable conditions of work but that it would also act as their voice in the workplace, and as such as an intermediary between the worker and the employer. Moreover, in 1976 the personal grievance process introduced in the Industrial Relations Act 1973 was beginning to be widely utilised. The unilateral and unchecked power of employers to dismiss had finally become subject to constraint through the requirement to justify such decisions – which initially at least was given an industrial meaning rather than a legal one. Workplace relations were viewed as a matter for joint agreement and joint regulation.

As the chapters in this book make clear, four decades later that picture has been almost totally reversed. Outside of the public sector and some larger industries, few workers have any voice in the terms under which they are employed and even less in the day-to-day working of the employment relationship. That relationship, at least at the point of any disagreement, is now seen as a purely legal one regulated by contract and in which the employee is legally subordinate.

As the authors show, this change has come at a high price for workers. Working conditions have deteriorated, labour's share of national income has declined significantly and employment security has been partially eroded through the juridification of the employment dispute process. Most importantly, of course, the massive fall in union density and collective bargaining coverage has left workers atomised and isolated, an effect aggravated by the growth in precarious work. Atomised workers are less likely to complain about working conditions, including health and safety violations, and are more vulnerable to retaliation should they do so.

These observations beg the question: will there be a reversal of current trends and the re-emergence of effective worker voice? This is a question we will return to in the concluding chapter.

Driving Transformation

The Changing Landscape of Workplace Relations

Ian McAndrew, Alan Geare and Fiona Edgar

Introduction

To understand how industrial relations (IR) have changed in New Zealand from 1976 to the present, it is necessary to first contextualise and consider how the world has changed and then how New Zealand society has changed within this ever-changing world.

In 1976, the world was dominated by two superpowers – the United States and the Soviet Union. Relations were tense and there was considerable angst over the possibility of nuclear war. This consternation is possibly less today than it was then – with the focus of concern now having shifted to international terrorism. Nobody in 1976 predicted that either the Soviet Union would collapse in fifteen years or that China would emerge as a new superpower. As for the planet, there was a general concern that it would run out of oil. Surprisingly, today the concern about oil is its over supply, and planetary concerns encompass issues pertaining to global warming, climate change and some worrying political developments on the world stage.

Two things that were taking place in 1976 have continued, but at a much faster rate than anticipated, namely globalisation and population increase. Globalisation is a major factor today and influences our way of life to a great extent. The world population has increased from around 4.5 billion to 7.3 billion and the number of 'mega cities' (conglomerations of 10 million plus) has gone from three to thirty-five.

Technological advancement, particularly around communications, has also been dramatic throughout this period. Although the origins of cellphones and the internet precede 1976, these were unknown to the general public. Today, however, they comprise a major part of most people's everyday lives. The advent of smart phones has, in many circles, seen landline telephones replaced with texting and, while bills still have to be paid, payment is today by EFTPOS, internet banking or credit card with much less emphasis on cash. Cheques today are a rarity. The internet has opened up entire businesses and access to huge amounts of information. E-mails today replace most of the so-called 'snail mail'.

In 1976, people listened to music on vinyl records or on the radio. The boom and then decline of the compact disc was yet to come. Today much music is downloaded from the internet. Concerts are still as popular today, however, with many bands reconnecting themselves with golden-oldie tours. Surprisingly some – the Rolling Stones, Bruce Springsteen – have remained popular for all the forty years.

Not surprisingly, with all these global changes, some aspects of New Zealand life have also changed markedly. In 1976, New Zealand was an insular, protected economy and, although the 'Mother Country' (United Kingdom (UK)) had just joined the European Economic Community (EEC), New Zealand was still highly dependent on exporting meat and wool to this region. Over the interceding years New Zealand has remained highly dependent on agricultural exports, with the only major change being that frozen meat carcasses have been replaced by chilled cuts of meat. At this time, no one would have predicted that wool exporting today would be of less significance than wine, and few anticipated the huge growth in the volume and value of dairy products in our exports – or indeed that Australia, China and the United States would now be our major trading partners. Most recently, the Brexit phenomenon has added a new and unpredictable twist to the economic matrix.

As already stated, the New Zealand economy was protected in 1976. A 'collectivist' welfare state ethos prevailed, reflected in relatively high taxes, extensive public services, state ownership of strategic enterprise activities such as energy and transport, and quite generous social welfare benefits. There was incredibly low registered unemployment (0.4 per cent) – although there was considerable 'under employment', particularly in areas of the public service and local government but also in the private sector. The major changes (and these were indeed major, sometimes being referred to as 'blitzkrieg' (Kelsey 1993)) came about in the early 1980s when the Labour Government opened up the economy. The concept of 'a job for life' disappeared; there were widespread redundancies and correspondingly much higher unemployment.

New Zealand's population has increased, though not at the same rate as the rest of the world, but with a significant change in demographics. As the economy was opened to the world so too was the country. In 1976, the population was 90 per cent European, 9 per cent Māori and 1 per cent Other. Today it is 74 per cent European, 15 per cent Māori, 12 per cent Asian, 7 per cent Pacific peoples and 2 per cent Other. Society is now much more cosmopolitan, globalisation influencing lifestyle elements such as restaurants and cafés as well as industry.

Some factions of New Zealand have remained fairly consistent. There was, and still is, an obsession with sport, although in 1976 the Rugby World Cup was still a distant dream. Most would have assumed New Zealand would win it when it was a fact of life – and few would have anticipated the actual results from 1991 to 2007. Although one-day cricket internationals were being played as far back as 1976, few again would have anticipated their growth and popularity.

Industrial Relations in New Zealand – 1976 to the Present

Probably, the major theoretical contribution to understanding industrial relations was made well before 1976, with the book by John Dunlop, *Industrial Relations Systems* (1958). Dunlop's ideas were later modified somewhat (Geare 1977) to produce an understanding that industrial relations may be considered to be the interrelation among and between three major parties – 1) managers, employers and their organisations, 2) the State, Courts and agencies concerned with the workplace and 3) employees and their organisations – to obtain, regulate and modify the rules that govern the work environment for the purpose of enabling the parties to achieve their industrial relations objectives. Industrial relations objectives will vary, but in most cases will relate to power, labour productivity and satisfaction with the factors that make up a job. These industrial relations objectives, in turn, help parties achieve their overall objectives – which in many cases could well be profitability, survival and growth (employers), re-election (MPs), and a happy and satisfying life (employees).

Using this adapted version of Dunlop's theory, we will consider changes in industrial relations in this country, concentrating on five time periods: 1976–1987, 1987–1991, 1991–2000, 2000–present, and the future. The first four periods reflect the principal legislative regimes governing work relations. This also reflects the reality that the State "is the dominant actor in industrial relations . . . it has the power resources that considerably outweigh those of the either labour or business" (Adams 1992, 517). With legislation, the State may decide to reduce the power difference between the other two parties – or allow employers and managers to dominate employees and unions.

1976–1987

This first time period marked the end of two eras: the Arbitration era for the private sector, and the era when there were two industrial relations systems operating; one for the private sector and a different one for the public. As with other social institutions, something of a collectivist or egalitarian ethic infused the structure of the industrial relations system for most of this period, but began to disintegrate quickly towards the end of the period, as the industrial relations system itself began to disassemble.

In the private sector, the principal legislation was the Industrial Relations Act 1973 (IR Act 1973). This was a significant relabelling, as the principal legislation since 1894 had been various Industrial Conciliation and Arbitration Acts (IC&A Acts). However, although there was public relations rhetoric from the government that this comprised the first major reconstructing of New Zealand's industrial relations since 1894, the Act was indeed in most respects "the old pattern revamped" (Woods 1974, 39). Thus, in retaining the conciliation and arbitration-based award system, the IR Act 1973 was little more than a continuation of the IC&A Acts, albeit that some changes around the edges represented some initial nibbling away at the foundations of the system.

The original IC&A Act 1894 was introduced in the aftermath of the Maritime Strike of 1890 and the public outcry against sweated labour. The view was that unions were needed to protect workers against their exploitation, but the fear was that strike action could end in the unions being destroyed – as occurred in the Maritime Strike. The Long Title of this Act was "to encourage the formation of industrial unions . . . and to facilitate the settlement of Industrial Disputes by Conciliation and Arbitration". Thus, the Act was primarily to protect employees by encouraging the formation of unions and removing the need for strike action. The legislation was paternalistic, possibly patronising, but intended to benefit employees. The Conciliation and Arbitration era not only supported but required centralised employer organising, with wide-application negotiations taking place, these often being conducted remotely from the average employer. The latter part of this period saw large employers increasingly targeted by unions to directly deal and negotiate.

When it came to organising employees, societies of workers were expected to register under the Act, and become 'unions'. Once registered, the unions had sole bargaining rights and could not be 'taken over' by a larger union wishing to expand. So-called 'blanket provisions' meant that any settlement made by a registered union could be extended to cover all other employers and employees in that industry (or later occupational group) and district or districts. Up to this period, only 15 workers were needed to register as a union. From 1936 to 1961 it was compulsory by law to be a member of a union, if one existed. From 1961 compulsion was by agreement between the union and employer(s) – but the effect was the same. This meant, of course, that the pressure to register was coercive. An unregistered (or a 'deregistered' former union) could only survive if it comprised 100 per cent totally committed members, otherwise a small breakaway group could register as a union and then, because of the blanket provisions and compulsory membership, all the workers in the society would have to join the union or leave the industry or occupation.

As detailed elsewhere (Geare 1983), there were only a small number of societies who would settle terms resulting in a 'voluntary agreement'. A registered union had a choice. It could negotiate outside the system and reach a voluntary settlement, with a single employer, resulting in a 'collective agreement'. This could contain all the terms and conditions, or could be supplementary to a principal document settled by conciliation or arbitration.

The other choice was to settle terms and conditions through conciliation. Conciliation, in this context, had a specialised meaning different to that in the United Kingdom or the United States. It was not a process close to mediation, but rather a formalised system of collective bargaining with a conciliator chairing the negotiations between employer and union negotiators (assessors). Mostly the end product of conciliation was termed an 'award'. This "illiterate nonsense" (Woods 1977, 24) proved very confusing to overseas observers who presumed most settlements were reached through arbitration by the Court. The Court could arbitrate if conciliation failed to reach agreement and the arbitrated settlement was also termed an award. Arbitration was used only occasionally, as the Court would refuse to arbitrate if it felt that the assessors had not made sufficient effort to settle in conciliation. About 5 per cent of awards involved arbitration. Even in these cases, arbitration would be involved in a very small number of issues (albeit usually the most important!). What is unclear, however, is to what extent the possible involvement of the Court would influence the assessors' negotiating positions on any particular issue. If both sides could accurately pick how the Court would rule if it had to arbitrate, then this would strongly influence their settlement ranges.

In 1970, a personal grievance procedure was introduced into legislation; this proved unworkable. It was modified in 1973 and with periodic amendments it has remained to the present day. The Industrial Mediation Service was established in 1972 and by 1976 had four or five mediators who were employed as independent statutory officers charged with intervening in disputes that arose in workplaces outside of established procedures; these were 'trouble shooters' working alongside and around the conciliators, settling local grievances and putting out fires pertaining to both interest and rights disputes. These mediators did not operate in isolation from government politicians and officials, as the government on occasions would also actively intervene in industrial disputes through such devices as Ministerial inquiries or compulsory mediator conferences. In this period (and the following) the grievance procedure was only available to union members. Common law determined what made a dismissal justifiable, as it was not until s 103A was inserted into the Employment Relations Act (ER Act) 2000 in 2004, that the statute incorporated the principles of common-law decisions. While reinstatement is a possible remedy for an unjustified dismissal, it was and still is rare, with most workers receiving lost wages and possibly compensation.

This period also saw the end of a somewhat unusual incomes policy, which went from 1922 until 1984, in which the Court could make a 'General Wage Order'

(GWO) which, in 1922 and 1930, reduced all wages under its jurisdiction while all later orders (except for the 1968 Nil Order) increased wages. From the 1970s, GWOs applied to the public sector as well as to the private sector. Although they did not, in theory, apply to managerial salaries, in practice most organisations passed on all GWOs.

The 1968 Nil Order came before this time period. It is mentioned here because it became something of an urban myth with ludicrous claims made about it, such as the one by Williams (1976) that it caused the "trade union movement (to) boycott the Court" (59). Others claimed it signalled the end of arbitration. It may have signalled that – but it took another 16 years to occur. The Nil Order did cause uproar and resulted in a second application to the Court and the unique situation of both the employers' and union representatives of the Court voting against the Judge for a 5 per cent order.

In addition to general wage increases, this period also saw wage restrictions and wage freezes when the Government tried to overcome price inflation and balance of payment problems by restricting wage increases. A wage freeze introduced in 1982 ended on 30 November 1984, virtually coinciding with the end of the Arbitration era.

The legislation in this period prohibited strikes and lockouts. Strike, under the law, covered more than the popular concept of a total stoppage of work by the workforce and included any reduction in the rate of work ('go-slows'), refusal to work usual overtime, or breaches in the contracts of service. Lockouts were in theory stoppages caused by employers who would refuse to allow the workforce to enter the place of work. However, given the high rate of inflation during this period, any employer who wanted a stoppage of work could easily induce the workforce to strike by any provocative action. Strikes were decriminalised in 1979 but remained illegal and subject to penalty. Nonetheless, strikes took place frequently during this period and indeed right through the 1980s.

Because of compulsory union membership (either by law 1936–1961, or by agreement 1961–1991), unionism in the private sector was high by international standards. As discussed earlier, unions in New Zealand had been very dependent on legislation for their creation and later their survival. However, their general approach had also been heavily influenced by the Court that ruled, in *Ohinemuri Mines and Batteries Employees' IUW v Registrar of Industrial Unions* [1917], that their activities were basically limited to representing workers over wages and conditions. This ruling was overturned by statutory amendment in 1964, but this was after nearly half a century of restrictions. Hence, private sector unions, for the period 1976–1987, were still very limited in focus.

A few unions during this time were involved in a high proportion of strikes. These were unions representing workers in meat freezing works, construction, waterfronts and transport, and these unions, along with the Federation of Labour

(FOL), the central union body, were perceived to have significant power. The FOL provided the representative of the Court and, with the Employers' Federation, took part in tripartite discussions with the State. To a great extent this power of the unions and the FOL, at least in terms of militant industrial power, was a mirage. Whenever there has been a major confrontation (for example, 1890, 1917, 1951) the unions involved have been shattered. The mirage of power was only maintained through this period because there was no major confrontation lasting a reasonable timeframe.

Also, as mentioned earlier, during this period there were two industrial relations systems – one for the private sector and one for the public sector. In the public sector, most of the 'unions' were referred to as associations, societies or institutes and still in those days many government employees would have considered themselves too middle class to be in a union, seeing themselves as being more akin to a lawyer in the Law Society or a doctor in the Medical Association. Thus the 'union' for primary school teachers was the New Zealand Educational Institute (NZEI). When originally formed back in 1883, the aims stated in its rules were quasi-professional "to advance the cause of education" (New Zealand Educational Institute 1895). Only later did it become more union-conscious and included the aim "to uphold and maintain the just claims of its members" (New Zealand Educational Institute 1985). By far the largest of the employee groups in the public sector has been the Public Service Association (PSA). Its size and dominance meant the theoretical central body, the Combined State Service Organisations, was largely ignored. The central body relabelled itself in 1978, becoming Combined State Unions. This reflected the increasing acceptance by those in the state sector that they were *not* too professional and upper-middle class to be in a union.

The State dominated industrial relations in the public sector to an even greater degree than it did in the private sector. Industrial relations were governed by two principal Acts: the State Services (SS) Act 1962, which was concerned with employment conditions other than wages, and the State Services Conditions of Employment (SSCE) Act 1977, which was concerned with wages.

A major issue at this time was whether appointments could be made on 'merit' without appeal. The State view was that as many appointments as possible should be exempt from appeal and be made on merit. Unfortunately, the State has a long and sorry history of making appointments in theory on merit, but in practice as political paybacks and patronage. While the PSA argued its case strongly, it was unsuccessful in reducing exempt positions.

In places, the SS Act 1962 reads like an autocratic company rule book, providing for offences under which a public servant could be fined (such as being negligent, insolent or incompetent) and others for which the penalty could be salary reduction, transfer and/or dismissal. Public servants could also be transferred, even against their will, because it suited the employer. Appeals against transfer were only allowable on the grounds of 'extraordinary personal hardship'.

Wages in the public sector were fixed and periodically adjusted. Wage fixing was determined primarily by relativities:

(a) external comparability with the private sector
(b) vertical relativities in the public sector
(c) horizontal relativities in the public sector and, finally
(d) the adequacy of the pay scale to meet recruitment and retention needs.

Wage fixing was a time-consuming and expensive exercise and would only take place every five years or so. In the interim, the wages for an occupational group would be adjusted to keep in line with the private sector. This was a time of high price inflation and so wage increases were also large. Given the surveys used to determine wage shifts in the private sector would take several months to complete, this meant public servants would often receive quite large sums of back pay. Notwithstanding this system achieved some degree of egalitarianism in wages and conditions, it also resulted in high consumer spending, resentment by employees in the private sector and further price inflation.

Between 1984 and 1987, in the spirit of deregulation, the government took a very 'hands off' approach to industrial relations. This was symbolised by commentators referring to the Minister of Labour as 'Sideline Stan' Rodgers and the eventual abolition of the Arbitration Commission. Near the end of this first period, the IR Am Act 1984 effectively finished the Arbitration era as interest disputes could only go to the Court for settlement with the agreement of both parties. Employers were in a strong position and simply refused to go to arbitration.

1987–1991

This was a period in which New Zealand was still undergoing significant change. Wool prices had dropped, the New Zealand dollar had devalued and, as already noted, in 1984 the Labour Government had taken the dramatic step of deregulating the economy, and in the process puncturing the collectivist ethos that had guided social policy, including industrial relations policy for decades. This saw an opening up of financial markets, a reduction in tariff protections, the corporatisation and privatisation of some public enterprises and some dismantling of the public services. Deregulation of industrial relations was both a consequence and a part of these changes. This began with the removal of compulsory arbitration (as noted earlier, in 1984); this broke the back of a wage system which up until this time had effectively ensured no workers were ever left behind. Now workers had to rely on their own bargaining power. Active resistance to unions ensued. By 1987, the Arbitration Court had become the Labour Court; the distinction between conciliators and mediators had been eliminated with the merging of the Industrial Conciliation Service and the Industrial Mediation Service – all were now mediators handling rights disputes. Conciliation of collective bargaining, collective bargaining interventions, and grievance and disputes committees did, however, remain, with the mediators assisting parties in all of those functions.

This period could be referred to as the 'Collective Bargaining Era' in that the State through its legislation – the Labour Relations (LR) Act 1987 – had a clear intent that the other two parties should use collective bargaining to settle interest disputes. The State attempted to strengthen unions by continuing to give them the protection they had had in the arbitration era, reintroduced compulsory unionism by agreement, removed the threat of deregistration for strike behaviour, made strikes legal and also required unions to have at least 1,000 members for registration. In addition, the introduction of the State Sector Act in 1988 effectively brought the two sectors together with the public sector now also to be covered by the LR Act 1987.

The LR Act 1987 was explicitly pluralist and the Minister of Labour had made it clear the Labour Government wanted industrial relations problems to be settled by employers and unions without continuous Court or Ministerial involvement. However, this contrasts markedly with the next era – the *laissez-faire* era. The State tried to decrease the power difference between the vast majority of employers and unions by increasing the size of unions and by supporting the principles of collective bargaining and unionism.

These legislative changes have to be put in context. The Fourth Labour Government came into office in 1984 under the helm of Prime Minister David Lange. While still supported by the union movement, Labour politicians were increasingly middle class and university educated. The LR Act 1987 was supportive of unions and the working class, but the major economic changes brought in by Labour had a devastating effect on employees and unions. The power in the Labour Government was in the hands of a group of Cabinet members led by the Minister of Finance, Roger Douglas. They were strongly committed to what appeared, to many, as a very right wing agenda to rapidly change the New Zealand economy from protectionist to open and competitive.

Opening up the economy resulted in rapidly increasing unemployment, widespread redundancies and a climate of uncertainty, which resulted in the union movement becoming nervous and apprehensive – but also receptive to good management if that would save jobs. For example, the Meat Workers Union accepted greatly increased mechanisation of the killing chain – an issue which had been refused for decades.

In October 1987 the stock market crash took place. The New Zealand market was affected to a much greater extent than elsewhere in the West (dropping around 60 per cent) and, consequently, it took much longer to recover. The crash further exacerbated unemployment.

The LR Act 1987 allowed for enterprise bargaining, but until 1990 it had to be initiated by the union. The vast proportion of employers were content to operate under a national or near national award – and to provide for 'above award' payments if market conditions required or if the employer made a strategic choice to pay above the market to attract a better skilled or motivated workforce.

Research by McAndrew (1992) on changes in bargaining outcomes from the period of the LR Act 1987 to the Employment Contracts Act 1991 (see Table 1) shows that the majority of private sector employers were operating under awards right throughout this period. These results were based on data from 557 firms (a response rate of 37 per cent) from a random sample of 1800. It should be noted that some significant moves towards enterprise collective bargaining did occur in this short period in the government sector under the stimulus of the State Sector Act 1988 and the Labour government's desire to promote enterprise bargaining.

Structure of Collective Documents 1991–1992

Major Document	Early 1991	Mid 1992
National (or near-National) Award	80%	10%
Regional Award	8%	2%
Contract exclusive to firm	9%	80%
Contract exclusive to parent company	3%	8%

Table 1.

The LR Act 1987 did not meet with the approval of supporters of the 'New Right', such as the New Zealand Employers Federation (NZEF) (the official national body representing employers) and the New Zealand Business Roundtable (NZBR) (an unofficial lobby group for employers, which at the time comprised mainly the CEOs of major organisations). By way of a series of papers, these two organisations attacked the union movement (NZEF 1990, NZBR 1991), compulsory union membership (NZEF 1986, NZBR 1989, 1991), wide coverage union documents (NZBR 1989, 1990), and the Court (NZBR and NZEF 1992). Both organisations stressed the need for flexibility to achieve 'efficiency'. What this meant in effect was that employers should be free to act as they wished, with minimal interference from unions or government.

The major changes to the New Zealand economy, referred to earlier, created an environment in which the New Right could be very hopeful of being able to push through their proposed changes. There was high and increasing unemployment caused by restructuring and redundancies and, despite union membership being compulsory during this period, it dropped by 80,000 during the late 1980s. Fear of more plant closures meant traditionally strong unions were entitled to be apprehensive.

1991–2000

This period is best characterised by an environment in which industrial relations was dominated by accelerated deregulation of the economy and society based on neoliberal principles. Corporatisation and privatisation of State assets continued and dismantling extended into the industrial relations arena with legislative supports for unions and collective bargaining removed. Employment relationships were redefined, becoming solely contractual relationships – the power continuing to shift from the working people to the corporate sector – with individual contracting more often than not being employer dictation rather than mutual negotiation.

The National Party came to power in November 1990 and very rapidly introduced the Employment Contracts Act (EC Act) 1991. As Macfie (1990) observed in the fairly conservative *National Business Review*, "Rarely has a lobby group wish-list been transformed so accurately into legislation" (1–2). Academics at home (Anderson 1991) and abroad (Dannin 1992) agreed that the Act heavily favoured employers. Whatever shared ideology there had been quickly evaporated; the sentiment was very much anti-union. Workers, as we noted earlier, were now wholly reliant on their bargaining power; those unions that withstood the de-unionisation drive were comprised of workers with inherent power, and those in the state sector who were already entrenched in enterprise level bargaining. Not surprisingly, the New Right element of society was adulatory. In a joint paper, the NZBR and NZEF claimed "The Act is making an outstanding contribution to productivity growth and its contribution to employment growth is likely to become increasingly apparent" (Dannin 1992, 1).

There were some apologists for the Act. Justice Hardie Boys of the Court of Appeal (later to become Governor General), for example, argued that "the Act is not anti-union; it may fairly be described as union-neutral" (*United Food Workers Union v Talley* [1993], 370). This statement is 'technically' correct, but the statement is also totally disingenuous if not mere sophistry. For nearly one hundred years, the legislation had supported unions and collective bargaining, encouraged union membership and, for over fifty years, made union membership compulsory. The EC Act 1991 removed all support for unions, made compulsory union membership illegal, removed support for collective bargaining and allowed employers to bargain individually if they wished and if they had the greater power – which in almost every case they did.

The practical reality was that the Act enabled employers to act virtually as they wished with very little opposition from a weakened union movement which had now lost State support. Certainly, the Act did not encourage or require exploitive or anti-employee behaviour and only a minority of employers were that way inclined. However, the totally *laissez-faire* stance of the Act did enable such behaviour. Large employers increasingly developed their own in-house capabilities to deal with unions, with human resource management (HRM) staff and proactive policies coming to the fore. Smaller employers sought their advice from regional or trade employers' organisations. It was this situation which saw the birth of a new occupational specialisation – the 'employment lawyer'.

Consistent with the notion, mentioned earlier, that employment relationships were strictly contractual arrangements, with all enforceable terms contract-based, a new institution emerged – the Employment Tribunal. This body ruled on any alleged contractual breaches, after first trying to reach a mediated solution. The Labour Court became the Employment Court as an appellate body. The EC Act 1991 made the personal grievance procedure available to *all* employees – not solely union members as was the case in the past. While this can, of course, be argued as simply extending employment protection to all, it was also a covert undermining of unions, as it removed one of their major selling points to attract members in a voluntary membership regime. And, while mediation of collective bargaining disputes was available from the Employment Tribunal, essentially this was pushed to the back burner.

Both academics and the judiciary have commented on the drafting of the EC Act 1991. Anderson (1991) observed that it contained "glaring ambiguities and inconsistencies" (129), while Geare (2001) considered the standard of drafting to be "abysmal . . . (but) may have been deliberate as part of a policy of *suggestio falsi* and *suppressio veri*" (292). The Chief Judge of the Employment Court in *NZ Airlines Pilots* stated that he felt bound to say that the framers of the Act "could not have intended to leave so much room for judicial doubt" (1995, 43) and in another judgement (*Ford v Capital Trusts* [1995]) the Chief Judge stated "fortune may favour the strong but justice must favour the weak" (66). This view is highly significant. An Act is not merely the printed statute but it is also the common law. As argued more fully elsewhere (Geare 2001), the abysmal drafting of the EC Act 1991 enabled the Employment Court in particular, but also the Court of Appeal, to reinterpret the Act through a progression of cases so that the EC Act in 2000 was almost unrecognisable to the EC Act in 1991. There were marked changes in case law over the period – favouring 'the weak' – in terms of what constituted 'harsh and oppressive' behaviour, what degree of influence and duress becomes 'undue', what bargaining strategies and tactics are permitted, and whether certain strikes and lockouts may be lawful yet open to punishment. In some cases the change in judicial decisions was extreme. In 1992, it was clear that employers do not "need to negotiate at all" (*Adams v Alliance* [1992], 1023), but by 1997 there was "a duty to bargain" and this was to be "in good faith" (*NZEI v State Services Commissioner* [1997], 391).

In summary, the EC Act 1991 rejected the philosophy underlying previous industrial law in New Zealand dating back to 1894 that employees were in an inherently weaker position than employers and that the State should help to at least partially redress this power imbalance by supporting employees through the support it gave to unions and collective action *via* legislation. The EC Act adopted the New Right philosophy that there was no inherent power imbalance favouring employers over employees and thus there was no need to support unions or collective bargaining. So, while the arbitration of interest disputes had already gone with the LR Act 1987, this Act saw the removal of the other well-established foundation blocks of New Zealand industrial relations:

(a) monopoly bargaining rights for unions;
(b) compulsory union membership either by law or agreement; and
(c) blanket coverage of agreements.

This Act also sounded the virtual death-knell for regional or national agreements as shown in Table 1 above. The Act did not make such agreements illegal, but it did make them very difficult to negotiate. Not surprisingly, employers and in particular employer groups (the NZEF merged with the NZ Manufacturers Association to form Business NZ) were very happy with the Act, employees much less so. Indeed, for most, terms and conditions of employment were increasingly becoming negotiated on an individual basis, with the contents largely dictated by 'minimums' laid out in the legislation (only about 20 per cent of the workforce continued to be covered by collective agreements).

As early as 1992, the Labour Opposition had proposed changes to the EC Act and an issue of the *NZJIR* was focused on these proposed reforms. A central issue addressed by these proposals concerned collective bargaining. While it was stated that an objective of the proposed Act (Objective 2) was to "promote collective bargaining" (Clark 1993, 154) there was little indication as to how this would be done. Certainly, collective bargaining was going to have to be done 'in good faith' – by statute as opposed to the common law contractual obligation of fair and reasonable dealing, but given employers could avoid collective bargaining this was a very weak form of promotion. In essence, the Labour Opposition's proposed reforms were "superficial rather than substantial" (Geare 1993, 203).

After three terms in opposition, Labour came back into power in November 1999 and remained in office for three terms. Their proposed Employment Relations Act (ER Act) was enacted in 2000.

2000–Present

Although the economic and technological environments in New Zealand remained largely unchanged, power distributions altered slightly in favour of the working people. In an interesting parallel to the political changes here, the Labour Party (recast as 'New Labour') regained power in the United Kingdom in 1997 after the neo-liberal Conservatives had had a lengthy period in office. A recent analysis was that in the UK, the New Labour government "explicitly accepted the principles and the bulk of the detail of the Law on trade unions and industrial action bequeathed by their Conservative predecessors" (Smith 2015, 352).

Certainly the ER Act 2000 ushered in a new ideology. Principled around 'good faith' and the promotion of positive employment relationships, it looked more union-friendly than did the EC Act 1991 (which did not even make reference to unions) and indeed s 3 which states its object is:

(i) to build productive employment relationships...
(ii) by a legislative requirement "for good faith behaviour";
(iii) by acknowledging and addressing the inherent inequality of power in employment relations; and
(iv) by promoting collective bargaining

It seems very laudable. Unfortunately the above observation made by Geare (1993) referring to superficiality rather than substance is particularly apposite to the supposed changes made by the ER Act 2000. As in the UK, Labour here basically accepted the EC Act 1991 – certainly as modified by common law decisions.

Notwithstanding the superficial changes, employer groups greeted the introduction of the ER Act 2000 with "howls of protest" (Cooper and May 2005, 4) but this was mere ritualistic game playing exposed when, in 2004, Labour proposed the ER Amendment Act 2004 (ER Am Act). These same groups again howled in protest but this time they protested the ER Act 2000 did not need fixing. Even after the amendments the ER Act represented only "moderate reform... within a clear ECA context" (Cooper and May 2005, 4).

The 'promotion of collective bargaining' was apparently to be achieved by requiring it occur – if it was going to occur at all – between the employer and a 'union'. Completely undermining the efforts of the 1984 Labour Government to ensure unions were stronger, this statutory move simply resulted in an increase in the number of 'paper' unions, created to fulfil this statutory requirement. If employers decided it would be quicker and easier on them to have a collective agreement rather than 20–50 or so individual agreements, they would assist in the paperwork to create a union to sign the document.

Year	Union membership (1)	Number of unions (2)	Potential union membership		Union density	
			Total employed labour force[2] (3)	Wage and salary earners[2] (4)	(1)/(3) % (5)	(1)/(4) % (6)
Dec 1991	514325	66	1509400	1199000	34.1	42.9
Dec 1992	428160	58	1514200	1190500	28.3	36.0
Dec 1993	409112	67	1545400	1215300	26.5	33.7
Dec 1994	375906	82	1612000	1269600	23.3	29.6
Dec 1995	362200	82	1686600	1331700	21.5	27.2
Dec 1996	338967	83	1741200	1375100	19.5	24.7
Dec 1997	327800	80	1750600	1401700	18.7	23.4
Dec 1998	306687	83	1739300	1387000	17.6	22.1
Dec 1999	302405	82	1766400	1395600	17.1	21.7
Dec 2000	318519	134	1800000	1425200	17.7	22.3
Dec 2001	329919	165	1846100	1482200	17.9	22.3
Dec 2002	334783	174	1906500	1540100	17.6	21.7
Dec 2003	341631	181	1955900	1579700	17.5	21.6
Dec 2004	354058	170	2024100	1637900	17.5	21.6
Dec 2005	377348	175	2084800	1702100	18.1	22.2
Dec 2006	382538	166	2134700	1759700	17.9	21.7
Mar 2008[1]	373327	147	2173000	1792000	17.2	20.8
Dec 2008	384777	141	2175900	1798000	17.7	21.4
Dec 2009	385280	145	2147000	1791800	17.9	21.5
Dec 2010	386276	145	2156600	1804100	17.9	21.4
Dec 2011	372891	134	2188200	1819100	17.0	20.5
Dec 2012	369200	133	2183500	1817000	16.9	20.3
Dec 2013	365927	126	2226900	1881400	16.4	19.4
Dec 2014[3]	361419	125	2305300	1951600	15.7	18.5
Dec 2015	358633	121	2357000	2005400	15.2	17.9

Source: HLFS – Persons Employed by Sex by Employment Status (Annual–Dec). Table reference: HLF005AA; Centre for Labour, Employment and Work Survey 2015.

Notes:
1 The 2007 figures are from the DOL Union Membership Return Data
2 Figures in column 3, 4, 5 and 6 are different from those reported in previous years due to the population rebase by Statistics New Zealand to take account of the latest census results.
3 A change in union membership accounting for one union decreased membership by close to 5000 compared with previous years.

Table 2: Trade Unions, Membership and Union Density 1991–2015.
Source: Ryall and Blumenfeld (2016)

Table 2 shows the significant impact the EC Act 1991 had on unions but from these data we can also see the insignificant impact the ER Act and its Amendment had on unions, aside from its influence on the actual number of unions, and in turn on collective bargaining. Given that an employer with sufficient power (and the vast majority have that) can still require individual bargaining if they so desire, *laissez-faire* still remains.

New Zealand's labour force had grown steadily over the past five or six years, but despite this growth union density continued to gradually decline. The industry demographics for union membership largely resemble earlier industrial relations periods. In 2013, the industry segments of transport, postal, warehousing, manufacturing, electricity, gas, water and waste services had the highest union density (ranging between 36 and 21 per cent), while the segments of wholesale trade, agriculture, forestry, mining, rental, hiring and real estate had the lowest (all under 5 per cent) (Ryall and Blumenfeld 2016). It is noteworthy within these demographics, however, that in a legislative regime which gives no real assistance to employees wanting to move into a collective relationship with employers, inherently strong groups at the top end of the labour market – police, teachers, airline pilots, nurses, and similarly skilled occupations – are among the most visibly effective unions in New Zealand today.

Most large and small employing organisations continue to remain opposed to unions and collective bargaining, with large employers increasingly utilising HRM strategies to manage their workplace relations. Not surprisingly, employment lawyers also continue to play a prominent role, particularly, but not exclusively in the resolution of rights disputes. The Employment Tribunal, considered too adversarial in both adjudication and mediation, and to have become too legalistic and costly, was disestablished by the ERA 2000, replaced in part by the Mediation Service. The Mediation Service, housed within the Department Labour, was staffed by State-employee mediators who were given a mandate to salvage and repair relationships – rather than manage them to 'divorce' as was often the norm with the Employment Tribunal. More recently, the Department of Labour has been disestablished with its functions absorbed into a 'super ministry', the Ministry of Business, Innovation and Employment, with the Mediation Service rebranded as Resolution Services. A new adjudicating body, the Employment Relations Authority (ERA), was also established; its objective was to conduct relatively informal inquisitorial 'hearings' without the direct appeal supervision of the Employment Court, contrasting with the more formal adversarial proceedings that had evolved in the Employment Tribunal. As with the Employment Tribunal, initially around half the membership of the ERA comprised lawyers; it is now staffed nearly exclusively by lawyers. The ERA was promoted as a final, accessible step of the employment relationship problem resolution system, not as the first step in a judicial system. The Department of Labour supported this, developing a comprehensive resolution framework, comprising wall-to-wall solutions including much-enhanced information services, early mediation intervention and relatively informal adjudication if required.

In November 2008, Labour suffered a crushing defeat by the National Party which has continued in office to the present. Given that the ER Act 2000 made relatively minor changes to the main structure of the EC Act 1991, it is not surprising that the National-led coalition government has not felt the need to make substantial changes either.

Unfortunately, there has been a continuous tinkering with the legislation; more than occasionally it would appear this is done to appease a small section of the electorate, rather than because the amendments were necessary or beneficial. Examples include changes in the ER Amendment Act of 2010 which restricted unions' right of access. As Anderson (2010) observes, "There was no rational reason for this change" (93).

A further controversial amendment was the introduction of the 90-day trial period for newly hired employees. This measure appears to have been introduced to appease employer groups who promoted the notion that there was a "grievance gravy train" (Woodhams 2007, 8) which was encouraged by advocates who advertised their services on a 'no win, no fee' basis. Although the 90-day trial period may be condemned because it disregards "the elementary human dignity of consultation before dismissal" (Hughes 2009, 3), the real objection to it should be that it panders to inept managers. As Rosenberg (2010) puts it:

> [The] legislation is encouraging poor personnel management practices such as failing to supervise employees adequately, failing to give them feedback to enable them to improve their performance, and using dismissal rather than good interview and employment practices to address the quality of the appointment process (80).

Although there were no significant changes to the nature of the interactions between the parties in terms of setting the work rules, some minor changes to employee protections and entitlements have either been made or look likely to eventuate in the coming years and we address some of these as we look to the 'future' of industrial relations in New Zealand.

The Future

So what are the big issues today? Contemporary industrial relations in New Zealand has largely seen the spotlight placed on matters related to workplace health and safety. A broad focus has been applied to this remit, with the gamut of identifiable issues ranging from the physical injury to the mental health of workers. The impetus for this spotlight was prompted by New Zealand's high incidence of workplace trauma (for example, there were 3,300 serious harm notifications and 48 deaths reported to Worksafe New Zealand for the 2014/2015 period – inexcusable statistics even by international standards) with numerous reports being commissioned over recent years (The Report of the Independent Taskforce on Workplace Health and Safety April 2013; Tynan, Milsom and O'Reilly 2013; Workplace Health and Safety 2012).

We capture the general sentiment of these reports with the comment made by the chief executive of Business NZ that, "The health and well-being of everyone in the workplace should be a key goal for all business. People's well-being is critical in its own right and a fundamental component of doing business in the workplace" (Tynan et al. 2013, 5). However, despite these reports offering a plethora of platitudes (for example, ". . . nine out of ten enterprises consider improving employee well-being to be either desirable or a priority" (Tynan et al. 2013, 6)) and recommendations, as yet little substantive reform has been evident.

Issues pertaining to equity and flexibility have also been placed high atop New Zealand's industrial relations agenda. It is pay that sits at the heart of the equity issue in the New Zealand context and as a consequence of the recent settlement with government of a very high profile employment case (*TerraNova Homes and Care Ltd v Service and Food Workers Union Nga Ringa Tota Inc* [2014]) this issue has been given a real boost. A joint working party has now been established to address pay equity with the Honourable Michael Woodhouse, Minister of Workplace Relations and Safety, quite rightly pointing out in a recent press release that "It is not practical or efficient for workers and employers to have to go to Court to seek principles for their particular industry one-by-one" (Woodhouse 2015). In terms of progress, while New Zealand is currently ranked in the top ten for pay gender equality, recently released statistics from the State Services Commission paint a somewhat less optimistic picture with men in public sector enterprises being paid 39 per cent more than women and with several others having pay differentials in the high twenties.

The issue of flexibility is still in its infancy. Flexibility lay at the heart of the EC Act 1991 and it comes as no surprise that, as the years have passed, the use of non-standard contracts has become quite prevalent. Given this longstanding propensity, it was somewhat surprising that in 2015 employers' use of zero-hours contracts was greeted with great condemnation. Indeed, the backlash for employers from the resultant media attention prompted some to stop using these arrangements altogether (such as KFC, Starbucks and Pizza Hut). Radical regulatory change may come eventually though if Labour returns to power. This is because current opposition MP, Grant Robertson, as we write, is steadfastly pursuing policy ideas at the Future of Work Forum for novel approaches to work and flexibility, drawing on Scandinavian models to do so.

These initiatives appear to indicate progress. However, what we are really witnessing is not leniency or benevolence towards workers; rather the heavy hand of the State (guided by employers) is continuing to incrementally carve out the industrial relations landscape. These initiatives create a façade whereby workers, at the lower end of the labour market at least, are powerless as the State erodes their rights, prompting greater income and work-life inequality. It is unlikely much will change for this group as, over successive years, their mechanisms for collective bargaining have been systemically eroded. If they don't have the power to compel the other party to sit at the table, and in most cases they don't, then substantive outcomes cannot accrue.

So, as we have argued through this chapter, the actor with the power to really influence industrial relations is the State. The two major governing parties, ideologically, usually sit just to the right of centre (National) and just to the left (Labour). The major tenor of employment relations today was set back in 1991 with the EC Act 1991, which Labour only slightly modified with the ER Act in 2000. We cannot foresee any major changes affecting the majority of either employers or employees. The majority of employers have always, and probably will always, behave approximately to the norm. A few are truly excellent and a few are truly despicable. We predict that, at least in the next forty years, the majority of employers will not become so exploitative that measures will have to be introduced by the State comparable to those of the 1890s.

Employment rights in the workplace will be increasingly the prerogative of the State and we see it most unlikely that unions will ever achieve the significance and perceived power that they were still holding back in the 1970s. New Zealand will probably experience a phenomenon similar to that experienced in the United Kingdom where "statutory employment rights are now a 'ceiling' rather than a 'floor'" (Smith 2015, 361). A cynical observer might even question whether this is the motive underlying recent, and largely unopposed, increases to some of our statutory entitlements (for example, paid parental leave). For there is also apparent an incremental chipping away at the legislative protections and entitlements that an increasing proportion of the New Zealand workforce now rely on, lacking as they do union protection. These have included, under the present government, the introduction of the 90-day probationary period without recourse to dismissal grievance protection, initially applicable to only small establishments, but then extended to all workplaces. Also included are provisions authorising employees to 'negotiate' to exchange (read 'surrender') a week of statutory annual leave in exchange for unspecified benefits (read 'to get a job'), the removal of legislatively guaranteed rest breaks in favour of 'negotiated' (read 'employer dictated, if any') rest breaks. None of this includes the government's virtual elimination of all employment entitlements and protections for workers in the film production industry at the insistence of the Hollywood movie conglomerates back in 2010 (McAndrew and Risak 2012).

In concluding, industrial relations in New Zealand has been relatively undramatic over the past decade or so. Collective bargaining aside, it would seem that big issues, as in the past, continue to be dealt with by the State, with minor ones being handled either in-house or through established institutions. The political landscape, such that it is, makes it difficult to envisage any radical changes to the current framework in the near future. To some extent, it could be argued that some workers are now using the media, as opposed to unions, as a platform for voicing their concerns. Notwithstanding, when it comes to the truly big issues – there is nearly always a union presence.

References

Adams, R. 1992. "The Role of the State in Industrial Relations." In *Research Frontiers in Industrial Relations and Human Resources*, ed. Lewin, D., Mitchell, D. S. and Scherer, P. D., 489–524. Madison, WI: IRRA.

Anderson, G. 1991. "The Employment Contracts Act 1991: An Employers' Charter?" *New Zealand Journal of Industrial Relations* 16 (2): 12–142.

Anderson, G. 2010. "Union Rights of Entry to the Workplace." *Employment Law Bulletin* 8: 93–94.

Clark, Rt. Hon. H. 1993. "Employment Relations – The New Direction Under Labour." *New Zealand Journal of Industrial Relations* 18 (2): 153–162.

Cooper, R. and May, R. 2005. "Union Revitalisation in Australia and New Zealand, 1995–2005." *New Zealand Journal of Employment Relations* 30 (3): 1–17.

Dannin, E. J. 1992. "Labor law reform in New Zealand." *New York Law School Journal of International and Comparative Law* 13: 1–39.

Dunlop, J. T. 1958/1993. *Industrial Relations Systems* (Rev. ed.). Boston, MA: Harvard Business School Press.

Geare, A. J. 1977. "The Field of Study of Industrial Relations." *Journal of Industrial Relations* 19 (3): 274–285.

Geare, A. J. 1983. "Formal Collective Agreements in New Zealand Private Sector Industrial Relations." *New Zealand Journal of Industrial Relations* 8 (1): 23–29.

Geare, A. J. 1993. "The Proposed Employment Relations Act." *New Zealand Journal of Industrial Relations* 18 (2): 194–204.

Geare A. J. 2001. "The Employment Contracts Act 1991–2000: A Decade of Change." *New Zealand Journal of Industrial Relations* 26 (3): 287–306.

Hughes, J. 2009. "The Introduction of the New Trial Period Law: Urgent or Expedient?" *Employment Law Bulletin* 1: 1–14.

Kelsey, J. 1993. *Rolling Back the State: Privatisation of Power in Aotearoa/New Zealand*. Wellington, New Zealand: Bridget Williams Books.

Macfie, R. 1990. "Labour Act Thrown out Window." *National Business Review,* December 21. 1–2.

McAndrew, I. 1992. "The Structure of Bargaining under the Employment Contracts Act." *New Zealand Journal of Industrial Relations* 17 (3): 259–282.

McAndrew, I. and M. Risak. 2012. "Shakedown in the Shaky Isles: Union Bashing in New Zealand." *Labor Studies Journal* 37 (1): 56–80.

New Zealand Business Roundtable. 1989. *Review of the Operation of the Labour Relations Act in the 1988/9 Wage Round*. Wellington, New Zealand: NZBR.

New Zealand Business Roundtable. 1991. *Submission of the Employment Contracts Bill*. Auckland, New Zealand: NZBR.

New Zealand Business Roundtable and New Zealand Employers' Federation. 1992. *A Study of the Labour/Employment Court*. Wellington, New Zealand: NZBR and NZEF.

New Zealand Educational Institute. (1895). *The Educational Institute of New Zealand: Its Work, History, and Constitution*. Wellington, New Zealand: Whitcombe & Tombs Limited.

New Zealand Educational Institute. (1985). *Constitution*. Wellington, New Zealand: NZEI.
New Zealand Employers Federation. 1986. *Response to Government Green Paper on Industrial Relations*. Wellington, New Zealand: NZEF.
New Zealand Employers Federation. 1990. *The Benefits of Bargaining Reform*. Wellington, New Zealand: NZEF.
Rosenberg, B. 2010. "No Evidence for the Prime Minister's Claim on 90-day Trials." *Employment Law Bulletin* 7: 79–80.
Ryall, S. and S. Blumenfeld. 2016. *Unions and Union Membership in New Zealand – Report on 2015 Survey*. Wellington, New Zealand: Centre for Labour, Employment and Work, Victoria University of Wellington.
Smith, P. 2015. "Labour under the Law: A New Law of Combination, and Master and Servant, in 21st-century Britain?" *Industrial Relations Journal* 46 (5-6): 345–364.
Tynan, P., Milsom, S., and O'Reilly, P. 2013. *Wellness in the Workplace Report 2013*. Wellington, New Zealand: BusinessNZ. Accessed April 22, 2016. https://www.businessnz.org.nz/__data/assets/pdf_file/0005/74615/.
Williams, G. 1976. "The History and Development of Wage Fixing Legislation in the Private Sector." *New Zealand Journal of Industrial Relations* 1 (3): 56–63.
Woodhams, B. 2007. *Employment Relationship Problems: Cost, Benefits, Choices*. Department of Labour Report. Accessed May 24, 2017. www.communityresearch.org.nz/wp-content/uploads/formidable/woodhams1.pdf.
Woodhouse, M. 2015. "Working Group to Pursue Pay Equity Principles for Workplaces. Government Release." Accessed May 24, 2017. http://www.beehive.govt.nz/release/working-group-pursue-pay-equity-principles-workplaces.
Woods, N. S. 1974. "The Industrial Relations Act 1993." *Occasional Papers in Industrial Relations, no. 11*. Wellington, New Zealand: Industrial Relations Centre, Victoria University of Wellington.
Woods, N. S. 1977. "The Industrial Relations Amending Legislation of 1976." *Occasional Papers in Industrial Relations, no. 21*. Wellington, New Zealand: Industrial Relations Centre, Victoria University of Wellington.

Cases
Adams v Alliance Textiles [1992] 1 ERNZ 982
Ford v Capital Trusts [1995] 2 ERNZ 47
NZ Airlines Pilots Assn v Airways Corp. of NZ [1995] WEC 72/95
NZEI v State Services Commission [1997] ERNZ 381
Ohinemuri Mines and Batteries Employees' IUW v Registrar of Industrial Unions [1917] NZLR 829.
TerraNova Homes and Care Ltd v Service and Food Workers Union Nga Ringa Tota Inc [2014] NZCA 516
United Food Workers Union v Talley [1993] 2 ERNZ 360

The Politics of Workplace Reform: 40 Years of Change

Margaret Wilson

Introduction

The 1970s was the decade that foreshadowed the radical restructuring of New Zealand's economic, social and political systems that began in the 1980s and continues today. As a result, this transformation of New Zealand society included the radical restructuring of the regulatory framework of the labour market and the day-to-day practice of the employment relationship in the workplace. This chapter will chart the ideological and political changes that became evident in the 1970s and provided a new regulatory framework that affected employment relations practice for the next 40 years. It will further identify the main drivers of this transformation as they have been reflected in the legislative framework. The main drivers of regulatory change have been not only the economy, but also the ideological position of the government of the day. It is therefore necessary to analyse the ideological and political shifts over the past 40 years in order to understand the impact of the changes in workplace practice.

Although this article is not an analysis of articles or academic research published in the *NZJIR*, the *Journal* from the outset provided a useful insight into the issues that have attracted analysis and research over the past 40 years. A quick review of the publication over the past four decades reveals that the Journal has reflected both the theory and the practice of employment relations. For example, the issues in the 1970s reflected the growing challenges to the existing industrial conciliation and arbitration system with its centralised collective wage fixing system. Unsurprisingly, wage policy was an important focus during the 1970s, but during this period there was an assumption that the state was to maintain a central role in the labour market. This included an article by Max Bradford, a future Minister of Labour in the 1990s, on options for wages policy. The emphasis was more on devising a new partnership, with several articles on worker participation models, including a paper by Sir Frank Holmes advocating the need for unions, employers and governments to work together to develop a new economic policy.

There were two articles that were prophetic in terms of the radical changes that were ahead of the whole industrial relations system The first prophetic article was written by John Deeks, who analysed the nature and role of ideology in New Zealand industrial relation. He opened his article with the statement:[1]

> It is a truism that there is in New Zealand culture a widespread if inarticulate suspicion of ideas, of theory, of ideology ... and a genial preference for the practically useful, for the matter-of-fact treatment of things, for the pragmatic.
>
> ... the main thesis of this article is that ideological questions are central to the practice of New Zealand industrial relations and that we cannot adequately understand industrial relations behaviour if we persist with the view that it is not influenced by beliefs, values systems, ideas, theories.

This insight foreshadowed the total collapse of the industrial conciliation and arbitration statutory framework in 1991 and its replacement with the Employment Contracts Act. This radical shift was driven by "beliefs, value systems, ideas and theories" that impacted on the practice of employment relations in such a way that there has been a fundamental reconstruction of the employment relationship.

Another prophetic article was written by James Farmer and entitled "Labour Relations – A Takeover by the State?" He foresaw the changing role of the law during the 1970s with increasing resort to litigation to counter increasing strike action and the challenge to the managerial prerogative to hire and fire employees. He noted that while employers were responding to this new environment, the trade unions were slower to adapt and relied on traditional industrial action. He also questioned the implications of any increasing worker participation schemes to the authority of unions. He concluded with the following conclusion:[2]

> The rights and entitlements of workers will therefore become the product of the State, exercising powers of patronage, which might be extended or withheld at will ... [a]ny decline in trade union industrial power will have a corresponding effect on the considerable political strength of the unions as one of the counterbalancing forces that offset Government or State power. Any resultant increase in the political ability of the State to pass new laws to achieve its policy objectives will accordingly have significance from the wider perspective of the rule of law as it operates in a Parliamentary democracy.

Farmer foresaw the changing role of the state and the impact it would have on the employment relationship and in particular the rights of employees. As the

---

1   John Deeks "Ideology and Industrial Relations in New Zealand" (1976) 1 NZJIR 2 at 26.
2   James Farmer "A Takeover by the State? A New Zealand Experience" (1978) 3 NZJIR 397 at 104.

state has withdrawn regulatory support for the union movement, the individual employee has come to rely more on the state to provide for their legal employment rights and for enforcement of those rights.

This chapter will examine the various regulatory frameworks that have been in force over the past 40 years. The analysis will include the Industrial Relations Act 1973 that remained the primary regulatory framework until 1987 when the Labour Relations Act 1987 replaced it. The later Act was designed to begin a serious transition of employment relations practice to reflect the new neoliberal public policy framework. The transition was short lived, however. The change of government in 1990 repealed the 1987 Act and replaced it with the Employment Contracts Act 1991. The 1991 Act marked a radical shift in labour market regulation in the workplace. It ended the notion of a tripartite partnership by the state withdrawing from its support for trade unions as the primary agency for the enforcement of employee employment rights. The new regulatory relationship was constructed as a direct market-driven relationship between the employer and the individual employee. The 1999 election bought a change of government with a promise of a new regulatory framework in the form of the Employment Relations Act 2000. Although this Act remains in force, it has been considerably amended and increasingly reflects a neoliberal conception of the labour market and workplace relationships.

An examination of the various regulatory frameworks requires a consideration of the ideological and political forces that shaped the statutory provisions. The past 40 years has seen political changes of government being shared by the main political parties, namely, the National Party and Labour Party. During this period, there have been 13 elections, with the National Party or National-led governments winning the election eight times and the Labour Party or Labour-led governments four times. While the Labour and National parties reflect different ideological positions, these differences are not as sharp as in previous history. The reality of globalisation and neoliberalism has blurred the number of differences between the legislative frameworks implemented by both political parties.

It is, however, important to note that there have been and continue to be ideological differences between the two main political parties and those differences are reflected in the regulatory frameworks they enact. Ideology, as noted by Deeks, has been recognised as an essential element of any system of employment relations.[3] The primary ideological tension in New Zealand has traditionally been characterised as being between a unitary and a pluralist approach. A unitary approach has been associated with the legitimacy and supremacy of

---

3 John Dunlop *Industrial Relations Systems* (Southern Illinois University Press, Carbondale, 1958); Alan Fox *Industrial Sociology and Industrial Relations* (Royal Commission on Trade Union and Employers' Associations, London, 1966).

management rights, while pluralism recognises there are competing interests in the workplace that need to be accommodated. The reality, however, has been that there has always been dissonance between workplace practice and the statutory framework. The differences in political ideology have been primarily reflected in the role of the state and the method for wage fixing. Generally, the National governments have supported a minimum role for the state and individual wage fixing through the contract of employment, whereas the Labour governments have supported a more active role for the state and collective bargaining to fix wages.

In a previous analysis of the different political ideologies, I raised the question whether there was emerging a consensus ideological position.[4] I noted that in the past New Zealand governments have asserted their right to govern in the public interest that is above sectoral interests. The industrial conciliation and arbitration system (IC&A) expressed the traditional position of the state. Although it was a tripartite system, the state always asserted the right to intervene in the interests of the country as a whole. I noted, however, that the ideological differences between political parties have become more pronounced after 1968 when the economic pressures on government increased with changes in the global economy. These differences have increased with neoliberalism playing a dominant role in the policies of the parties of the right, while the parties of the left contest those policies, seeking a more pluralist approach in the workplace. Currently there appears to be little space for a cross-party ideological consensus to emerge in the foreseeable future.

The Foundation of the Industrial Conciliation and Arbitration System

Before the various frameworks are considered, it is important to understand the nature of the foundational statutory industrial conciliation and arbitration system. It is important because, while there have been radical changes in the statutory frameworks, aspects of the foundational system still resonate within the current framework. Although it is beyond the scope of this article, it may be argued that there is an underlying culture of values that have found shape in various statutory systems. For example, there has been an assumption of a 'fair go' frequently expressed in dismissal procedures. There is also an expectation of a 'fair wage', as has been witnessed in the struggle over zero-hour contracts. Although the values of neoliberalism pervade the current legal framework, the challenges to this framework reflect the more traditional values traditionally associated with the New Zealand workplace.

4   Erling Rasmussen *Employment Relations Workers, Unions, and Employers in New Zealand* (Auckland University Press, Auckland, 2010) at 9–23.

New Zealand's industrial relations system was enacted in 1894 within a politico-legal framework. This framework recognised that there was a fundamental conflict between the interests of labour and capital, but the state had a responsibility to balance those interests in the overall public interest. The three parties to the relationship – the state, employer organisations and trade unions – developed a policy of tripartism, with the state being represented by the Arbitration Court in the day-to-day conduct of the relationship. It was a representative system that depended on individual workers and employers being members of representative organisations that were represented on the various state conciliation and arbitration institutions. However, employer organisations were just as important as trade unions for the smooth running of the system.

The dominant partner was always the state, because it had the legitimacy to act over and above the interests of the other parties. It kept control of the relationship through the use of legislation. Through legal control, the state influenced the shape as well as the operation of trade unions and employer organisations. Noel Woods, a former long-term and influential Secretary of Labour, described the effect of this control on the development of trade union organisations. He observed after a visit to Great Britain, "When I returned ... end of 1937 the contrast hit me ... New Zealand was, with some exceptions, primitive stuff; hundreds of small unions kept small and ignorant and poverty-stricken by the law."[5]

When some trade unions attempted to shrug off the 'leg iron of labour' early in the 20th century, the government of the day reacted by enacting legislation: the Labour Disputes Investigation Act 1913 that effectively prevented trade unions wage negotiations outside the institutions of conciliation and arbitration. The failure of this early attempt not only stifled the development of collective bargaining in New Zealand but it also contributed to internal dissension within the union movement and inhibited the development of a strong unified movement.[6]

While there were always elements within both the trade unions and employer organisations that sought the removal of legal restrictions, the reality was the system worked well enough for all the parties, including the state. For unions it was a trade-off between the security of achieving widespread membership, an outcome in bargaining and the avoidance of recognition disputes with employers, and the uncertainty of dealing directly with employers without the support of legal enforcement. For employers, however, it provided a level of certainty and stability and protection against competition. The level of support depended to

---

5   Noel Woods "Comments on the Industrial Conciliation and Arbitration Act 1894" (1994) 1 NZJIR 1 at 3.
6   Herbert Roth *Trade Unions in New Zealand: Past and Present* (AH & AW Reed Publications, Wellington, 1973) at 17–40.

some extent on the economic and political conditions of the time. This included conservative governments being more responsive to the demands of the employer lobby and in 1935 the first Labour government greatly enhancing the bargaining power of unions through compulsory unionism that extended union organisation into white-collar occupations.

It was not until the 1960s, and the changing economic conditions occasioned by the entry of the United Kingdom into the European Economic Community, that the challenges to the system became more insistent. The accommodation of these pressures was tried through the development of ruling rate agreements, but the increasing complexity of bargaining arrangements and the increase in industrial action started a process of construction of a new industrial relations framework.

New Institutional Framework – Industrial Relations Act 1973

The breakdown of the IC&A system became obvious with the 1968 General Wage Order. The nil-order of the Arbitration Court to an application for a general order, followed by the employer and union representatives on the Court awarding a five per cent general wage order formally signalled what had been apparent for some time. The wage fixing system, conducted formally through centralised awards and informally through ruling rate agreements with periodic interventions through the mechanism of the general wage order, no longer produced either industrial or economic stability in the 1960s. The economic and social pressures of the time placed too much strain on institutions that were not designed to cope with the increasing complexity of the economy. For the next 15 years various attempts were made to amend the IC&A framework to accommodate the changing economic and political pressures.

The first such attempt was the Industrial Relations Act 1973. Although there was a change of name from Industrial Conciliation and Arbitration to Industrial Relations, the Act maintained much of the philosophy and provisions underpinning the IC&A Act.[7] There were signs of greater flexibility in bargaining in the form of Voluntary Settlement Collective Agreements that could be negotiated outside the restrictions of the IC&A Act. Another important departure was the recognition of the distinction between disputes of rights and disputes of interest. The recognition of interest and rights disputes, as being different in nature and requiring dispute resolution procedures that reflected this difference, was an important step in separating collective from individual rights. Individuals now had access to a legal remedy in a way that had not been available previously. Although the changes did not seem a substantial change

---

7   *A Description of Wage Fixing and Industrial Relations in the Private Sector* (Long Term Reform Committee, Wellington, 1983).

from the past, Young was correct when he described the passage of the Act as "... as a significant shift in the underlying philosophy ... The full ramifications of this change have yet to develop. They have certainly not been grasped by the wider community and even by some within the ranks of the social partners."[8]

Whether the changes would have enabled a more flexible framework to evolve through experience will never be known. The economic conditions of the time provoked the governments of the period to embark on a policy of direct intervention in the bargaining process through statutory wage controls. This policy was first enacted in the Stabilisation of Remuneration Act 1971 and a series of regulations that came and went in various forms until the 1982 Wage Adjustment Regulations that prevented all wage bargaining and remained in force until 1984. This exercise of direct control by governments of the day produced a negative reaction from the trade unions that resented the controls on their right to bargain. Work stoppages rose from 71 in 1961 to 523 in 1979. It was not surprising that the increasing level of industrial conflict politicised industrial relations. This was most apparent during the 1975 election campaign when the National Party used dancing Cossacks to associate the unions with communism. The conflict between the union movement and the National government of the period went beyond ideological difference as was observed by Boston who noted:[9]

> To put it bluntly, there were many in the union movement were unwilling to reach an accommodation with the Muldoon administration, regardless of the apparent advantages of so doing. This reluctance was not merely the product of ideological convictions. It also stemmed from a fundamental lack of trust between the union movement and the National Government. The Muldoon Administration had conducted an active anti-union campaign throughout its term in office. It had demonstrated little desire to consult with the FOL or to foster a climate of understanding and goodwill.

Throughout this period, attempts were made to find agreement on a new statutory framework, but they proved unsuccessful for the reasons outlined.[10] While this work was proceeding in the industrial relations area, there was a growing understanding that a more fundamental policy shift was required to address the economic problems facing New Zealand. The result of this policy work emerged after the 1984 election in the Treasury briefing document *Economic Management*. It was in effect a neoliberal policy agenda for New Zealand of which industrial relations was one part of the overall change.[11]

---

8   John Young "New Zealand Industrial Relations: Retrospect and Prospect" (1976) 1 NZJIR 3.
9   Jonathan Boston *Incomes Policy in New Zealand* (Victoria University Press, Wellington, 1984) at 227.
10 Rob Campbell and Alf Kirk *After the Freeze* (Port Nicholson Press, Wellington, 1983).
11 Alan Bollard "New Zealand" in John Williamson (ed) *The Political Economy of Policy Reform* (Institute for International Economics, Washington, 1994) at 73–110.

The Road to a Neoliberal Statutory Framework – Labour Relations Act 1987

While the election of the Labour government in 1984 signalled a period of rapid change, the influence of the Labour Party and the trade unions ensured the government undertook a period of consultation on the future direction of industrial relations in the new market-focused economy.[12] It was clear, however, that the government intended to enact legislation with greater business focus. The mantra of 'improving productivity', through greater flexibility in the workplace, resounded through the discussions between the union movement and the government. The government released a Green Paper in 1985 that set out the issues that required reform with the general policy direction clearly stated in the White Paper *Government Policy Statement on Labour Relations*. Stan Rodger, the then Minister of Labour, noted in the introduction to the White Paper:[13]

> It is clear from the submissions that, while a climate for substantial reform exists, there is little consensus on the nature of that reform. The differences are sharpest between union and employer interests, but even within these sectors, discernible differences exist on important issues. In the absence of any consensus, the responsibility for making decisions shifts squarely onto the Government. In arriving at its position, the Government has been careful to preserve those features of the present arrangements, which it believes remain valid. It has also brought together elements, which have received significant support from both unions and employer submissions. The resulting reforms will constitute the most significant reshaping of industrial relations since 1894.

The government was again explicitly asserting its right to control the nature of the industrial relationship. The statutory result of this reform exercise was the Labour Relations Act 1987. It was an attempt to create a new flexibility in the bargaining environment with a move from the restrictions of national awards to industry or enterprise agreements. Employers had argued for greater flexibility in the conditions of employment to meet the conditions of the market in a timely fashion. The dilemma for the unions was they did not wish to abandon the security of minimum but extensive coverage under the national award system for the uncertainty of negotiating an industry or enterprise agreement without a commitment that the employers would conclude such an agreement. Harbridge and McCaw found through their research that the risk was real for unions through the experience of the Engineers Union and the Timberworkers Union.[14]

---

12 Margaret Wilson *Labour in Government 1984–1987* (Port Nicholson Press, Wellington, 1989).
13 New Zealand Government *Policy Statement on Labour Relations* (Department of Labour, New Zealand, 1986).
14 Raymond Harbridge and Stuart McCaw "Award, Agreement or Nothing? A Review of the

While the Engineers Union had greater success than the Timberworkers Union at negotiating agreements, the reality was that the environment was against serious negotiations and many agreements were never concluded. Employers, like everyone else, knew the government was about to change at the next election and that the National government had promised a reform of the system that reflected a fundamental departure from the system of conciliation and arbitration.

Although much of the focus during this period was directed to the changes in the private sector, the Fourth Labour government made substantial changes to the state sector that ultimately led to a unitary statutory framework applying to both the public and private sector employment relationships. These changes affected both institutional structures and practices. The structural changes were affected primarily through the State-Owned Enterprises Act 1986, the Labour Relations Act 1987 and the State Sector Act 1988. For example, the State-Owned Enterprises Act freed the new state-owned trading corporations from the constraints of the State Sector Act in terms of personnel procedures relating to appointment, promotion, transfer, discipline, occupational classification and grading of public officials. The State Sector Act made each department permanent head (now called a chief executive) an employer in their own right so that departments negotiated their own agreements and thereby replaced occupationally based bargaining. The new chief executives also were given the right to hire, promote, discipline and fire employees, providing the personnel policy complied with the principle of being 'a good employer'.

The fundamental assumption behind these changes was that the private sector managerial model was more efficient and should be adopted by the public sector. This approach led to the integration of the public- and private-sector labour relations procedures under the Labour Relations Act 1987. This change also led to the public-sector trade unions becoming subject to the provisions of the Labour Relations Act in terms of their membership and rules. Similarly, the disputes and personal grievance provisions of the Act now applied to the state-sector trade unions and employees. The only distinction between the two sectors was the provision for final offer arbitration being available for those covered by the State Sector Act. This provision was not used before the Act was repealed in 1991.

John Deeks undertook a thorough analysis of the implications of the Labour Relations Act and the changes in the public sector.[15] He observed that traditionally in New Zealand most industrial relations practitioners had operated within a pluralist framework in practice to ensure the organisation kept operational. Deeks argued, however, that this approach was inadequate to address the

Impact of s 132(a) of the Labour Relations Act 1987 on Collective Bargaining" (1992) 1 NZJIR 17.

15 John Deeks "New Tracks, Old Maps: Continuity and Change in New Zealand Labour Relations 1984–1990" (1990) 1 NZJIR 15 at 99–116.

economic and technological challenges facing New Zealand business. He noted the "... system maintenance role of traditional labour relations practitioners has been downgraded in value ... labour market have been a key focus of ideologists ... reinforc(ing) a unitarist frame of reference in corporate affairs."[16] Deeks also identified the underlying rationale for the various statutory and policy changes as being greater market flexibility and deregulation. There was evidence of greater flexibility being affected through large-scale redundancies and more flexibility in wage bargaining. He did conclude however with the observation that "The ultimate logic of complete labour market flexibility is absolute freedom of action for management, and a total loss of individual rights and collective protections of employees."[17] Whether the Labour Relations Act would have achieved a transition to greater flexibility in industrial relations will never been known, as it was repealed before it had time to be fully implemented.

Neoliberalism Arrives – Employment Contracts Act 1991

The enactment of the Employment Contracts Act 1991 marked the real break with the past and the IC&A system.[18] The centre of the statutory framework was the individual contract of employment and enterprise bargaining. The focus of the Act was to make the workplace business friendly through flexibility. In practice, this meant individualising the employment relationship that enabled the individual employee and employer to agree on wages and conditions without the intervention of a third party. Where there was a union presence, an enterprise agreement was the likely outcome of negotiations. The removal of the statutory infrastructure for awards meant they expired in the normal way but were not renewed. The Act applied to all employees in the public and private sectors. The result was a decline in union membership and union organisations.[19] Greater flexibility also resulted in lowering of wages and a decline in conditions of employment.[20]

The government in effect removed itself from the employment relationship. This trend had begun under the previous Labour government when the Minister of Labour declined to intervene in industrial disputes. The individualisation of the employment relationship totally marginalised the role of the government

---

16 At 112.
17 At 109.
18 Raymond Harbridge *Employment Contracts: New Zealand Experiences* (Victoria University Press, Wellington, 1993).
19 Andy Charlwood and Peter Haynes "Union Membership Decline in New Zealand 1990–2002" (2008) 50 NZJIR 1 at 87–110.
20 Raymond Harbridge "Collective Employment Contracts: A Content Analysis" in Raymond Harbridge *Employment Contracts: New Zealand Experiences* (Victoria University Press, Wellington, 1993) at 70–88.

in the day-to-day relationship. Although the government no longer supported a collective relationship between unions and employers, there was still an expectation that it was responsible for ensuring minimum standards were maintained in the workplace. The removal of awards exposed the fragility of employment conditions such as sick pay, holidays, safety and even the minimum wage. The minimum wage in particular stood in opposition to the ideology of neoliberalism. Rather than repeal the minimum wage, however, throughout the nineties the government did not regularly adjust it.

There was one area, however, that survived this radical restructuring of the employment relationship: the retention of the personal grievance process. The notion of an unjustified dismissal was retained, which required the employer to justify the dismissal of an employee. The Act also provided a remedy for employees who had been subjected to discrimination in the terms provided for in the Act. If the employee proved to the satisfaction of the Tribunal or Court a personal grievance, the remedies provided for were reinstatement, reimbursement and/ or compensation. The employee was required to pursue their remedy and the employer to defend their action through a legal process before the Employment Tribunal and then appeal to the Employment Court. This process soon became time consuming and costly for all parties. It also introduced the role of the lawyer into the settlement of personal grievances. Until this time, the legal profession had little interest in employment relations, but the decline of both trade unions and employer organisations meant their officials were no longer available to negotiate the settlement of such grievances. The combination of replacing the contract of employment for the collective agreement as the principle instrument of employment legal regulation and the change in the process of settlement of personal grievances legalised the relationship. This represented a sharp contrast with the previous statutory framework that was primarily dependent on a representative model from within both the trade unions and employer organisations.

By the end of the 1990s the consequences of the fundamental shift in employment relations was becoming obvious. There was certainly greater flexibility and employers had more control over their employees' wages and conditions. The lawyers replaced the union representative in disputes of rights with a consequential increase in costs and delays. With the decline in union membership and collective agreements, the union movement turned towards political lobbying for change in the legislation. It sought a new system of collective bargaining that provided a more even playing field. It did not seek a return to the old IC&A system, having recognised the reality of the marketplace. It was in effect seeking statutory support for collective bargaining in the new economic environment. For the individual employee who was not a member of a trade union, the issue was how to negotiate a contract with an employer that protected both wages and conditions of employment. For those interests that felt disadvantaged under the new system, the issue was how to effect greater protection under a system that was designed to remove many of the traditional employee protections.

A Challenge to Neoliberal Framework – Employment Relations Act 2000

The only hope of change for the union movement was a change of government. Although there were still reservations about working with the Labour party after the experience with the Fourth Labour government, the Labour party had spent the 1990s reconstructing itself and re-established a relationship with the union movement that was cemented with the party making an unequivocal promise in the 1999 election manifesto to repeal the ECA. Another important political factor was the MMP electoral system, which before the 1999 election saw an agreement between the Labour party and the Alliance, a left-leaning party to work together in coalition after the election. A united campaign from the opposition and a disunited campaign from the government and its support parties saw the election of a Labour-led government in 1999.

The commitment in the election manifesto recognised both the importance of collective bargaining but also the need for a new minimum code of employment rights. It read:[21]

> Legislation should recognise that the balance of power or influence between workers and employers is not equal. Labour believes that the best way to redress this imbalance is to encourage the collective organizations of workers and to foster collective bargaining as a preferred means of establishing the rights and obligations of workers. These beliefs are shared very widely internationally and form the basis of core ILO Conventions.

The Employment Relations Act 2000 was the government response to its election commitment.[22] The purpose of the legislation was stated in the Act as follows:

(a) to build productive employment relationships through the promotion of good faith in all aspects of the employment environment and of the employment relationship –
by recognising that employment relationships must be built not only on the implied mutual obligations of trust and confidence, but also on a legislative requirement for good faith behaviour; and

---

21 New Zealand Labour Party *Working Together Labour on Employment Relations* (1999).
22 Erling Rasmussen *Employment Relationships: New Zealand's Employment Relations Act* (Auckland University Press, Auckland, 2004).

(b) by acknowledging and addressing the inherent inequality of bargaining power in employment relationships; and
(c) by promoting collective bargaining; and
(d) by protecting the integrity of individual choice; and
(e) by promoting mediation as the primary problem solving mechanism; and
(f) by reducing the need for judicial intervention; and
(g) to promote observance in New Zealand of the principles underlying International Labour Organisation Convention 87 on Freedom of Association and Convention 98 on the Right to Organise and Bargain Collectively.

The Act was an attempt to provide a better balance between the market forces and the right of unions to bargain collectively. It was a retreat from the neoliberal approach of the ECA but attempted to acknowledge the legitimate role of the market, but not an unconstrained role. It also recognised the reality of the workplace that most workers were no longer protected by collective agreements but were subject to individual contracts of employment. The mechanism of good faith that was intended to provide a better balance was therefore applied to the negotiation of contracts of employment as well as collective agreements. The Act demonstrated the reluctance of government to require an outcome from the negotiations. It was more comfortable in setting the rules and the framework within which the parties themselves reached an agreement.

Although the Act stopped the decline in union membership and collective agreements, it has not greatly increased them either.[23] While union membership increased under the ERA, union density (the proportion of union members in the labour force) has been static at around 17 per cent. Much of the growth has also been in the public sector with private sector union membership clustering in the traditional unionised sectors of manufacturing, transport and storage. The recent Labour Department survey also found that only 15 per cent of the total employed workforce are covered by a collective agreement. Again, most of the agreements are in the public sector or traditional unionised industries in the private sector.

The reasons for this are complex but include the changing nature of the economy; a decline in sectors of traditional union membership such as manufacturing; the large number of small businesses that make organising employees not cost efficient; the rise in human resource capital management[24]

---

23 *The Effect of the Employment Relations Act 2000 on Collective Bargaining* (Department of Labour, New Zealand, 2009).
24 Alan Geare, Fiona Edgar and Ian McAndrew "Employment Relations: Ideology and HRM Practice" (2006) 17 IJHRM 7 at 1190–1208.

with its emphasis on employee identification with the enterprise; and the slow recovery of unions to adapt to the new business environment. The growth of insecure or precarious employment has also become an increasing factor in the decline of union membership and the designation of employees as legally dependent or independent contractors, which made these employees ineligible for collective bargaining.

Although the attempts to promote collective bargaining met with limited success, the government was active in developing the emerging role for government in employment relations, namely, legislating for a minimum code of employment standards to protect the interests of employees. It embarked on a programme of strengthening the Health & Safety in Employment Act, the Holidays Act, the Paid Parental Leave and Employment Act 2004, the Human Rights Amendment Act 2001 establishing an Equal Employment Opportunities Commissioner, the Employment Relations (Rest Breaks, Infant Feeding & Other Matters) Amendment Act 2008, and the Employment Relations (Flexible Working Arrangements) Amendment Act 2007. Regular reviews were also made to increase the minimum wage. Policy work was also undertaken on Pay Equity, work/life balance, and Partnership for Quality arrangements in the public sector. While the government was reluctant to directly intervene in the employment relationship, it was comfortable with creating a regulatory environment and with ordering inquiries or investigations on matters of concern, for example, the Ministerial Inquiry into Tranz Rail Occupational Safety & Health 2000, an Inquiry into Hazardous Substances in the Workplace and the Public Advisory Group on Restructuring and Redundancy 2007.

The change of government in 2008 was not accompanied by the rhetoric of major employment relations statutory change. The manifesto-foreshadowed changes were designed to further undermine collective bargaining – restricting the right for unions to meet employees in the workplace, and removing the monopoly unions had on the right to negotiate a collective agreement.[25] Since the National-led government was elected in 2008 there have been seven Amendments to the ERA. The first Amendment in 2008 introduced the 90-day rule, whereby employees were denied access to the personal grievance procedure if they were dismissed. This Amendment was followed by several other Amendments that were enacted to provide employers with further flexibility in the employment conditions they offered employees, for example, the need for employees to negotiate their rest breaks. New restrictions on the right to strike and lockout during collective bargaining placed further constraints on the collective bargaining process.[26]

---

25 *National Party Policy* 2008 (New Zealand National Party, 2008).
26 Margaret Wilson "Strike Ballots: The New Zealand experience" (2016) 29 AJLL at 194–209.

The current government policy is one of gradual and significant changes to the ERA that have undermined the legal status of both collective bargaining and individual employment rights. There is some evidence that there may be a retreat from the minimum employment standards statutory code, but a clearer picture of the government's policy will emerge after the current policy work on the Holidays Act. The lack of radical change to the statutory framework has been interpreted by some as a new consensus achieved in employment relations. If this is the case, then that new consensus centres on a declining role for unions and collective agreements. It may be too early to draw a firm conclusion.

Conclusion

The evolution of New Zealand's employment relations statutory framework has resulted in the government still having a substantial role in the employment relationship, but the nature of that relationship has changed. It has now assumed the responsibility of maintaining a code of minimum standards. The strengthening of a statutory minimum code of employment rights may be a cause or an effect of the decline in collective bargaining. What we may be witnessing is the reinvention of the role of the state in the regulation of employment relations. Although governments have continued to provide for the notion of collective bargaining in the statutory framework, in reality collective bargaining has become confined to the public sector and traditionally unionised private sector industries. Whether the decline in collective bargaining has stabilised may depend on the union movement to attract members and on its ability to devise new bargaining strategies. The current financial and economic conditions may provide the union movement with some opportunities as employees seek the protection of the collective and employers seek stability in an uncertain business environment.

Whatever may be the trend in unionised collective bargaining, there will be opportunities for the union movement to develop collective strategies to engage governments on behalf of employees for the protection and furthering of the codes of employment standards. The mobilisation of individual employees' support for statutory change will require unions to rethink their organising strategies. The union movement has always engaged with governments and state agencies on behalf of workers and employees, so the extension of this role to the working community as a whole would be a natural evolution of their traditional role. It would also be a role that would reassert the role of unions in civil society as a protector and activist in pursuit of the rights of citizens in a democratic society. Unions in New Zealand in the 1880s, 1890s and the 1930s were in the forefront of the struggle for individuals to participate in democratic decision-making. Although their role has been confined to the workplace through statutory controls, as those controls have been relaxed, there is now an opportunity for unions to reinvent their role. That role may be more political than in the past, but that is also appropriate as the effects of neoliberalism on political process and institutions is beginning to be better understood.

New Zealand has always been and remains a country of small employers. This reality has meant that collective bargaining has always been a somewhat crude instrument through which to negotiate wages and conditions of employment. The development of ruling rate agreements in the 1960s was a response to changing market conditions. Today the challenges come from globalisation and the increasing use of technology and artificial intelligence in the workplace. The growth of dependent and independent contractor arrangements to avoid the legal incidents attached to the employment contract is also likely to prove a greater challenge to devising a regulatory framework that reflects both the reality of the labour market and the rights of individual employees.

Reliance on the notion of flexibility or traditional collective bargaining techniques is unlikely to provide an adequate response to either of these challenges. It may be that the time has come for a fundamental rethinking of the values and principles that need to underlie a new regulatory framework. A return to the idea of a public interest as opposed to a sector interest to be incorporated into such a regulatory framework may be worth consideration.

Administering Workplace Relationships: From IR to HR

Jane Bryson

Introduction

This chapter argues that over the last forty years two major drivers underpin fundamental and ongoing change in the administration of workplace relationships. The first is the neoliberal political economy agenda, which emerged in response to the oil shocks and other crises in the 1970s and catalysed a range of consequential changes. These ranged from economic deregulation, and labour market and state sector reform (all in the 1980s and 90s) to the commoditisation of employment, organisations and individuals (in the 1990s and 2000s) as neoliberal policies changed the ideology and approach to workplace relationships. Second, the revolutionary growth in information and communication technologies (ICT), and their ever-expanding capabilities, continues to enable the pervasiveness of these changes.

In New Zealand organisations, neoliberal policies, bolstered by ICT capabilities, established a shift from administering awards to managing employer risk and organisational image. A core element of that shift was the reinvention of personnel management (and industrial relations) as human resource management (and employment relations), notionally a move from a quasi-pluralist to a more unitary approach to workplace relationships.

This chapter presents a brief snapshot of the workplace administration picture of the 1970s and 2016; it then proceeds to discuss in more detail some key features of the transformation including the role of legislation in the changing role of IR to HR; the professionalisation and feminisation of HR; the changing scope of the HR role; and HRM, managing risk and organisational image. This is followed by a brief mention of two features of workplace administration that have not changed greatly in the last 40 years and in conclusion the chapter speculates on the future and the possibility of a pluralist HRM.

Snapshot – Then and Now

In the 1970s the personnel department or staff section administered pay and rations according to national industrial awards – hopefully a fair day's pay for a fair day's work. The work of the personnel officer was labour intensive and included manual recording and processing of work attendance records, time sheets, pay slips, allowances, and apprenticeship and training records. Workers were a necessity to be administered. Trade union density was high in many industries and thus industrial negotiation was a feature of workplace relations. Throughout the 1960s to the 1970s, advances in personnel management were led by the small number of larger organisations in New Zealand with overseas headquarters. These organisations brought with them personnel management systems and expectations, skilled personnel managers and training in personnel and industrial relations matters for line management (Ransom 1966). At this time New Zealand organisations were made up of predominantly smaller workplaces; only large public works projects, a variety of manufacturing enterprises and a growing pulp and paper industry created a local demand for personnel and IR managers.

In 2016 the world is a different place, and so is New Zealand. All is transformed by information and communication technology. It enables communication from anywhere at any time with anyone. It provides access to a world of information and informers. The technology is simultaneously liberating and constraining, permissive and judgmental; it enables good things to happen and it can harm. It changes the type of work we do, and how we do it. It changes how we relate to others and it blurs work and private life, space, time and information (Lam 2016; NZ Law Society 2013; Thornthwaite 2016). In 2016 it is not enough to just do your job. Nowadays the HR department, on behalf of the CEO, wants you to be a totally engaged employee: loyal to the organisation in all your work and private life dealings, committed to exert discretionary effort for the organisation, willing to fulfil the sustainability or corporate social responsibility agenda of the organisation so as to boost its employer brand and social legitimacy. The HR department administer the terms and conditions of your employment which were given to you as part of your individual employment agreement. Although it is an individual agreement, the terms and conditions are generally identical to all your colleagues. Information technology has reduced most manual processing. Wage and salary levels are predominantly determined through (consultant led) benchmarking processes, not negotiation. Trade union density is low, except in the public sector. Leave and training recording may be done online by the line manager or employee. The modern HR department is primarily concerned with managing risk for the employer. Workplace relationships are a liability to be managed. As a result, the emphasis is on HR policy and compliance, on employer reputation, organisational image and the workers' contribution to organisational goals.

From Personnel Management and IR to Human Resource Management and ER

The economic and societal restructuring of the 1980s and 90s was given effect through radical legislative and public policy change outlined in earlier chapters. HRM was an integral part of the US-inspired neoliberal agenda. The core tenet of HRM encompasses the aim to build and improve the performance of workers so that they contribute to positive organisational outcomes. HRM serves the goals of the organisation, and shapes employees to also serve that end.

Theoretically, at least, industrial relations and HRM have been portrayed as representing pluralist and unitarist ideology respectively. The pluralist perspective acknowledges differing interests in workplace relationships, the likelihood of conflict and the need for the State to cater for that to be handled in a balanced manner for all concerned. The unitary perspective rests on "an organisational logic of a unified authority and loyalty structure which legitimates managerial authority" (Kramar and Parry 2014, 402), conflict is seen as unnecessary and all workers should contribute to organisational goals under management direction. Managers deal directly with staff in order to inspire loyalty and build a unified culture. As Geare, Edgar, McAndrew, Harney, Cafferkey and Dundon (2014) observe: "Unitary and pluralist frames are more than style choices; they cut to the heart of how employers view, perceive and approach the management of the employment relationship" (2278). There is no doubt that the Employment Contracts Act 1991 paved the way, indeed encouraged, a more unitary approach to employment relationships.

However, the transformation from personnel management and from IR to HRM was initially led by the state sector in New Zealand in the 1980s. A key plank of state sector reform, the State Sector Act 1988, introduced HRM to the state sector virtually overnight. In an abrupt end to centralised control of many personnel matters in the public service, the Act empowered the (newly labelled) chief executives of government agencies to manage their organisations and, in particular, their employees. The Act also, for the first time, deemed state servants to be subject to the same workplace legislation as the private sector. Importantly, however, the Act also included the requirement to be a 'good employer' (Section 56), an element of the reforms that raised the bar for people management higher than that for the private sector (Bryson and Anderson 2007; Edgar and Geare 2007). Newly labelled state-owned enterprises (SOEs) had led the way in 1986–7 as they were transformed from large government departments to commercially focused businesses. Their focus on organisational restructuring, de-unionisation of the workforce and individualising the employment relationship in order to enable unfettered labour flexibility, and, for some agencies, privatisation, is evidenced in the massive reduction in jobs in SOEs from 84,000 to 22,000 in a ten-year period (1988–1997) (State Services Commission 1998). The drive of 'new public management' was all towards separation of policy from operations and funder from provider functions, letting managers manage, and systems of performance accountability (Boston, Martin, Pallot and Walsh 1996). HR was an important component in the implementation of that model.

Free of centralised personnel policies, each government agency sought to develop their own HR department, usually advised to do so by a consultant. The State sector reforms fuelled a burgeoning in consulting companies providing all manner of HRM advice, organisation review and design, HRM products, training, performance management systems, salary benchmarking, team building, recruitment and selection, and psychometric assessment tools. In an attempt to emulate US-inspired private sector best practice HRM, the public sector, and their eager management consultant advisers, embedded the importation of HRM to the New Zealand organisational landscape.

This public sector transformation was rapidly followed by the deregulation of the labour market and workplace relations, with the introduction of new governing employment legislation for the public and private sector in the form of the Employment Contracts Act 1991 (ECA). The ECA cemented an individualistic approach to employment relations, effectively disenfranchising collective employee voice and the role of trade unions. In the private sector the incidence of collective employment contracts fell from 72 per cent in 1991 to 44 per cent in 1998 (Deeks and Rasmussen 2002). In 2014 only 12 per cent of wage and salary earners in the private sector were unionised, although 59 per cent were unionised in the public sector (Blumenfeld, Ryall and Kiely 2015). This massive decrease in union presence and collective negotiation completed the shift away from personnel and IR management roles to focus on HRM roles emphasising individual employment relationships.

The other key aim of the labour market deregulation agenda was to create flexible labour in order to increase productivity. The dominant approach to work organisation changed consequently to non-standard employment arrangements such as part-time, fixed-term, temp and casual work, which increased significantly in the decade to 2001 (Spoonley, Dupuis and de Bruin 2004). This, too, resonated with best-practice approaches to strategic HRM that organisations were keen to adopt. These non-standard modes of employment enabled numerical and contractual flexibility for the employer, making it easy to dispense with staff. As a result, by the mid-1990s the name change to HRM was more evident (Cleland, Pajo and Toulson 2000), as was a focus on the strategic contribution of HR and the growth of HRM as a profession in New Zealand.

Professionalisation and Feminisation of the HR Role

The last forty years have been marked by massive professionalisation of the HRM workforce. This has taken the form of increased levels of tertiary qualification of HR staff: in 1968 only 13 per cent had tertiary qualifications, whereas by 1997 85 per cent had tertiary qualifications (Cleland et al. 2000). This increase in education levels of HRM staff has been facilitated by an accompanying growth in the student demand for management, employment relations, HRM, organisation and work psychology courses in universities and polytechnics. The shift from Industrial Relations to HRM courses was also due to institutional pressure from university international (US) accreditation agencies such as The Association to Advance Collegiate Schools of Business (AACSB) (Ng and Spooner 2007).

The presentation of HRM as a professional occupation has been created not only by the existence of specialist tertiary education, but also by the development of a professional association, the Human Resource Institute of New Zealand (HRINZ). The Institute of Personnel Management (IPMNZ) had its genesis in the 1950s in Wellington and Auckland, and then as a nationwide sub branch of the NZ Institute of Management in 1969, but broke away as an independent body in 1985. The change of name to HRINZ occurred in 1999, reflecting the move away from personnel management and industrial relations. HRINZ gave its HR practitioner members a collective professional voice to lobby or have input to government policy change in the workplace space; input to the establishment of national standards related to HRM on the national qualifications framework; and the capacity to deliver professional development short courses, professional accreditation, national conferences and regular meetings through its network of branches for cross fertilisation of ideas and issues. Its current membership is in the region of 3,000. Not all HR practitioners are members; the most recent Statistics New Zealand National Census (2013) when analysed by occupational group shows more than 17,000 people in HR-related roles (see Table 1).

Two other consequential trends in the HR profession are important. First, in the 1970s personnel management and industrial relations were male-dominated occupations; the transformation to an HR profession has also heralded a feminisation of the HR occupation. Nowadays HR related roles tend to be around 70 per cent female occupied (see Table 1). The main exception to this trend is the Workplace Relations Adviser role, which is closer to a 50/50 gender split. This particular role includes specialisations such as Trade Union official and union organiser, and notably has suffered a decline in numbers since 2006 along with training and development professionals. In both these cases it is likely that deliberate action to de-unionise the workplace and to reduce training investment have resulted in dissipation of these roles.

Occupation	Male	Female	2013 Total	2006 Total	% change
Human Resource Manager	1,770	2,838	4,614	4,083	13%
Workplace Relations Adviser	330	306	645	684	(5.7%)
Recruitment Consultant	873	1,926	2,808	2,763	1.6%
Human Resource Adviser	792	3,123	3,942	3,231	22%
Training and Development Professional	846	1,176	2,058	2,256	(8.8%)
Human Resources Clerk	87	234	330	315	4.8%
Payroll Clerk	351	2,763	3,132	3,033	3.3%
Grand Totals	5,049 (29%)	12,366 (71%)	17,529	16,365	7.1%

Table 1: People working in HR related occupations in the NZ national census 2013 (and 2006).

These statistics reflect those in both full-time and part-time roles. Not fully represented in these statistics are the many HR consultants and contractors (both self-employed and employed in consultancy organisations), organisational psychologists, and the many employment lawyers and advocates, all of whom provide essential HR services to organisations (Johnson and Mouly 2002; Anderson, Bryson and Sizeland 2013). Overall, the activity of managing workplace relationships has become a significant one in terms of the numbers of people whose occupations are centred on it. The most common activities in which external provision is sought include recruitment and selection, training and development, human resource information systems and legal advice (Johnson and Mouly 2002; Rasmussen, Andersen and Haworth 2010).

Secondly, up until the 1970s there was a skill shortage in personnel management and industrial relations, thus existing staff were appointed with little specialist training but having worked elsewhere in the organisation (Ransom 1966). Now career HR staff are appointed without the benefit of having worked in other parts of the organisation, thus knowledge of the business may be limited, which affects the internal credibility of HRM and the quality of advice (Cooper 2012). Alternatively, staff may come with knowledge of HR from other businesses, which leads to a diffusion of similar practices across organisations, a phenomenon reinforced by use of a small community of HR consultants, employment lawyers and other advisors.

Change in the Scope of the HR Role

The scope of the HR role in practice has changed over the last twenty years; two key themes emerge here. One is whether HR has developed a more strategic role over time, and relatedly what the role of line management is in HR. The other is the tension between a policy and compliance role versus a culture change and organisation development role.

The tasks of personnel management and industrial relations in the 1970s were largely operational or tactical activities administering employment conditions. These tasks have not disappeared, although technology may have alleviated many. However, the focus has shifted to the strategic contribution HR can make to organisational goals through ensuring labour flexibility, and generating employee commitment or the current catch-all of employee engagement. One of the theoretical hallmarks of HRM distinguishing it from personnel management is its strategic nature.

Recent surveys of HRM practice in New Zealand have attended to this question of strategic contribution. In 2000, Cleland et al. (2000) reported that HR professionals in New Zealand organisations were seeking to become business partners that contribute to the success of the organisation, but they questioned the reality of this strategic orientation. Their survey showed very few "believed the HR function was accorded high prestige by the organisation's top managers. In addition, nearly two-thirds of the organisations had no director on the board who was responsible for HR" (Cleland et al. 2000, 155). Thus, it seems that HR was more involved in implementation and administration (Cleland et al. 2000; Hunt and Boxall 1998; Johnson and Mouly 2002). Rasmussen et al. (2010) report on New Zealand results in Cranet 2004, a HRM survey regularly conducted in multiple countries. They note growing awareness of people issues, an increase in influence of HR practitioners on strategic decision making and improved professional status. Formalised HR strategies, however, were less prevalent, and many organisations still had no HR department. Additionally, there was no increase in the percentage of HR managers reported as being part of the senior management team, and they concluded with uncertainty about the actual strategic status of HRM. Kramar and Parry (2014) report on the 2009 Cranet findings for Asia Pacific. They conclude that Australia and New Zealand HR displays increasing elements of the US unitarist model of SHRM, which they characterise as embracing three elements: 1) HR involvement in business strategy, HR partnership with line managers and evaluation of the HR function; 2) management of staff capability through performance management systems, performance based pay and training; and 3) HR facilitating direct relationships with employees via communication and collaboration systems (that is, with no trade union presence). However, they also report evidence of short-term orientation of private-sector business models which are cost driven with low training investment (Kramar and Parry 2014). This finding corroborates the reduction in training and development professional numbers identified in the national census (see Table 1).

Thus, evidence of the strategic orientation and contribution of HR is mixed, likely partially due to the large number of small and medium-sized enterprises (SMEs) in New Zealand. It should be noted that, despite the high number of small enterprises, over 55 per cent of paid employees work in organisations employing more than 50 staff (MBIE 2014). Additionally, evidence from the core public service is also mixed, despite comprising larger organisations with dedicated HR expertise. Administrative services in the core public service, including HR, are benchmarked annually against a range of measures and they show a clear current view on public service HR: "transactional HR activities continue to consume far too much time and takes away from strategic value-adding work" and "HR as a strategic partner . . . requires a repositioning of the profession" (The Treasury 2016, 37).

The complement of the strategic HR orientation is often seen as the devolution of functional HR activities to line management, thus freeing the HR specialist to set and monitor policy and provide advice. Johnson and Mouly (2002) found that devolution of HR to line management was directly related to the size of the organisation. The smaller the organisation the more involved managers were in HR, but this was largely because smaller organisations tended not to have HR staff at all, or very few. Hence as Rasmussen et al. (2010) note there are "doubts about whether devolution and outsourcing may indicate a strategic approach to people management. This cannot be assumed *a priori*" (116). Indeed, it may be a reflection of organisational size, or a lack of expertise in the HR department. More importantly, regardless of devolution of functional activities, HR is dependent on line management to implement its policies and embody the organisations' approach to workplace relationships.

There is no doubt that the advent of an HRM approach in workplaces has seen a shift in emphasis from administration to supporting organisational strategy and managing employer risk. This has taken several forms: standardisation of employment policies and practices in order to be efficient and economical; ensuring functional, numerical and contractual flexibility of labour; a focus on performance management; and a consequential emphasis on organisational culture and change management. The role has clearly emerged as a specialist agent of management focused on the contribution of human resources to organisational goals.

However, since the early 2000s there have been murmurings of a 'crisis of trust in HRM' (Kochan 2004). That crisis has been two-pronged: lack of full confidence in HR from the senior executive on one side and suspicion of HR motives and competence from the workforce on the other. Worker cynicism is the legacy of HR's role in ensuring labour flexibility for the firm whilst also trying to engender loyalty and engagement in the workforce. When HR purports to represent employee interests whilst carefully reducing job security in order to manage employer exposure to financial or legal risk, it becomes clear that the role serves employer interest first and foremost. Consequently, Kochan (2004) has argued that "HR professionals lost any semblance of credibility as a steward of the social contract" (at work) (134). Australian research confirms the tension HR managers experience between serving employee and organisation interests, and the dominance of the HR role as strategic business partner (Brown, Metz, Cregan and Kulik 2009). In New Zealand researchers cite a "consistent erosion of employee rights within the enterprise" (Delaney and Haworth 2016, 200), and surveys confirm employer support for reductions in employment rights (Foster, Rasmussen and Coetzee 2012).

In recent years there has been a move away in some large organisations from the HRM nomenclature. In a random sample (for this chapter) of 15 large New Zealand organisations who publicly list their senior management team on their websites, six refer to HR directors and departments and nine to People and Culture groups, and Chief People Officers. This is clearly an attempt to rebrand HR, maybe to renew trust, or maybe to signal a more strategic orientation towards 'culture' rather than administration.

For much of the 1990s and early 2000s HR in many organisations had a role to play in managing change, both restructuring and downsizing, and culture change. The strategic expression of the HR role may have been largely through these types of change initiatives and organisation development. Both sets of initiatives now travel under the culture umbrella and are epitomised by a focus on employee engagement.

Employee engagement has become something of a totem of the high performing workplace, the pinnacle of HR achievement. The label is ubiquitous, a key part of everyday HRM vocabulary signifying everything from job satisfaction and organisational commitment to some sort of barometer of workplace climate and organisational image. Its appeal lies in this breadth, its focus on performance from a behavioural and an attitudinal perspective, and the set of metrics it offers HR in order to measure the level of employee engagement in the organisation (Arrowsmith and Parker 2013). Metrics have been important in HR's bid to prove their contribution to organisation performance and to be recognised as credible by senior management. One might question the overall value of these popular measures, given that researchers have struggled for over two decades to definitively measure the link between HRM and business performance (Purcell and Kinnie 2008).

HRM, Managing Risk, Flexibility and Organisational Image

HR has had an important role to play in managing risk for employers. Initially, in the phase of economic and labour market deregulation of the 1980s and 90s, HR was focused on managing the financial risk of human capital costs. This entailed ensuring staff were employed on flexible arrangements favourable to the employer, for instance with minimal or no redundancy provisions, or on fixed-term contracts or as independent contractors, or open-ended contracts without overtime. This focus on flexibility to manage costs has continued and an added concern of managing legal liability and potential damage to organisational reputation has increased over the 90s and 2000s. This is due in part to legislative change, and in part to improved mass communication technologies.

The ECA 1991 disempowered trade union representation of groups of employees and effectively individualised the contract of employment and the interactions associated with employment. It also changed processes for resolving disputes between employer and employee. These significantly increased employers' potential exposure to litigation by introducing the right for all employees to take a personal grievance (PG) against the employer, that is, both union and non-union, white and blue collar, managerial and non-managerial. Also, in contrast to other countries the risk is arguably higher in New Zealand because there is no minimum qualification period before one can lodge a PG, and they can be used for disputes whilst one is still employed by the organisation. These provisions and processes were retained in the Employment Relations Act (ERA) 2000 and an obligation to bargain in good faith with trade unions was added. As Rasmussen et al. (2010) note, "Overall, these changes have increased the incentive for employers to implement appropriate HRM systems to avoid costly litigation and adverse media coverage" (106). However, management of this legal risk has been variable. Recent research into employee experiences of grievances under different levels of HRM devolution highlights problems: "the role of HR staff in grievance processes can be ill defined and shows wide variation, causing problems for both line managers and employees" (Walker and Hamilton 2011, 409).

As well as the numeric and contractual flexibility afforded under the ECA, the HR specialist was quick to latch on to the concept of functional flexibility. HR, advised and encouraged by key management consultants, overrode any job demarcations by focusing job descriptions around lists of generic competencies rather than specific tasks and responsibilities. Staff were encouraged to be functionally flexible, that is, to be prepared to work across a variety of tasks, projects and groups. Just as contractors and casuals are key to numeric and contractual flexibility, competencies are key to functional flexibility.

In the decade to 2016, labour flexibility has grown with both temporal and geographical flexibility enabled by technology. The ability to work from home or any other location has proved extremely useful in times of natural disaster, for example, after the Christchurch earthquakes (Donnelly and Proctor-Thomson 2015). Mobile technologies have revolutionised some jobs by enabling not only working at distance, but also instant ordering of product, access to important information and rapid communication of information. However, it has also provided risks and challenges for HRM. Most importantly are potential issues of health and safety of employees whom it is now possible to communicate with about work at any time of the day or night. This runs the risk of allowing no down time, particularly for those in management or specialist roles. It also provides another medium through which miscommunication and conflict can occur. Many HR departments have responded to these risks with email and telework policies, but active management, particularly of the need for downtime, is not apparent. More obvious is the take-up of the ability for organisations to monitor work performance through checking email and internet usage, GPS tracking of mobile devices, and other reporting mechanisms or technologies (Lin 2016; Taylor 2015).

Allied with this growth in ICT enabled flexibility and monitoring has been the rise of social media. It is in this space that further blurring of work and private life has occurred (Lam 2016; NZ Law Society 2013; Thornthwaite 2016). This has had three major impacts on HRM: one has been the need to develop organisational policy on accessing social media sites during working hours if it is not in the course of work; the second has been concerns about the portrayal of the organisation or its employees in social media; and the third has been the enabling of a radical change in recruitment and selection practices.

In the contemporary workplace HRM and marketing have overlapping interests in the image of the organisation, the development of employer brand and the dissemination of that brand. This interest stems from a desire to attract good employees, customers and suppliers, as well as establishing social legitimacy in the public eye (Boxall and Purcell 2008). This legitimacy rests on being perceived as a good employer (Anderson and Bryson 2012). One way in which HR both measures and publicises the quality of the organisation is through entering consultant-driven competitions like IBM's 'Best places to work' in New Zealand, or the EEO Trust Diversity awards, or the NZI Sustainable Business Network awards. The staff surveys these competitions use are a popular way of benchmarking against other employers, stimulating organisational change, measuring the progress of change and being seen in a socially legitimate light. Employer branding on a day-to-day basis happens through organisation websites and social media presence (Facebook, Twitter, LinkedIn, and the like). The challenge for HR can be the social media presence of employees in their private capacity out of the workplace. There have been a small number of employment cases centred on the Facebook posts of employees or former employees who in their capacity as private individuals have commented negatively about the employer or have engaged in behaviour which the employer regards negatively (see Lin, 2015). This could be seen as evidence of the behavioural and attitudinal management of employees by HR extending beyond the work space in a unitarist bid to dispel dissenting views of the organisation.

HR has a particular concern with the career and recruitment content of the organisational website, as these can attract or repel potential employees. Since 2010 the intersection of social media with recruitment activity has increased significantly (LinkedIn Talent Solutions 2016). HR uses social media to publicise job vacancies and potential careers, to maintain relationships with potential employees and former employees, and to find job applicants. Additionally, many recruiters will view job applicants' social media profiles to assess their suitability as an employee, a practice that is shown to be inconsistent and unreliable (van Iddekinge, Lanivich, Roth and Junco 2016). Arguably it is in this social media space that the unitarist face of HRM is clearly in evidence, expecting employees to be loyal to the employer and compliant with managerial authority in all public facing aspects of their lives. Despite the prognostications and encouragement of management consultants for organisations to engage in gathering personal information about employees from social media, the employees of the current and next generation remain sceptical of the need for employers to know about their private lives (Kenny and Foreman 2014).

What Hasn't Changed?

While one can argue there has been significant change in the management of workplace relationships over the last forty years, there are also ways in which there has been very little change.

Others have noted that New Zealand, unlike the United Kingdom, never had a 'welfare' tradition in personnel management, rather it was purely administrative. This is attributed to the small size of many organisations in New Zealand and the fluid lower-skilled nature of the colonial labour market (Ransom 1966). The lack of an industrial welfare tradition continues to haunt New Zealand workplaces, particularly as greater governmental pressure is brought to bear on workplace health and safety following the Royal Commission on the Pike River Coal Mine Tragedy (2012). The Royal Commission's report sparked a concern with health and safety, and the subsequent report of the Independent Taskforce on Workplace Health and Safety (2013) changed legislation for workplaces and established a new monitoring agency, WorkSafe New Zealand. However, as noted by the Taskforce, to embed any meaningful focus on health and safety will require a significant cultural change for many New Zealand employers.

The greatest job growth in the early 2000s was in SMEs (Bryson 2006). Yet most smaller organisations continue, as they always have, without personnel or HRM expertise other than occasional specialist advice contracted as required, and often largely in ignorance of employment obligations or good practice. Massey, Lewis, Cameron, Coetzer and Harris (2006) surveyed the HR practices of New Zealand SMEs and found that the majority use informal, undocumented practices. The larger the organisation, the more likely they were to have formal, documented HR practices. Many of these organisations are beyond the reach of trade unions and HRM specialists. In the academic literature these types of workplace are referred to as 'black holes', as they have neither HR nor IR to inform workplace relations (Guest and Conway 1999). Workers in such organisations are at the mercy of the individual beliefs and quality of their supervisors and employers.

What Next?

The most likely scenario is that workplace relationships and their management will continue along the now well-established path of HR implementing the unitary model focused on individualisation of the employment relationship, various forms of labour flexibility to meet the needs of the business, HR policy and advice to management, and practices to ensure worker compliance and commitment. The concern for employer brand and organisational image will remain vital, and integral to that will be a continuation of the move away from the term 'human resources' to 'people' and 'culture' or 'capability'. Whatever the title, the task is to serve the goals of the organisation.

In the immediate future the recent focus on well-being at work will continue. This well-being trend has its genesis partly at a much broader level in United Nations concerns with social well-being of the populace and attempts by various governments to incorporate measures of social well-being in national statistics.[1] It is also one way in which HR are responding to the New Zealand government's renewed interest in workplace health and safety. Well-being is not health and safety, however, it could be that translated to the workplace this offers hope for a more pluralistic focus on the interests of workers rather than solely those of the employer and shareholders. How much hope is debateable given the method of implementation in most organisations appears to be a paternalistic 'this is good for you' well-being policy, rather than an employee expression of the range of their well-being needs at work. Additionally, these policies tend to place the responsibility for well-being on the individual, for example through managing your own stress levels, making healthy living choices in diet and exercise,

---

1   See http://www.nationalaccountsofwellbeing.org/.

employer sponsored gym memberships and employee assistance programmes. How often do such policies acknowledge HR and employer responsibility for workplace well-being through ensuring good quality, well designed jobs; reducing the incidence of role conflict or ambiguity; effectively managing bullying situations; embedding mechanisms for employee voice and meaningful involvement; and fair living pay rates that are equitable across all levels in the organisation? Not often. Although HR will accept these examples, seldom will they be articulated in the context of employer responsibility for well-being in the workplace. At worst, internationally, employers are moving to using well-being as an excuse to increase surveillance of every aspect of employees' lives (Moore and Piwek 2017).

Over a decade ago, Kochan (2004) opined that "to meet contemporary and future workplace challenges, HRM professionals will need to redefine their role and professional identity to advocate and support a better balance between employer and employee interests at work" (132). However, it seems that the vast majority of organisations only respond to actions which are perceived as either good for business or an unavoidable legal requirement. Notions of organisations having a wider responsibility to society, with a few notable corporate social responsibility exceptions, are few and far between. Hence, it is hardly surprising that in this context notions of HR having any wider responsibility for the social contract in the workplace are seldom raised or applauded.

There is no doubt we are in a world of increasing social and economic inequality, punctuated by the breakdown of alliances and communities, unstable democracies, environmental concerns and unknown work futures. Any one of these factors is difficult, but in combination they create an increasing likelihood of a sense of individual alienation. Hence, there is an even greater need for security, tolerance and pluralism in our workplace dealings. Is this a likely prospect, is there a possibility for pluralist HRM? Two recent pieces of New Zealand research offer some insight. Arrowsmith and Parker (2013) in an organisational case study found that HR adopted an employee advocacy role in order to have effective employee engagement strategies that responded to the issues raised by employees. They argued that this was "something different from both the classic pluralism of personnel management (as arbitrator) and the conventional characterisation of HRM as essentially unitarist (management agent)" (Arrowsmith and Parker 2013, 2708). Rather, they styled it as a neo-pluralist approach focused on mutual gains through genuine prioritising of employee concerns. However, given this was an organisation that worked in partnership with its employees' trade union, they were uncertain of the viability of such an approach in "less collectivised (and perhaps more commercially aggressive) environments" (Arrowsmith and Parker 2013, 2708). Geare et al. (2014) surveyed managers and employees, in both New Zealand and Ireland, regarding their workplace values and beliefs.

They found that, relatively speaking, New Zealand managers held moderate pluralist beliefs at societal level and 'soft' moderate unitarist orientation at the workplace level, and that New Zealand employees had a 'soft' moderate pluralist orientation at both societal and workplace level. Hence, they found support for a pluralist undercurrent in HRM in New Zealand.

What this illustrates is the impact of normative pressure in the workplace on the behaviour of management and HR. Despite more pluralist personal orientation, the common management behaviour is more unitarist. This outcome is likely influenced by perceptions of what successful businesses or managers do, the advice of management consultants and other advisors, the business management rhetoric of the day in various media, the economic environment, and the institutional signals expressed through workplace, employment and company legislation. International, and particularly US, large corporate HRM practices will continue to be highly influential as they permeate consultancy trends, popular business media and case-study learning examples. In most cases, HR is unlikely to re-establish the social contract with workers until there is institutional pressure to do so. Legislation is an unequivocal signal of what a society values in the workplace relationship. HR practices and management behaviour give life to that signal.

References

Anderson, G. and Bryson, J. 2012. "The Good Employer: The Image and the Reality." *Victoria University of Wellington Legal Research Papers* 2 (10), 2 VUWRLP 43/2012

Anderson, G., Bryson, J. and Sizeland, J. 2013. "The Interface Between the Law and the Workplace: The Role of Human Resource Managers." Barcelona, Spain: LLRN Conference.

Arrowsmith, J. and Parker, J. 2013. "The Meaning of 'Employee Engagement' for the Values and Roles of the HRM Function." *International Journal of Human Resource Management* 24 (14): 2692–2712.

Blumenfeld, S., Ryall, S. and Kiely, P. 2015. *Employment Agreements: Bargaining Trends & Employment Law Update 2014/2015*. Wellington, New Zealand: Centre for Labour, Employment and Work, Victoria University of Wellington.

Boxall, P. and Purcell, J. 2008. *Strategy and Human Resource Management*, 2nd edition. New York, NY: Palgrave Macmillan.

Boston, J., Martin, J., Pallot, J. and Walsh, P. 1996. *Public Management: The New Zealand Model*. Auckland, New Zealand: Oxford University Press.

Brown, M., Metz, I., Cregan, C. and Kulik, C. 2009. "Irreconcilable Differences? Strategic Human Resource Management and Employee Well-being." *Asia Pacific Journal of Human Resources* 47 (3): 270–294.

Bryson, J. 2006. "HRM in New Zealand." In *Perspectives of Human Resource Management in Asia Pacific*, ed. Nankervis, A., Coffey, J. and Chatterjee, S., 111–142. Melbourne, Australia: Pearson.

Bryson, J. and Anderson, G. 2007. "Reconstructing State Employment in New Zealand." In *Public Sector Employment in the Twenty-first Century*, ed. Pittard, M. and Weeks, P., 253–279. Canberra, Australia: ANU E-press.

Cleland, J., Pajo, K. and Toulson, P. 2000. "Move It or Lose It: An Examination of the Evolving Role of the Human Resource Professional in New Zealand." *International Journal of Human Resource Management* 11 (1): 143–160.

Cooper, K. 2012. "The Business of HRM." In *Human Resource Management in the Workplace*, ed. Bryson, J. and Ryan, R., 257–299. Auckland, New Zealand: Pearson.

Deeks, J. and Rasmussen, E. 2002. *Employment Relations in New Zealand*. Auckland, New Zealand: Prentice-Hall.

Delaney, H. and Haworth, N. 2016. "Battling in a Bleak Environment: The New Zealand Context for Partnership." In *Developing Positive Employment Relations: International Experiences of Labour Management Partnership*, ed. Johnstone, S. and Wilkinson, A., 181–205. Basingstoke, United Kingdom: Palgrave Macmillan.

Donnelly, N. and Proctor-Thomson, S. 2015. "Disrupted Work: Home-based Teleworking (HbTW) in the Aftermath of a Natural Disaster." *New Technology, Work and Employment* 30 (1): 47–61.

Edgar, F. and Geare, A. 2007. "Legislating for Best Practice HRM: The New Zealand Approach." *Public Personnel Management* 36 (3): 103–196.

Foster, B., Rasmussen, E. and Coetzee, D. 2012. "Ideology Versus Reality: New Zealand Employer Attitudes to Legislative Change of Employment Relations." *New Zealand Journal of Employment Relations* 37 (3): 50–64.

Geare, A., Edgar, F., McAndrew, I., Harney, B., Cafferkey, K. and Dundon, T. 2014. "Exploring the Ideological Undercurrents of HRM Workplace Values and Beliefs in Ireland and New Zealand." *International Journal of Human Resource Management* 25 (16): 2275.

Guest, D. and Conway, N. 1999. "Peering into the Black Hole: The Downside of the New Employment Relations in the UK." *British Journal of Industrial Relations* 37 (3): 367–389.

Hunt, J. and Boxall, P. 1998. "Are Top Human Resource Specialists 'Strategic Partners'? Self-perceptions of a Corporate Elite." *International Journal of Human Resource Management* 9: 767–781.

Independent Taskforce on Workplace Health and Safety. 2013. *He Korowai Whakaruruhau: The Report of the Independent Taskforce on Workplace Health and Safety*. Accessed November 10, 2016. www.hstaskforce.govt.nz.

Johnson, E. and Mouly, S. 2002. "The Human Resource Function in New Zealand Organisations: The Cranfield Survey." *New Zealand Journal of Human Resource Management* 2 (1). Accessed September 10, 2016. http://www.nzjhrm.org.nz/Site/Articles/2002.aspx.

Kenny, K. and Foreman, M. 2014. "Nosy Employers Not Welcomed by All." Stuff. Accessed October 10, 2016. http://www.stuff.co.nz/business/better-business/10399708/Nosy-employers-not-welcomed-by-all.

Kochan, T. 2004. "Restoring Trust in the Human Resource Management Profession." *Asia Pacific Journal of Human Resources* 42 (2): 132–146.

Kramar, R. and Parry, E. 2014. "Strategic Human Resource Management in the Asia Pacific Region: Similarities and Differences?" *Asia Pacific Journal of Human Resources* 52 (4): 400–419.

Lam, H. 2016. "Social Media Dilemmas in the Employment Context." *Employee Relations* 38 (3): 420–437.

Lin, T. 2015. "Poor Facebook Behaviour Could Amount to Justified Dismissal in New Zealand." Stuff. Accessed February 10, 2016. http://www.stuff.co.nz/business/industries/74652550/Poor-Facebook-behaviour-could-amount-to-justified-dismissal-in-NZ.

Lin, T. 2016. "Surveillance of Workers Risks Breaching Privacy Laws." Stuff. Accessed February 10, 2016. http://www.stuff.co.nz/business/industries/75839806/Surveillance-of-workers-risks-breaching-privacy-laws.

LinkedIn Talent Solutions. 2015. "Australia and New Zealand Recruiting Trends 2016." LinkedIn. Accessed December 21, 2015 https://business.linkedin.com/content/dam/business/talent-solutions/regional/APAC/grt-2016/GRT16_AustraliaNewZealandRecruiting_102215.pdf.

Massey, C., Lewis, K., Cameron, A., Coetzer, A. and Harris, C. 2006. "It's the People that You Know: A Report on SMEs and their Human Resource Practices." New Zealand Centre for SME Research. Accessed August 9, 2017. http://www.newnzforum.co.nz/massey/fms/sme/businessmeasure/Summary_Report_HR_FINAL.pdf.

MBIE (2014). "Small Businesses in New Zealand: How do they Compare with Larger Firms?" Ministry of Business, Innovation and Employment fact sheet, May 2014.

Moore, P. and Piwek, L. 2017. "Regulating Wellbeing in the Brave New Quantified Workplace." *Employee Relations* 39 (3): 308–316.

New Zealand Law Society. 2013. "Social Media's Legal Criteria." *Law Talk* 812 (16 July). Accessed October 10, 2016. https://www.lawsociety.org.nz/lawtalk/lawtalk-archives/issue-812/social-medias-legal-criteria.

Ng, S. and Spooner, K. 2007. "From IR to HRM: Thank God for AACSB!" *New Zealand Journal of Employment Relations* 32 (2): 69–86.

Purcell, J. and Kinnie, N. 2008. "HRM and Business Performance." In *The Oxford Handbook of Human Resource Management*, ed. Boxall, P., Purcell, J. and Wright, P., 533–551. Oxford, United Kingdom: Oxford University Press.

Ransom, S. W. N. 1966. "Background of Personnel Management." In *Personnel Management in New Zealand*, 3rd edition, ed. Hanley, G., 9–21. Wellington, New Zealand: Sweet & Maxwell.

Rasmussen, E., Andersen, T. and Haworth, N. 2010. "Has the Strategic Role and Professional Status of Human Resource Management Peaked in New Zealand?" *Journal of Industrial Relations* 52: 103–118.

Spoonley, P., Dupuis, A. and de Bruin, A. (eds.) 2004. *Work and Working in Twenty-First Century New Zealand*. Palmerston North, New Zealand: Dunmore.

State Services Commission. 1998. *Public Sector Reform in New Zealand: The Human Resource Dimension*. Wellington, New Zealand: State Services Commission.

Taylor, C. 2015. "Employee Surveillance: What's Legal." HRM New Zealand. Accessed October 7, 2016. http://www.hrmonline.co.nz/news/employee-surveillance-whats-legal-203142.aspx.

The Treasury. 2016. *Administrative and Support Services Benchmarking, 2014/15*. Wellington. Accessed September 24, 2016. http://www.treasury.govt.nz/statesector/performance/bass/benchmarking/2014-15.

Thornthwaite, L. 2016. "Chilling Times: Social Media Policies, Labour Law and Employment Relations." *Asia Pacific Journal of Human Resources* 54 (3): 332–351.

van Iddekinge, C., Lanivich, S., Roth, P. and Junco, E. 2016. "Social Media for Selection? Validity and Adverse Impact Potential of a Facebook-based Assessment." *Journal of Management* 42 (7): 1811–1835.

Walker, B. and Hamilton, R. T. 2011. "Employment Rights Disputes: What is the Role of HR Professionals?" *Asia Pacific Journal of Human Resources* 49 (4): 409–424.

Measuring Transformation

A Brief History of Labour's Share of Income in New Zealand 1939–2016

Bill Rosenberg

Introduction

The share of the income that an economy generates that returns to labour and the owners of capital has long been a subject of interest among labour historians and economists (who term them 'factors of production') as far back as David Ricardo in the early 19th century. It is an important measure of income inequality, because the returns to capital tend to be concentrated in relatively few hands, while labour provides easily the largest source of income for the great majority of households.

Internationally, the analysis of the labour share of income stagnated under the dominance of policies based on neoclassical economics, which considered it had resolved the issues of income share with its assumptions of perfect competition in the labour (as in other) market and an aggregate 'production function' linking quantity and quality of labour and capital to the quantity of production. This approach implied wages and returns to capital were shared according to their marginal productivity. This was provided sustenance by a common assumption (known as Bowley's law) that the labour share of income was essentially fixed and any variations were due to changes in technology, the nature of that change (labour substituting or complementing) and 'imperfections' in the labour market.

However, there are other economic approaches which do not give such decisive weight to productivity in income distribution, view capital in different ways, and give greater emphasis to social context, power relationships and institutions. In fact, labour income shares have fallen across the OECD since the 1980s and this has reawakened interest in the labour income share, with perhaps the most well-known recent analysis internationally that of Thomas Piketty. His best-selling *Capital in the Twenty-first Century* includes an extensive historical analysis of labour's and capital's shares of income across many countries. His view of capital is that the income passing to it is a result of the power of its owners to withhold assets from production. The returns to it are thus determined by the power relationships society is prepared to tolerate. At the very least, most economists would concede that some return to capital is in the form of 'rent' – in this sense, returns to capital that can be extracted because of power (whether market, political or physical), rather than the capacity of productive assets. Not all income to capital is the same. The degree to which incomes to capital are rent rather than returns to production differs according to the economic approach taken, but, with widespread evidence of the power of financial markets and of the ability of wealth-owners to withhold capital, especially with the internationalisation of markets, I take the approach that it is not credible to expect income distribution to be simply determined by productivity.

Piketty's (2014) view was expressed as "In every country the history of inequality is political – and chaotic" (286). His explanations emphasise the effects of war, economic cycles, policies such as privatisation, and "perceptions of social justice and norms of fairness" (286) which lead to government actions such as rises in the minimum wage and supportive changes in labour laws.

It is largely this approach which will be taken in this article. It could be described as an 'institutional approach', in the sense that it puts greater emphasis on the sets of rules and conventions that impact on the economy. But, more broadly than this, it takes into account social changes and values. I show that many of the changes in the labour income share can be easily understood in terms of changes in employment law, patterns of major industrial disputes, government actions and external events that affect returns to New Zealand producers. It is not to dismiss effects due to changes in technology and the nature and intensity of capital utilised in production, but they are not dominant. Analysis of the fall of the labour income share by the International Labour Organisation (for example, International Labour Office 2013), for developed countries finds the fall can be explained by increased financialisation (46 per cent), globalisation (19 per cent), technology (10 per cent) and loss of employee bargaining power, de-unionisation and falling government spending (25 per cent).

This article looks at the history of New Zealand's labour and capital income shares for the period over which sufficient official data are available: since 1939. It focuses largely on changes in the labour share, but that implies complementary changes in the capital income share. It sets the scene with an overview and then describes some existing New Zealand research literature, followed by technical issues that need to be understood. The article then provides a narrative of the changes in terms of changes in the economy, employment regulation and events impacting on the labour income share before concluding.

Overview

The precise details of the different measures will be described below, but to outline the narrative and argument, Figure 1 shows the relationship between labour productivity (measured by GDP per hour worked) and real wages adjusted by employer revenue (the real product wage), which under standard neoclassical assumptions outlined above should follow the same paths.

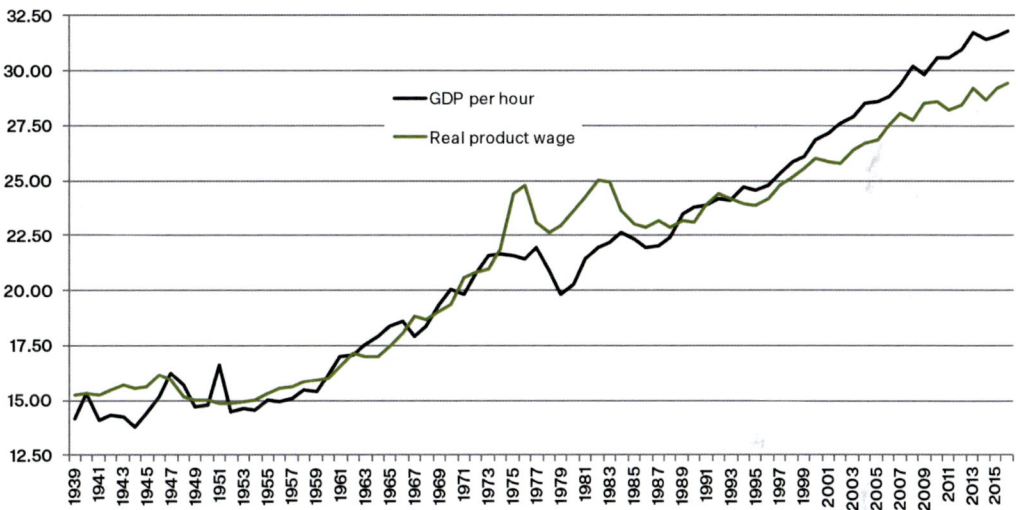

Figure 1.

It shows them tracking closely from 1947, around the end of the highly regulated period during and following the Second World War, to around 1974. An exception was a brief boom in wool prices in the year to March 1951 due to the Korean War. This was a period of highly regulated employment relationships under the Industrial Arbitration and Conciliation system of court-approved awards negotiated between unions and employer associations, and regular general wage orders for pay increases for all workers up to prescribed pay levels. Economic growth was strong, averaging 3.6 per cent per year, and unemployment averaged around 1 per cent.

From the late 1960s unions were losing confidence in the system, leading to increased organising and stoppages to achieve pay settlements outside the arbitration system. There was a one-year breakaway in the year to March 1975 when the real product wage increased by 11 per cent. The real wage again followed the productivity path until the year to March 1984 when a wage freeze reversed the gains made. From about 1992 onwards, the real wage path steadily fell behind

Labour income share if wages had followed labour productivity compared to actual share

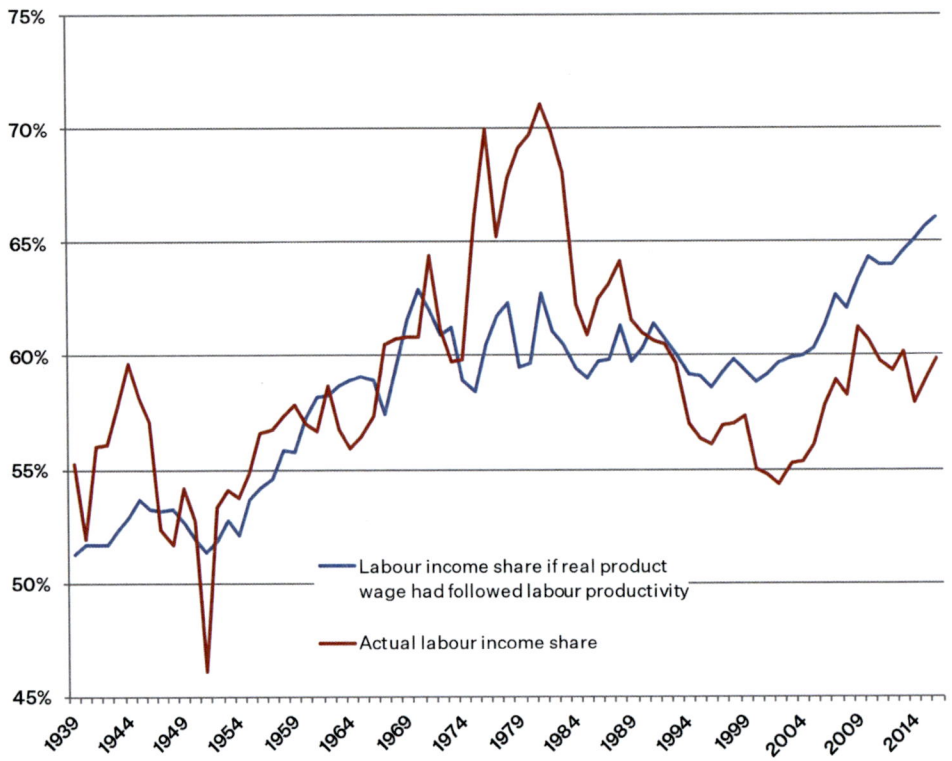

Figure 2.

labour productivity increases in the neoliberal regime which began in 1984, but directly attacked organised labour in 1991 with the Employment Contracts Act, which largely deregulated employment relationships. Its successor regime under the Employment Relations Act 2000 was only slightly more regulated. Ironically it was in a deregulated regime designed to come closest to the neoclassical assumptions where the relationship between wages and productivity most persistently broke down.

The resulting labour income share for wages and salaries can be seen in Figure 2. The actual share rose steadily throughout the period from 1947 to 1974, in large part because of a reducing income share of the self-employed. The 'plateau' in the actual share between 1976 and 1983 corresponds to the sharp increase in the real product wage in the March 1975 year and the precipitate fall in the March 1984 year. After a brief respite in the year to March 1988 following intensive industrial activity (the most worker-days of stoppages in New Zealand's history occurred in 1986) it began a long fall to 2002. A recovery to 2009 under the 2000 legislation is now being reversed.

In contrast, the path the labour income share would have traced if the real product wage had followed labour productivity can be seen in blue. Its slope follows the rising actual share until the early 1970s, then levels out until the early 2000s. It then continues to rise. By 2016 the gap between the theoretical and actual labour income shares was worth approximately $6,000 or 11 per cent on top of the annual income of the average wage and salary earner. It is notable that over the whole period from 1939, the theoretical trend would be an increasing one, largely a result of the shrinking of self-employment.

Previous New Zealand Research

Easton (1983), in his definitive volume *Income Distribution in New Zealand*, devoted a chapter to factor shares of income from 1947 to 1981 (though mainly to 1976). He focused on the share of income of wages and salaries plus the labour (earned) income of the self-employed. This total, sometimes called the adjusted labour income share, represents the total income from labour in the economy.

Easton (1983) found a statistically significant rise in the labour income share between 1947 and 1976. It was dominated by the rise in the share of wages and salaries which rose by 0.44 percentage points a year from around 52 to 66 per cent, while the share of the labour income of the self-employed (calculated using a different method to this paper – see the online appendix) fell by 0.23 percentage points a year from over 18 to under 15 per cent (Easton 1983, 40–42).

Bertram (2000) updated earlier papers on the subject and looked at the period 1962 to 1998 in response to claims that a rising wage and salary income share in the 1970s had led to a "profit squeeze" among companies, reducing their ability to invest to increase productivity and capacity, thereby leading to slower economic growth and unemployment. He found an unequivocal fall in the share of wages and salaries during the post-1984 free market reforms (after Easton's series ends), though no evidence of a specific effect of the Employment Contracts Act (ECA). He found no shift in the income share of corporate profits but a "massive transfer" from local into foreign hands. Self-employed income "suffered a massive squeeze from the early 1960s to the late 1970s" in after-tax terms. Most of the apparent rise in capital's share of income was attributable to rising house prices and hence the imputed rents of home ownership.

More recently, the New Zealand Productivity Commission analysed the labour share in the part of the market economy for which current productivity data exists back to 1978 (Conway, Meehan and Parham 2015). Their main focus was the relationship between productivity and real wages.

The real wage in this context is the nominal wage adjusted (deflated) by the price level that determines employer revenue, sometimes called the 'real product wage'. It represents the wage seen as a cost to the employer. The most readily available index of these prices is the GDP Deflator, which tracks the price level for the whole economy. Evidence in New Zealand (for example, Rosenberg 2010) is that, particularly since the 1990s, real product wages have failed to keep up with labour productivity. The labour share will fall if real product wages fall behind productivity growth.

This is in contrast to the 'real consumption wage', which is the wage adjusted (deflated) by the consumer price index (CPI) and is the most common use of the term 'real wage'. It represents the wage as income to employees, adjusted for their cost of living. In the long run (over decades) the CPI and the GDP Deflator rise at similar rates, but they can be very different in the short run. Bertram and Wells (1983) point out that both forms of the real wage should also take company and personal taxation into account. I do not address this matter here for lack of space, but both they and Easton (1983) find a falling after-tax labour income share.

The Productivity Commission's researchers (Conway et al. 2015) found a fall in the adjusted labour income share of 8.5 percentage points between 1978 and 2010 in the sector of the economy they investigated and that the real product wage grew more slowly (1.7 per cent on average) than labour productivity (2.2 per cent). They noted a fall in the early 1980s due to a price and wage freeze which "proved more a wage freeze than a price freeze" (Conway et al. 2015, 37). Following the neoliberal reforms beginning in 1984, labour productivity rose strongly driven by widespread lay-offs of workers creating a deepening of capital. Initially strong wage growth raised the income share but another fall in the income share occurred in the early 1990s: "Wage restraint following the earlier period of high wage growth and labour shedding and the introduction of the Employment Contracts Act (1991) were possible likely key factors" (Conway et al. 2015, 38) Compared to Australia, they wrote, "New Zealand's earlier and deeper foray into labour market reform may be an important contributing factor" (38) to the fall in share when Australia's did not despite extensive structural economic changes. Another fall in the early 2000s was due to wages not keeping up with product price inflation.

Bridgman and Greenaway-McGrevy (2016) analysed the fall in labour share between the mid-1980s and mid-1990s from the point of view of the neoliberal reforms of the period. They found a steep decline in the labour share of the state-owned part of the market sector of the economy (that part subject to commercial pricing) as a result of commercialisation. They concluded that this accounted for almost all the decline in labour share over this period. The labour share in the subsector fell from 57 per cent in 1984 to 36 per cent in 1994 according to my own calculations (though it had been falling before 1984 and continued to fall until 2000). However, they did not explain why the labour share also fell sharply during the same period in the private part of the market sector.

Methodology

There are a number of challenges to integrating several statistical series over a period of almost 80 years since 1939, and these need to be borne in mind in interpreting the results. The various series do show very similar trends where they overlap. It is therefore assumed that while the different statistical methods used over the years may lead to different *levels* of aggregates, *changes* from year to year will be similar, so linking series together on that basis is valid. The details are described in a separate online appendix. I simply deal with some essentials here.

The modern use of National Accounts emphasises Gross Domestic Product (GDP), a measure of production. The income derived from that production is measured as Gross Domestic Income (GDI), which is the most frequently used denominator used for calculating income shares. It is before the deduction of consumption of fixed capital ('Gross'). This is provision for wearing out, obsolescence and damage to assets, similar to but wider than depreciation. GDI includes net payments made to overseas residents ('Domestic'). Given that provision is required to replace worn out, obsolete or damaged assets before an economic profit can be made, the economically appropriate aggregate for calculating the labour share is after consumption of fixed capital has been deducted from Operating Surplus (the income to capital). This is Net Domestic Income (NDI), and unless otherwise stated all income shares will be as a percentage of NDI. Certain indirect taxes (GST, tariffs on imports and stamp duties) are not able to be attributed to industries or income shares, but affect market prices. Without them, prices are referred to as 'factor prices' and all components of NDI will be at factor prices (calculating income shares factor prices is equivalent to sharing the above taxes proportionately between labour and capital income).

Total wage and salary income, plus other employer costs of employment such as superannuation and accident compensation (ACC) contributions, is called Compensation of Employees (COE) in the national accounts. The labour income share is COE as a proportion of NDI. It is often adjusted to take into account the labour of the self-employed. However, their labour income is rarely explicit. There are various methods that are used to impute it and I use one favoured by Piketty (2014) and Inklaar and Timmer (2013), two economists responsible for the widely used Penn World Tables. This apportions total self-employed income ('mixed income') into labour and capital income in the same ratio as the rest of the economy. I will use the terminology that the wage and salary income share is the 'labour income share'; while including the labour of the self-employed it is the 'adjusted labour income share'.

It is worth remembering that farming is the dominant form of self-employment in New Zealand, averaging 55 per cent of self-employment income from 1939 to

1971. The proportion has fallen since then, but it still received an average of 21 per cent since 1987.

A measure of labour productivity is calculated: GDP per hour of labour. This should be regarded as approximate (and small movements should not be over-interpreted), but it tracks other estimates reasonably well, such as GDP per full-time equivalent worker and the official Statistics New Zealand series for the market ('measured') sector from 1996 though rises more slowly than both this and labour productivity in the narrower 'former measured sector'.

The concept of real product wages and real consumption wages have been described in the previous section. Unless otherwise stated, 'wages' will refer to average hourly wages including overtime.

Note that national accounts years are to the end of March, so 2016 is the year from 1 April 2015 to 31 March 2016. It is therefore more influenced by the 2015 calendar year than 2016.

Figure 3 to Figure 7 will be referred to extensively throughout the remainder of this article: the labour income share and adjusted labour share (which includes bars indicating recessions from peak to recovery); the division of NDI into types of income; the path of real average hourly wages both in consumption and product terms alongside labour productivity; union membership and work stoppages as a proportion of employees; and the terms of trade, which have a strong influence on economic activity, prices and corporate and self-employed income. (The terms of trade show the value of imports that can be purchased from a given volume of exports.)

The Progress of the Labour Share

The Second World War and Immediate Aftermath: 1939 to 1951

The first Labour Government, elected in 1935, had embedded and extended the system of industrial conciliation and arbitration that had its beginnings at the end of the 19th century. It introduced a raft of legislation protecting and enhancing working conditions including compulsory union membership, a minimum wage (which by 1946 was for males 76 per cent of the average ordinary time hourly wage, though only 46 per cent for females), paid holidays for all workers, and maximum work hours based on a 40-hour week, backed by a greatly enhanced system of social security, state housing and rent regulation. Rates of pay and conditions for the majority of workers were set in awards determined by the Arbitration Court if bargaining between employee and employer unions did not reach a settlement. The Court could also make general wage orders, an increase in all wages covered by awards. It worked in a tripartite manner jointly with union and employer representatives.

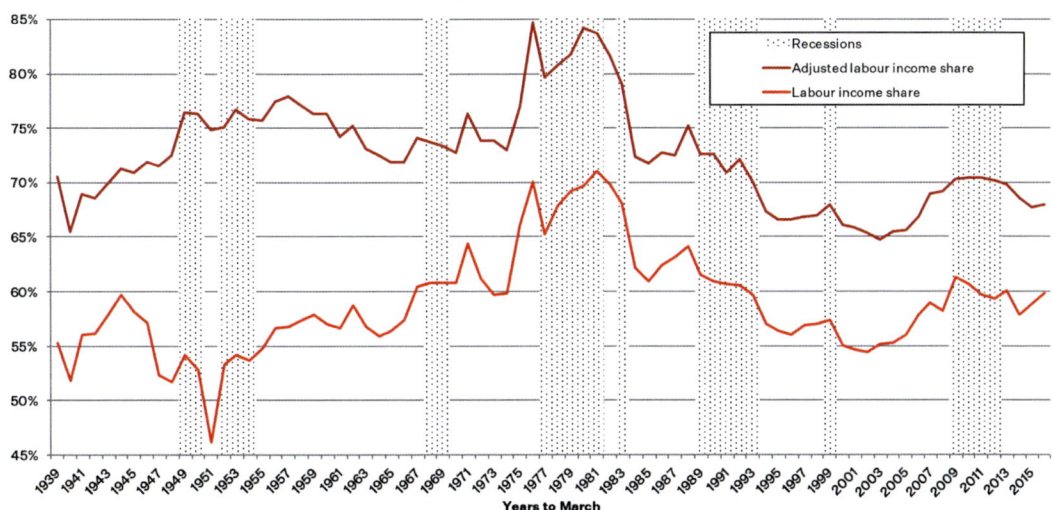

Figure 3.

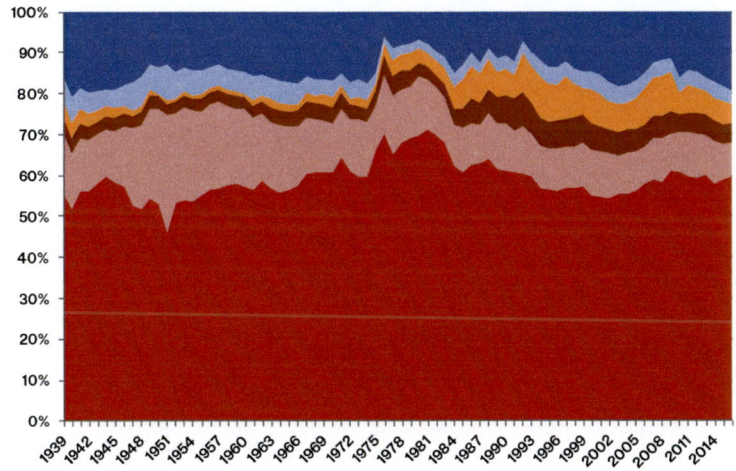

Figure 4.

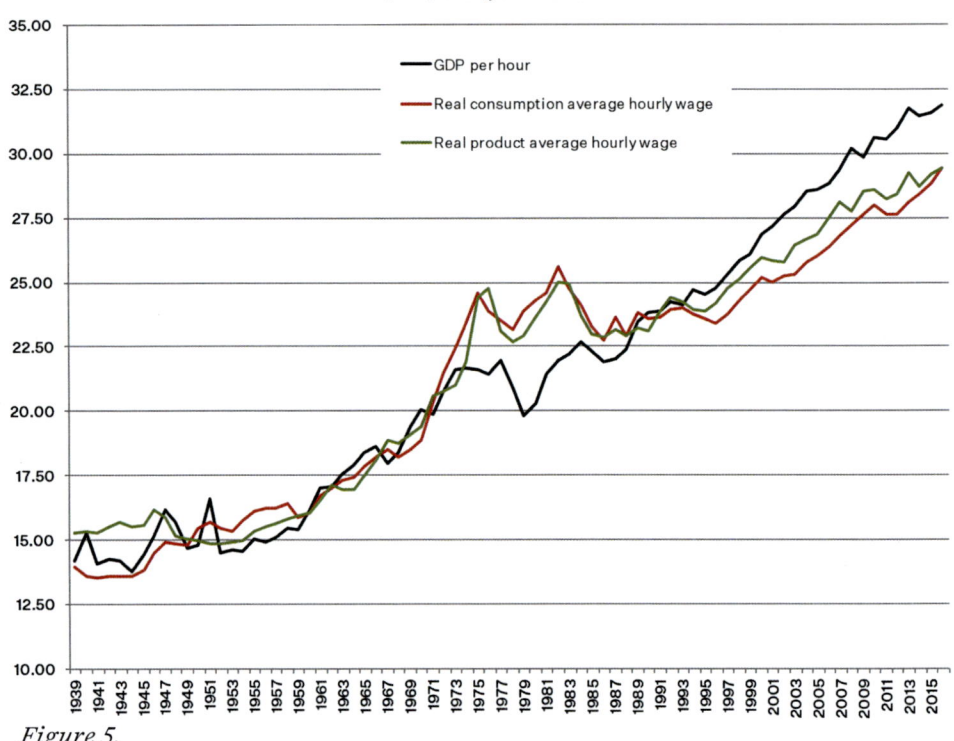

Figure 5.

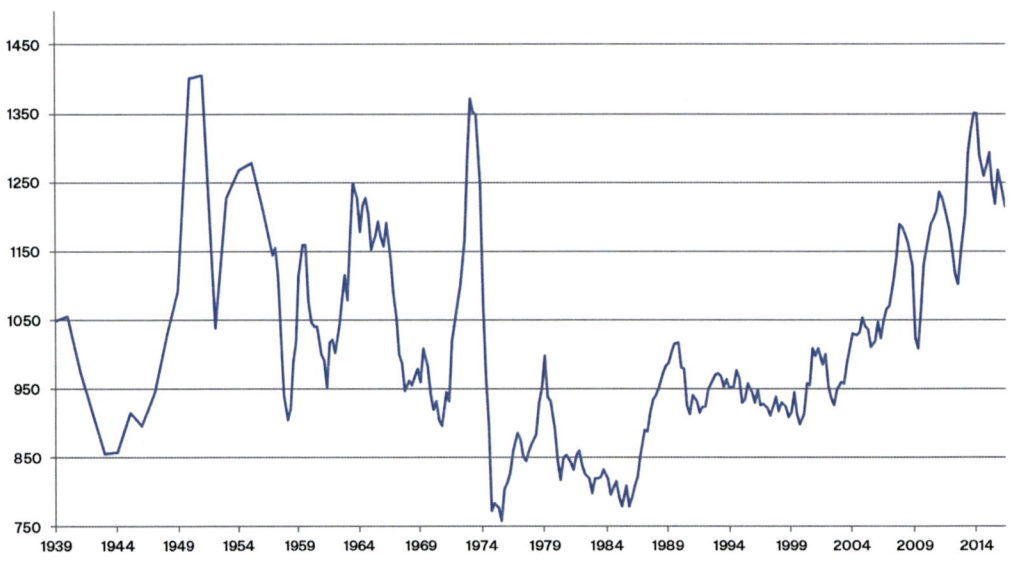

Figure 6.

A Brief History of Labour's Share of Income in New Zealand 1939–2016

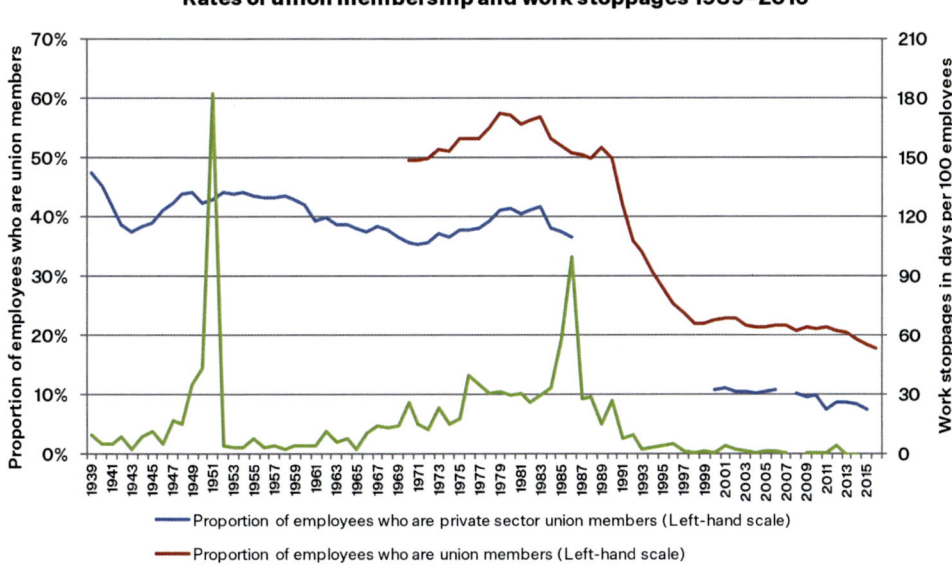

Figure 7. Note that 'work stoppages' include only those classified by the Department of Labour as 'industrial' and for registered unions (which generally excluded public sector unions until 1988). See the technical appendix and Boraman (2016).

Many controls were put on wage settlements and other aspects of working conditions during the war, and there was widespread price control and an additional 'national security tax' on incomes to finance the war activities. These remained in place for varying numbers of years after the war ended. However, wage increases still took place during the war. General wage orders raised all wages in 1940 and 1942, and there was strike action at times. The real consumption wage was flat during the war, but the real product wage was rising. Easton (2010) describes how government authorities avoided wage orders by manipulating the price index, but perhaps the price controls tended to reduce revenue to employers even more, contributing to the increase in the labour share.

The war's most direct effect on the labour income share was the mobilisation of large numbers into the armed forces, creating a peak in 1944 in the wage and salary labour share. According to the national accounts, by the year to March 1944, pay to the armed forces was $117 million, not far from half of the remaining salary and wage payments of $281 million. With mobilisation, men (mainly) moved into the armed forces from unemployment, education and self-employment such as farming. This included enlisted Māori, who were then largely rural and to the extent that they had a subsistence living would have been significantly under-represented in national income (censuses excluded them in labour counts until 1951). In addition, more women were brought into the labour force to replace men as they enlisted. Consistent with a movement from self-employment into the armed forces, the adjusted labour share increased, but, unlike the wage and salary share, remained high as the war ended.

At the end of the war, though prices were still controlled (inflation was negative in the year to December 1946), pressure was building for pay rises. Reductions in wartime subsidies in 1947 and in 1950 following the 1949 election of the Holland National Government added to the pressure, creating annual CPI inflation above 10 per cent. In the year to March 1948, the labour income share fell below its 1940 level. The first post-war recession hit the country from 1948 to the beginning of 1950 (Hall and McDermott 2016). However, registered unemployed numbers barely changed, peaking at a monthly average of 92 in 1949.

Industrial action almost tripled from approximately 100,000 working days lost in each of 1947 and 1948 to 271,500 in 1950 in demands for wage rises. The labour share recovered sharply in the year to March 1949. With general wage orders in June 1950 and February 1951 totalling 15 per cent, by the year to March 1951 real consumption wages had risen 8 per cent above their level at the end of the war (year to March 1946): from $14.47 to $15.68 in June 2016 dollars.

However, the real product wage fell 8 per cent over the same period, reflecting a strong and steady rise in employers' revenue. A contributor was the Korean War, which began in June 1950 and led to a short-lived boom in commodity prices, with wool export prices in 1951 averaging $0.81 per pound, over double the already high $0.38 in 1949 and $0.37 in 1952. The consequent rise in profits benefited the self-employed (mainly farmers): a ravine in the labour income share in the year to March 1951 was due not to falling wages (though real wages were under pressure from 12 per cent inflation) but to windfall profits. The income share of the self-employed went from 30 per cent to 37 per cent to 28 per cent. Indeed, 1951 was the peak income share of the self-employed (see Figure 8).

New Zealand's bitterest industrial dispute began in February 1951, sparked by a clash over how the 15 per cent general wage order would apply to waterside workers. After the workers refused to work overtime, they were locked out by the employers. The long and bitter dispute lasted 151 days until July, with draconian powers taken by the government, intervention of the armed forces and suppression of normal civil liberties. The long stoppage and sympathy strikes by other workers made the lion's share of the 1.16 million working days reported lost in 1951 by the Department of Labour. However, the corresponding loss in wages is difficult to identify in the labour income share for the year to March 1952, which was dominated by resumption to normal profits after the 1950 commodity price boom. In dollars of the day, the loss in wages would have been in the order of $0.5 million (waterside workers on ordinary cargo earned on average a minimum of $1.60 per week at 31 March 1950 and $1.95 per week at 31 March 1952), which was about 0.1 per cent of the country's total wage pay-out for the year and would have been partly balanced by reduced profits.

The Long Boom: 1951–1968

This period until 1967 is what Easton (1997) describes as the "long boom" (88). The recession which began in 1951 was over by 1954 and the average growth in GDP between 1953 and 1967 was a strong 4.4 per cent. Unemployment over this period according to the Census was between 1.0 per cent and 1.4 per cent (slightly higher for women) (Easton 1997, 196). Wages grew steadily in real terms – the real consumption wage rose at an annual rate of 1.4 per cent between 1953 and 1967 (from $15.34 to $18.52 in June 2016 dollars) and the producer wage by 1.7 per cent. The latter closely followed labour productivity growth. Wage rises were helped by a series of general wage orders between 1954 and 1959, totalling a 24 per cent increase. The last, in 1959, followed new Economic Stabilisation Regulations under the Nash Labour Government elected in 1957. Industrial action was at a low for the post-war era under the industrial conciliation and arbitration legislation, averaging less than 40,000 working days lost per year between 1952 and 1965.

The terms of trade were strong over the period, at an average level only reached again since the 2000s. However, as is the fate of a commodity-based export economy, they were very variable. There was a sharp fall in 1957 resulting from a collapse in dairy and wool prices (Easton 1997, 74). This triggered a fall in the labour share of the self-employed, while the share of salaries and wages continued to grow steadily. It is likely to have been boosted by self-employed moving to waged or salaried jobs. The New Zealand Official Yearbooks of this period (for example, 1973) note a tendency during this quarter century (which likely continues) for sole traders or partnerships to convert to company ownership, reducing self-employment.

The fall in the terms of trade bottomed out in June 1958, rising to its previous level by September 1959, but collapsed again. The so-called 'Black Budget' of the Labour Government in response to the fall in farm incomes and rising current account deficit was its death-knell electorally and National returned to Government in 1960 under Prime Minister Holyoake.

The incoming Government had the good fortune of another steep rise in terms of trade from September 1961 and they stayed high until another collapse in September 1966. Three general wage orders between 1962 and 1966 increased wages by a total of 14 per cent, in the face of 20 per cent inflation from April 1959. There was growing unhappiness among workers at the effectiveness of the arbitration system.

As a result, direct bargaining between unions and employers on large sites grew during the 1960s, according to Franks (2009). Between the years to March 1959 and 1967, the real consumption wage rose 17 per cent. Labour shortages "meant that many employers, particularly in the cities, paid higher wages than the minimum rates in Arbitration Court awards. There was growing dissatisfaction with the Court's conservative approach to margins for skill and ruling rates" (Franks 2009).

The labour of the self-employed was particularly important over this period. Its labour income share peaked at 24 per cent of income in the year to March 1950 and then again at 29 per cent due to the Korean War in the year to March 1951. Given that the dominant portion of self-employed were farmers, that is not a surprise with record commodity prices such as wool and meat. Total self-employed income had a share of 30 per cent and 37 per cent in the two years. Those levels have never since been reached: their share has steadily declined (see Figure 8).

There were other influences at work leading to the rise in the wage and salary labour income share. A strong union-led movement forced the Labour Government to pass the Government Service Equal Pay Act in October 1960, requiring equal pay for all female government employees by April 1963. This differential rise in women's wages and salaries is probably barely perceptible in the labour share, but was a precursor of the 1972 Equal Pay Act. It recognised growing participation of women in paid work and growing demands for equal rights and recognition.

Hill (2009) describes a "massive migration" of Māori from rural to urban areas in the third quarter of the 20th century; "By some definitions, more than 80% of Māori eventually ended up living in urban environments – as opposed to less than 10% in 1926" (2). Most will have found jobs as employees, which in itself would not have necessarily raised the labour income share, but to the extent they moved from self-employment with taxable income (such as farming or fishing) their move will have increased the wage and salary share at the expense of the self-employed labour income share.

Finally, there were changes in the structure of the economy. Manufacturing grew from 14 per cent of National Domestic Income in the year to 1940–41 to 20 per cent in 1966–67.

It had a higher labour share than the average 56 per cent for the whole economy, though falling from 72 per cent to 65 per cent over the period. The rise in manufacturing would consequently increase the labour income share. Easton (1997) notes a rise in the proportion of the economy engaged in services, particularly finance, insurance and communications, which typically have a relatively high labour income share, particularly before technology became a large factor. At the same time the GDP share of the self-employed-dominated agriculture sector was falling steeply (according to Easton (1997), from 22 per cent of GDP in 1952–53 to 12 per cent in 1969–70).

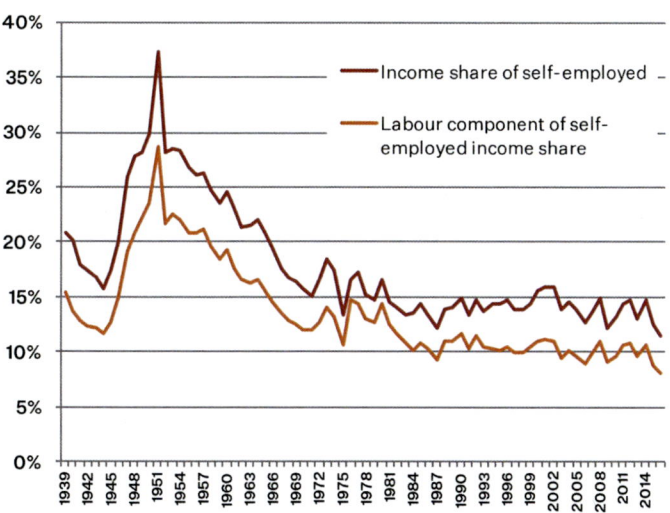

Figure 8

The High Plateau: 1968–1984

The sharp fall in the terms of trade starting in September 1966, again led by a collapse in wool prices, led the Government to introduce counteracting measures in 1967, including a 19.45 per cent devaluation of the New Zealand dollar. CPI inflation, which had from 1960 to 1966 averaged only 2.4 per cent, began to rise: in the 1967 calendar year it was 6.6 per cent, and at the same time the economy was entering its first recession since the early 1950s. The union peak body, the Federation of Labour, applied for a general wage order of 7.6 per cent in March 1968. Under political pressure, the Arbitration Court judge rejected the case and in an unprecedented decision the Court refused to grant any increase, the employer representative voting in favour and the workers' representative against.

The outrage at this 'nil wage order' led to widespread industrial action. FOL President Tom Skinner persuaded the Employers Federation to take a new case to the Court. In what then Minister of Finance Robert Muldoon called an "unholy alliance", the worker and employer representatives on the Court overrode the judge to grant a 5 per cent wage increase in August 1968. While the immediate problem was mitigated, the decision "undermined the credibility of the Arbitration Court and marked the end of its pre-eminence in wage fixing", says Franks (2009). While the industrial protest against the Nil Order was short-lived, it was followed by a wave of industrial action over the next two years, as unions engaged in extensive second-tier bargaining outside the arbitration system. In 1970, the equivalent of 12 per cent of workers were involved in strikes. From the late 1960s to the late 1980s, strike action reached levels that were unprecedented since 1951. It was apparently popular: the number of employees in private sector unions rose 45 per cent from 1968 to its peak in 1982 of 527,797, and 723,000 including the state sector, an estimated 56 percent of employees.

It would be tempting to attribute the sharp rise in the labour income share between the nil wage order and the early 1980s to this breakdown in the Arbitration system and greater activity by workers pursuing better pay and conditions, but if that was the case, the effect was not immediate. The labour income share remained flat between 1968 and 1970, through a recession that began at the start of 1967, to recovery at the end of 1968.

There was only one appreciable break away of the real product wage from the increase in labour productivity before 1974: the March 1971 year when labour productivity fell and the real product wage rose 6 per cent. But the blip was as much due to a further fall that year in the already low terms of trade, which bottomed out in the March 1971 quarter, reducing self-employed incomes and corporate profits in real terms.

By 1972 a rapid recovery in the terms of trade was occurring, raising product prices, particularly for meat and wool. While the real consumption wage rose on average by 10 per cent between the March 1971 and March 1973 years, the real product wage rose only 2 per cent because of rapid increases in product prices: the GDP Deflator rose 26 per cent. As a result, in the March years from 1972 to 1974 the labour share fell lower than the level before the temporary March 1971 peak. Both self-employed (farming) and corporate incomes benefited, each rising from 15 per cent of National Domestic Income in the year to March 1971 to 17 per cent in the 1974 year.

After years of struggle for equal pay for women, the Equal Pay Act was passed in October 1972 by the outgoing Government, requiring equal pay to be reached in five steps by 1978 (brought forward to 1977 by the next Government). The impact of these changes on the labour income share are difficult to determine, but would have contributed to the increase over the implementation period.

A rise in wages was initially helped by the election of the Kirk Labour Government in November 1972. It moved immediately to repeal the previous government's Stabilisation of Remuneration Regulations, bringing a return to the Industrial Conciliation and Arbitration Act 1954 and free collective bargaining. It raised the minimum wage in May 1973 to 58 per cent of the average wage (though only 44 per cent for women), with annual increases while it was in office.

Accelerating wage increases in early 1973, however, led to new Economic Stabilisation Regulations. By the end of the year the Government was confronted by the first oil shock following the October 1973 Yom Kippur War in the Middle East when OPEC oil-producing states raised their crude oil prices by over five times. The consequent collapse in the terms of trade was intensified by a simultaneous fall in the previously booming meat and wool prices (Easton 1997, 159). By 1975 the terms of trade had fallen from its highest level to its lowest level between 1951 and the present. The Economic Stabilisation Regulations were replaced in June 1974 by 'long term wage stabilisation measures' allowing limited collective bargaining. General wage orders were suspended, but restricted general wage adjustments totalling 14 per cent were made from July 1974 and January 1975 with CPI inflation raging at 13 per cent in the March 1975 year.

In all, the real consumption wage rose steeply without break beginning in 1970 and peaking in 1975. In June 2016 dollar terms it rose 30 per cent over that period, from $18.86 in the year to March 1970 to $24.59 in the year to March 1975. The real product wage rose 26 per cent. In the year to March 1975 it rose 11 per cent, easily a record between 1939 and the present. It was this that created the labour income share plateau from the point of view of employers.

If the Kirk Government thought the initial freeing of collective bargaining in 1973 was a mistake which it quickly corrected, that did not show up as a blowout in the labour income share. It initially fell and did not rise until a leap from 60 per cent to 66 per cent in the year to March 1975 and then a peak of 70 per cent in the year to March 1976. The steep rises in the two years to March 1976 were partly due to industrial pressure, as seen in the increasing number of work stoppages and the strong rise in the real consumer wage prior to 1975. But they were also partly due to the fall in commodity prices, loss in profitability due to the huge increase in the price of oil, and the beginning of a five-year recession. CPI inflation reached a record 17.2 per cent in the year to March 1976 and the real consumption wage fell by 2.8 per cent while the real product wage rose by 1.4 per cent.

While the self-employed saw a fall in income share from March 1974 to the following year, it had recovered by the year to March 1976. It was the income share of locally owned corporates that was hit hardest. From 17.4 per cent in the year to March 1974 the corporate income share fell to 15 per cent the following year and then crashed to 6 per cent in the year to March 1976 (from which it recovered only a little before 1982).

Not all of the 9 percentage point 1976 fall in the corporate income share went to wages and salaries, whose share rose from 66 per cent to 70 per cent. Consumption of fixed capital made a permanent increase in that year from 16 per cent to 20 per cent of NDI, due to rocketing replacement values of assets (a 22 per cent increase in the year), effectively subtracting 4 percentage points of NDI from all operating surpluses. This is likely to have affected corporates disproportionately to the extent that they are more highly capitalised than the self-employed. The share of income going to overseas investors (net of relatively small receipts from New Zealand investment overseas) rose by over two-thirds from 1.7 per cent to 2.9 per cent, a permanent increase that continued to rise. With a rapid rise in rents in the middle of house-price boom (15 per cent in the year to March 1976), the income share of the imputed rents of owner-occupied property rose 22 per cent from 3.8 per cent to 4.6 per cent. The fast-rising rents and a housing construction boom (relative to the population, the greatest New Zealand has seen since 1966 (Statistics New Zealand, 2016)) doubtless contributed to the incomes of the self-employed in the housing sector.

The fall in corporate profits coincides with a slowing economy. Hall and McDermott (2016) date the start of a long recession from the third quarter in 1975. GDP did not return to the same level of activity until the June quarter 1981. A fall in company incomes is therefore not unexpected, but the size of the fall is.

The sizeable 9 percentage point fall in corporate income share is very different to Bertram (2000), who found 4.5 percentage points fall in the year to March 1975, which recovered partially the following the year and fully the year after. There are some technical reasons that could at least partly explain this. The difference in years could be because the ONA series which he was using was not on an accrual basis. The ONA made a different, lower allowance for deterioration in asset values than the modern series (depreciation vs consumption of fixed capital) and there was a rapid rise in the latter in the year to March 1976, which could account for almost the entire difference between 9 and 4.5 percentage points fall. The measurement of the corporate sector operating surplus is problematic. Some incorporated firms are 'closely held' companies, which are a form of self-employment. I include those as self-employed in order to recognise the reality of the relationship rather than the form, following Statistics New Zealand's practice. Since both Bertram and I calculate corporate income as a residual in National Domestic Income, it is not equal to the various official series for net corporate operating surplus (which in any case are incomplete). The fall is smaller and shorter lived if income on overseas investment in New Zealand and corporate profits are taken together (though part of this was rising overseas debt, much of it government debt). The difference requires further research.

At any rate, the March 1976 peak in labour income share was again short lived. It fell from 70 per cent to 65 per cent in the year to March 1977 before beginning another rise. In the November 1975 general election, Labour was voted out and National became Government under Prime Minister Robert Muldoon. It introduced a series of further regulations and amendments to Labour's Industrial Relations Act 1973, restraining wage increases other than general wage orders and in late 1976 a price and rent freeze.

CPI inflation was 14 per cent for the year to March 1977 – but the GDP Deflator rose even faster, at 22 per cent, contributing to the fall in labour income share. The real consumption and product wages both fell in that and the two subsequent years. Though industrial action had slowed to an average of 220,000 working days lost per year under the Labour Government, they rose to an average of 400,000 under the National Government.

A recovery in the terms of trade began in 1976 which peaked in June 1979. It was set back by the second oil crisis which began in February 1979 after revolution in Iran and oil prices did not return to pre-crisis levels until the mid-1980s. Wool, meat and dairy prices all fell, and the terms of trade declined until 1986. In the year to March 1981, the labour income share rose to 71 per cent, its highest point.

It then began a precipitate decline. The Government increasingly intervened in disputes under changes to employment legislation, which also weakened compulsory unionism. Wage orders continued but for lower rises than before despite annual CPI inflation at 15 per cent to 16 per cent. But the real consumption wage rose 4.1 per cent in the year to March 1982. Though the self-employed income share continued to fall, the corporate income share continued to rise strongly.

In June 1982, a one-year wage, rent and price freeze was imposed, later extended until February 1984. This was a much more effective wage than price 'freeze'. The CPI still rose 8.3 per cent in the first year of the freeze and 3.5 per cent in the year to March 1984. The average hourly wage rose just 2.8 per cent and 1.9 per cent in those years. In each March year 1983 to 1985 it fell steeply in real consumption and product terms, a total of 9 per cent and 8 per cent respectively. Though the labour income share was already declining in the year to March 1982, the wage freeze extended it to a four-year collapse from 71 per cent to 61 per cent. Apart from a few years of recovery it was the beginning of a long fall.

Neoliberalism: 1984–Present

The Muldoon Government was replaced by a Labour Government under Prime Minister Lange and Finance Minister Douglas in July 1984. It quickly began implementing a radical neoliberal programme, which would have been a surprise to most of the electorate, particularly Labour voters. It removed the wage and price freeze, the New Zealand dollar was floated, domestic and cross-border finance deregulated, subsidies withdrawn from agriculture, import controls removed and tariffs greatly reduced. 'New Public Management' principles were applied to the state sector, with widespread commercialisation and privatisation of state functions. As will be seen, these had a direct effect on employment and income shares. The Government fell in internal acrimony in the 1990 election, to be replaced by the even more right-wing neoliberal National Party.

During its period in office, however, the Lange-Douglas Labour Government made only relatively modest reforms to employment law (for which it was criticised by those on the right who were otherwise enthusiastic about its programme). The Labour Relations Act 1987 strengthened conditions for compulsory union membership, raised to 1,000 the minimum size for unions to be registered (affecting two-thirds of unions according to the 1988–89 Yearbook) which led to a degree of deunionisation, for the first time included State Sector unions on a similar basis and opened up competition between unions for coverage. Automatic links of public sector wages to the private sector were broken. Corporatisation and privatisation of the public sector also made marked contributions to reducing union membership and employment conditions.

The minimum wage, which had fallen to 27 per cent of the average hourly wage in 1984, was increased in December 1985 to 49 per cent of the average wage. Despite annual increases it had fallen to 44 per cent of the average wage by the time the Government had been voted out of office.

Union activity ramped up from 1984 to try to recover lost wages. From around 400,000 days lost per year in stoppages since 1977, there were 756,000 in 1985 and 1,329,000 (the most since the 1951 Waterfront lockout) in 1986. The real consumption wage fell 2 per cent, while the real product wage rose just 1 per cent over the March 1984 to March 1991 period of that Government. The labour share rose from its March 1985 year low of 61 per cent to 64 per cent in the year to March 1988. It was an appreciable rise – a partial recovery from the wage freeze – but well below its 71 per cent peak. The share then began an almost uninterrupted 14-year fall to March 2002.

There was little difference in the behaviour of the adjusted labour share. Farmers over this period lost heavily as a result of the removal of subsidies. Real income per self-employed person fell to a low in 1987 not seen since the late 1940s. As farmers went out of business, and the remainder tended to intensify production, agriculture's share of the self-employed shrank. By occupation, agriculture and fisheries workers fell from 35 per cent of the self-employed in 1991 to 18 per cent in 2011 according to Statistics New Zealand's Household Labour Force Survey, while professionals grew from 5 per cent to 16 per cent and managers, administrators and legislators increased their representation from 11 per cent to 16 per cent.

The terms of trade bottomed out in 1986 and rose until 1990, after which they began a trend of a slow decline until the commodity boom starting in 2000. A share market crash in October 1997 – an almost inevitable result of irrational exuberance following the deregulation of finance – triggered a recession which began that quarter and ran straight into another recession beginning at the end of 1990. The whole recessionary period did not recover until the first quarter of 1993. Easton (2011) calls the period from 1985 to 1995 a ten-year stagnation because output per capita had by 1995 only regained its 1985 level. He describes the recession as self-imposed, beginning at a time of improving terms of trade. He contrasts that to all other medium-term stagnations, which can be attributed to external 'shocks'.

Unemployment rose to 8.9 per cent by the end of the 1984–1990 Labour Government (seasonally adjusted) and then continued to rise to 11.2 per cent in September 1991. It remained above 10 per cent until June 1993 and then fell only slowly, never falling below 6.2 per cent in the 1990s decade. This was easily the highest unemployment seen since the Great Depression of the 1930s: census data show between 0.8 per cent and 1.4 per cent between 1945 and 1971, rising to 2.1 per cent in 1976 and 4.5 per cent in 1981.

The incoming National Government in 1990 wasted no time in making further major changes. Most notably for our purposes it enacted the Employment Contracts Act in May 1991. This deregulated employment relationships, emphasising 'choice' in representation and between individual and collective agreements. Unions, which were mentioned only in transition provisions, became 'bargaining agents' with no different status to lawyers or any other group or individual, and voluntary membership. There was no extension of the benefits of collective bargaining to all workers in an industry as there had been in awards. Individual 'contracts' were encouraged and collective agreements made difficult to obtain. Private sector employers refused to negotiate multi-employer collective agreements, let alone national agreements, and they all but disappeared except in the state sector.

Union membership, which was 52 per cent of employees in 1989 (648,825 people in both private and public sectors), had halved to 25 per cent by 1996 (338,967) and 23 per cent by 2000.

At the same time, the Government made substantial cuts to social security benefits and toughened conditions for receiving them, reducing support for people suffering from the extensive changes, and further undermining wage levels.

It continued the programme of privatisation of public assets and almost complete removal of tariffs and protection of manufacturing. This triggered a continuous decline in manufacturing until the present in share of GDP (from 26 per cent in 1984 to 12 per cent in 2015) and jobs (from 21 per cent in 1989 to 10 per cent in 2016). Its labour income share, averaging 70 per cent over this period, is high and its loss would tend to lower the share for the whole economy (for more detail see Conway et al. 2015, 48).

Real wages largely stagnated between their trough in 1986 and 1996. In the year to March 1986 the real consumption wage was $22.76 in June 2016 dollars and was only 3 per cent higher in the year to March 1996, while the real product average hourly wage rose somewhat more but still only 6 per cent over the decade. Real wages then began to rise, but only by 2004 had the real consumption wage returned to its 1982 peak (the real product wage matched its 1982 peak in 1998). Stillman, Le, Gibson, Hyslop, and Maré (2012) find that households increased their work hours to compensate for declining real earnings over this period, over which one of the greatest increases in household income inequality in the OECD occurred (mid-1980s to mid-1990s).

An important aspect of capital deepening during this period has been pointed out by Bridgman and Greenaway-McGrevy (2016). They argue that "the decline [in labour share] from the mid-1980s onwards is due to public sector reforms. Corporatisation re-oriented the public trading enterprises away from a broad range of social and trading objectives towards generating profits" (22). The point of their argument can be seen clearly in the path of the labour income share for the publicly owned market sector, seen in Figure 9a. The labour share, which first fell with the rest of the economy from 1982, crashed between 1989 when it was at 55 per cent to 2000 when it was at only 32 per cent. It recovered a little with a change of government, but remained around 40 per cent.

The change from a social to a commercial purpose required these operations to make a commercial rate of profit, increasing the capital share of income, and at the same time they reduced employment and the wages and salaries of employees, a two-fold downward pressure on the labour income share. It is likely that the same effect occurred on privatised operations, but the data is not readily available to quantify this.

Bridgman and Greenaway-McGrevy (2016) assert that this accounts for "most of the decline in aggregate labour share from the mid-1980s onwards" and that "there is a smaller, short-run decline in private sector labour share that is reversed over the long run reforms" (18). However, as Figure 9b shows, the private market sector also experienced a decline only slightly less than (but in the same proportion as) the whole economy, which requires explanation. Privatisation could be part of that explanation. The reversal is only partial and, as will be seen, can be accounted for by other factors and now appears to be declining again. Nevertheless, the point they make is important and reinforces the view that the decline in the labour share was in significant part a result of deliberate political choices.

The Clark Labour-led coalition Government was elected in 1999. It reversed a small number of privatisations but retained most of the commercialised structure.

It replaced the Employment Contracts Act with the Employment Relations Act 2000, which was far from a return to arbitration, compulsory union membership and awards. It is based on good faith relationships and reserves collective bargaining to unions, but has been ineffective in returning to multi-employer collectives. A 2004 amendment, which attempted to make multi-employer collectives more achievable, was largely unsuccessful. Union membership continued to fall as a proportion of employees. The Government raised the minimum wage faster than wages generally between taking office in December 1999, when it was at 40 per cent of the average hourly wage, to 50 per cent of the average hourly wage in its last year in office in 2008.

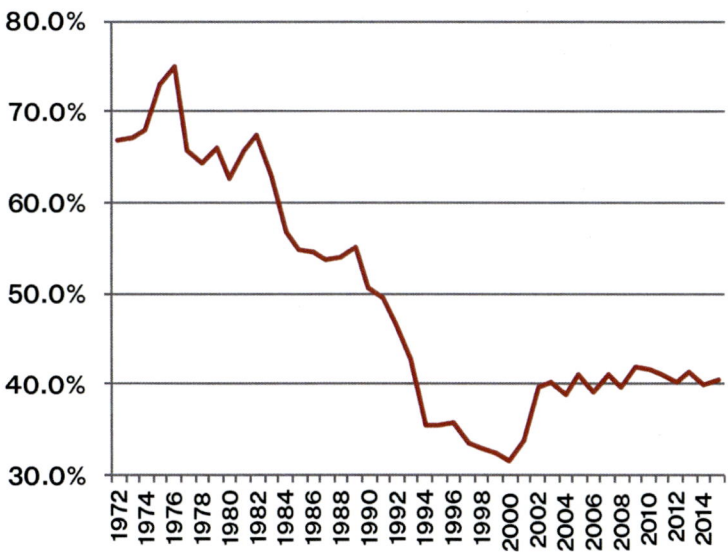

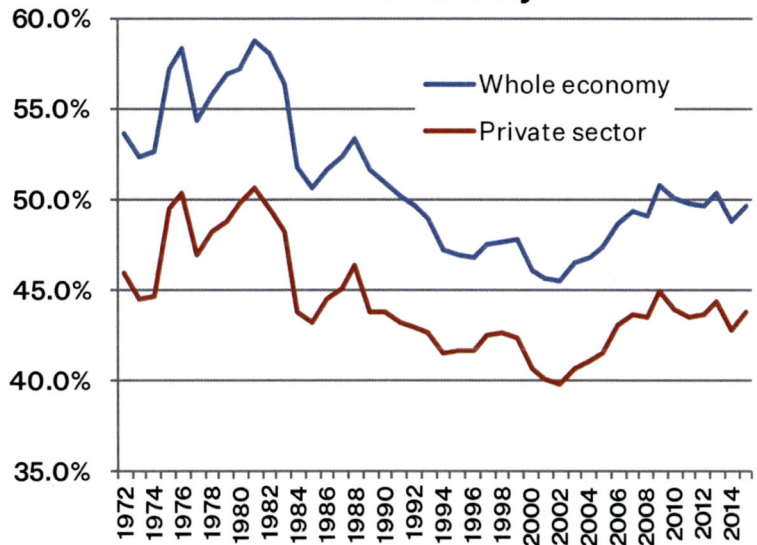

Figures 9a and 9b.

Terms of trade were on a strongly rising trend from 2000. Following the recession caused by the Asian Financial Crisis from mid-1997 to late 1998, there was strong economic growth until the Global Financial Crisis. New Zealand was already in recession from late 2007 due to a drought, but the full recession lasted through to mid-2011 and unemployment was still higher in 2016 than before the recession.

The labour income share bottomed out in the year to March 2002 at 54 per cent, 17 percentage points below its 1981 peak and at a level not seen since 1954. It began to rise, perhaps as a result of industrial campaigns by unions and with the help of the strong rises in the minimum wage. Both consumption and product real wages rose 10 per cent between the March years 2000 and 2009.

A National Party-led Government under Prime Minister John Key and Finance Minister Bill English won the 2008 election. They made a number of amendments to the Employment Relations Act, making collective bargaining more difficult to conclude, and withdrawing the 2004 amendment supporting multi-employer agreements. The minimum wage continued to be reviewed annually, though rising at a slower rate than before (at September 2016 it was 51.2 per cent of the average wage).

The labour income share increased sharply by three percentage points during the Global Financial Crisis, perhaps as a result of declining profits at the outset of the crisis, reaching 61 per cent in the year to March 2009, the level it was last at in 1991. From that point it has declined. In the year to March 2016 it was at 60 per cent. The adjusted labour income share fell below its immediate post-war level of 72 per cent in 1993 and in 2003 was at a record low of 65 per cent. In the year to March 2016 it was at 68 per cent. The self-employed then had their lowest share of income since 1939. The largest beneficiary has been corporate profits, which rose to a 19 per cent share in 2016, a level reached before only in 1940 under wartime conditions (and shaky statistics).

Conclusion

There is much more to the labour share of income, adjusted or not, than capital/labour ratios and shifts in the composition of the economy. These do have their effects, but it is clear from the above that often the biggest drivers are employment relationships, political decisions and balances of power. As Piketty emphasises, the relationship between capital and labour, and their relative incomes, is a social one, not just a mechanical one. There is therefore no 'natural' level of the labour income share, adjusted or not. It reflects those social and power relationships. Bertram (2000) takes the approach of provisional acceptance of the Ricardian hypothesis that in a growing economy not settled into a stationary state there is a degree of indeterminacy in the relative shares of labour and capital in the product, over a range bounded by the "subsistence wage rate" and the zero-investment threshold rate of return (3).

The view that the high plateau in the labour income share of the late 1970s and early 1980s was too high should be evaluated in this light. Perhaps it did squeeze corporate profits too much – it is not possible to know without examining their rates of return – but other factors contributed to that and the labour income share was not at a level unusual in other advanced economies. According to data from the European Commission's AMECO database,[1] New Zealand's labour income share of Gross Domestic Income has historically been somewhat lower than the median of other OECD members, but it has been dramatically lower since the 1980s. Virtually all followed a similar trajectory upwards in the late 1970s, but New Zealand fell much further after that period (see Figure 10). In this sense, New Zealand is now a low-wage economy.

Denmark, a country with similar agricultural background to New Zealand but very different employment relationships and institutions since the 1990s, and greatly reduced dependence on agriculture, has a labour income share 10–14 percentage points higher than New Zealand's – higher than New Zealand's peak and rising – and an adjusted share 5–9 percentage points higher. The general increase in labour income share in the OECD in the late 1970s points to external factors such as the oil shocks and 'stagflation' of the time being major causes rather than labour institutions as such. They responded to the impacts, rather than caused them.

The Employment Contracts Act 1991 could be seen as revenge by employers against the labour movement for perceived reduced profits and loss of control during the plateau period (Anderson 1991). It was much more than a rebalancing. As already noted, the fall in the labour income share accelerated after the act was passed. The economic restructuring did not necessitate this, as the counterexample of Australia shows. Aspects of the restructuring itself also reduced the labour income share. It was around this period that official measures show real product wages departed most persistently from productivity growth.

As discussed in relation to Figures 1 and 2, the 'more market' employment laws that have dominated since 1991 appear to have been less effective at tying real wages to productivity than the system of arbitration, conciliation and awards at their most effective in the two decades from 1952. But the circumstances of the introduction of the Employment Contracts Act suggest that this was deliberate, and the Employment Relations Act (particularly with its most recent

---

1   See https://ec.europa.eu/info/business-economy-euro/indicators-statistics/economic-databases/macro-economic-database-ameco_en, November 2016 update. The data from this study is used for New Zealand. The main difference using AMECO data is that it shows a lower labour income share between 1960 and 1972 and lower adjusted income share between 1986 and 2009. It does not have data earlier than 1986 for the adjusted share.

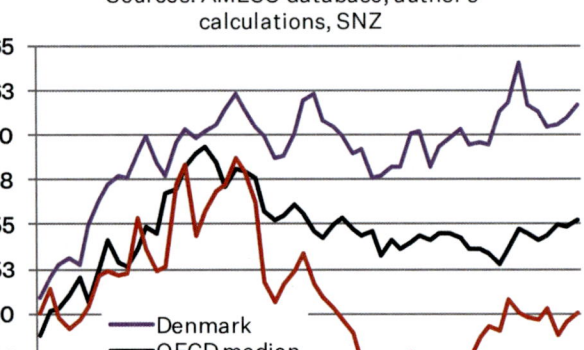

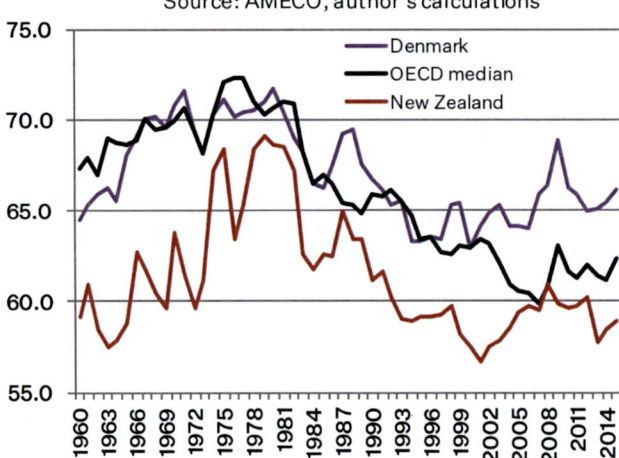

Figures 10a and 10b: New Zealand labour share compared to the OECD and Denmark.

Note that this compares labour income to Gross Domestic Income (GDI) at factor prices, because Net Domestic Income is not available. AMECO adjusts the labour share by the number of self-employed as a proportion of the labour force rather than the mixed income apportioning method used in the above analysis, so this is used for New Zealand in 10b. For New Zealand, at least, this overestimates the labour income of the self-employed (see the technical appendix). AMECO uses the convention that March years are identified as the previous year (for example, the year to March 2016 is identified as 2015).

amendments) has not been up to the task of returning wages to the productivity track.

In retrospect, New Zealand had two forks in the road of employment relations during this period. The first one was after the nil wage order in 1968. While the cooperation between the union and employer parties was remarkable in an attempt to resolve the failure of the arbitration system, the cat was then out of the bag following the loss of faith in the system. Both the then Holyoake National Government and the Kirk/Rowling Labour Government from 1972 to 1975 (admittedly hit by the first oil crisis and Kirk's death) had the opportunity to get it back on track, but resorted to patching the system rather than trying to fix it. It was left to the polarising Muldoon, who was never likely to find a sustainable path forward. While the system lasted for another 20 years, it was ailing.

The second fork was at the time of the radical restructuring of the state and economy post 1984. In other countries such as Denmark the response to the destabilising problems of globalisation and domestic structural change was closer cooperation between unions, employers and government, recognising that this was necessary to retain skills and obtain all three parties' buy-in to the changes. Instead, the New Zealand response was firstly to tinker with the old system under the 1984–1990 Labour Government, and then completely destroy it under the National Government. Its deregulated system ignored the reality of large imbalances in bargaining power between employers and employees, with predictable outcomes.

Perhaps that reflected the polarised relationships that had long been evident. Alongside cuts to welfare benefits and deregulation of the industry training system, this dug New Zealand into a low-wage, low-skill rut with poor productivity performance. The employment laws since that period have failed to provide an environment that fairly shares the income generated by workers and encourages the development of skills and productivity-enhancing management and investment. The labour income share is falling again.

Notes: I would like to acknowledge the very helpful comments on a draft of this chapter from Brian Easton and Geoff Bertram. As usual they bear no responsibility for its content and any errors.

An online appendix explaining technical issues and a data spreadsheet are available at *https://www.researchgate.net/publication/317868928_A_brief_history_of_labour%27s_share_of_income_in_New_Zealand_1939-2016.*

References

Anderson, G. 1991. "The Employment Contracts Act 1991: An Employers' Charter?" *New Zealand Journal of Industrial Relations* 16: 127–142. Accessed August 8, 2017. https://ojs.victoria.ac.nz/nzjir/article/viewFile/3104/2759.
Bertram, G. 2000. "The Factor Shares Debate: An Update." Presented at the Ninth Conference on Labour, Employment and Work. Wellington, New Zealand.
Bertram, G. and Wells, G. 1983. "The Real Wage Controversy." In *Inflation and Economic*

Adjustment: Proceedings of a Seminar, ed. R. A. Buckle, 68–117. Wellington, New Zealand: Victoria University of Wellington.

Boraman, T. (2016). "Merging politics with economics: Non-industrial and political work stoppage statistics in New Zealand during the long 1970s." New Zealand Journal of Employment Relations, 41: 64–82. Accessed 10 September 2017. http://www.nzjournal.org/NZJER41%281%29.pdf

Bridgman, B. and Greenaway-McGrevy, R. 2016. "The Fall (and Rise) of Labour Share in New Zealand." *New Zealand Economic Papers* 1–22. Accessed August 8, 2017. https://doi.org/10.1080/00779954.2016.1219763.

Conway, P., Meehan, L. and Parham, D. 2015. *Who Benefits from Productivity Growth? The Labour Income Share in New Zealand* (Working Paper No. 2015/1). Wellington, New Zealand: New Zealand Productivity Commission. Accessed August 8, 2017. http://www.productivity.govt.nz/working-paper/who-benefits-from-productivity-growth-the-labour-income-share-in-new-zealand.

Easton, B. 1983. *Income Distribution in New Zealand*. Wellington, New Zealand: New Zealand Institute of Economic Research.

Easton, B. 1997. *In Stormy Seas: The Post-war New Zealand Economy*. Dunedin, New Zealand: University of Otago Press.

Easton, B. 2010. "The Political Economy Of the Consumer Price Index." Presented at the A Research Gathering: Viewing New Zealand's Social, Economic and Political History Through the Eyes of the CPI. Accessed August 8, 2017. http://www.eastonbh.ac.nz/2011/07/the-political-economy-of-the-consumer-price-index/.

Easton, B. 2011. "Five Great Stagnations of the NZ Economy." Presented at the Guest Lecture, Treasury. Wellington, New Zealand. Accessed August 8, 2017. http://www.treasury.govt.nz/publications/media-speeches/guestlectures/easton-jul11.

Franks, P. 2009. "The Nil Wage Order." Labour History Project. Accessed August 8, 2017. http://www.lhp.org.nz/?p=155.

Hall, V. B. and McDermott, C. J. 2016. "Recessions and Recoveries in New Zealand's Post-Second World War Business Cycles." *New Zealand Economic Papers* 50 (3): 261–280. Accessed August 8, 2017. https://doi.org/10.1080/00779954.2015.1129358.

Hill, R. S. 2009. *Māori and the State: Crown-Māori Relations in New Zealand/Aotearoa, 1950–2000*. Wellington, New Zealand: Victoria University Press.

Inklaar, R. and Timmer, M. P. 2013. *Capital, Labor and TFP in PWT8.0*. Groningen, Netherlands: University of Groningen. Accessed August 8, 2017. http://piketty.pse.ens.fr/files/InklaarTimmer13.pdf.

International Labour Office. (2013). *Global Wage Report 2012/13: Wages and Equitable Growth* (Global Wage Reports). Geneva, Switzerland: International Labour Organization. Accessed August 8, 2017. http://www.ilo.org/global/research/global-reports/global-wage-report/2012/WCMS_194843/lang--en/index.htm.

Piketty, T. 2014. *Capital in the Twenty-first Century*. Cambridge, MA: The Belknap Press of Harvard University Press.

Rosenberg, B. 2010. "Real Wages and Productivity in New Zealand." Presented at the 14th Conference on Labour, Employment and Work in New Zealand. Wellington, New Zealand: Industrial Relations Centre, Victoria University of Wellington.

Statistics New Zealand. 2016. "Dwelling Consents, and Population and Dwelling Estimates – Tables." Statistics New Zealand. Accessed August 8, 2017. http://stats.govt.nz/browse_for_stats/industry_sectors/Construction/dwell-consents-popln-and-dwelling-estimates-tables.aspx.

Stillman, S., Le, T., Gibson, J., Hyslop, D. and Maré, D. C. 2012. *The Relationship Between Individual Labour Market Outcomes, Household Income and Expenditure, and Inequality and Poverty in New Zealand from 1983 to 2003* (Working Paper No. 12-02) (p. 78). Wellington, New Zealand: Motu Economic and Public Policy Research. Accessed August 8, 2017. http://motu.nz/our-work/population-and-labour/firm-performance-and-labour-dynamics/the-relationship-between-individual-labour-market-outcomes-household-income-and-expenditure-and-inequality-and-poverty-in-new-zealand-from-1983-to-2003/.

Collective Bargaining Across Four Decades: Lessons from CLEW's Collective Agreement Database

Stephen Blumenfeld and Noelle Donnelly

Introduction

Collective bargaining, the outcome of which is a collective agreement, is a voluntary process used by employers, workers and their organisations to determine wages, hours and other terms and conditions of employment. Enshrined in international labour law and reinforced through International Labour Organisation (ILO) conventions, collective bargaining has long been regarded as the more efficient and appropriate means of determining wages and conditions of employment. This chapter examines the development of collective bargaining in New Zealand over the past four decades. It focuses largely on the coverage, structure, and scope of collective bargaining since enactment of the Industrial Relations Act (IRA) in 1973.

Much of the data presented derives from the Employment Institutions (EI) Project database of collective employment contracts and agreements, compiled by the Centre for Labour, Employment and Work (CLEW), formerly the Industrial Relations Centre (IRC). The IRC first began gathering data on collective bargaining shortly after enactment of the Employment Contracts Act (ECA) in 1991 as part of the EI Project[1] and has documented changes to New Zealand's industrial relations environment since then. Key juncture points over this timeframe include the enactment of the ECA, which precipitated a dramatic restructuring of collective bargaining and a swift decline in collective bargaining coverage, and the introduction of the Employment Relations Act 2000 (ERA), following which the scope and outcomes of collective bargaining have continued to change.

---

1   Initially supported with funding by the Public Good Science Fund administered by the Foundation for Research Science and Technology (FoRST), CLEW continues to collate data without Government funding today.

The extent to which collective bargaining influences labour markets varies considerably across countries. As Figure 1 indicates, the role and significance of collective bargaining, measured as the percentage of wage and salary workers covered by collective bargaining agreements, has declined considerably in most industrialised countries since the late 1970s and early 1980s. A drop in collective bargaining coverage has occurred, in particular, in countries where collective bargaining has become more decentralised, typically shifting to the enterprise level, even though relatively large numbers of workers may still be covered by multi-employer agreements, most notably in the public sector (Schmitt and Mitukiewicz 2011). Such a description perhaps fits best the labour markets of New Zealand and Australia over the past two decades, as well as that in the UK since the 1970s, albeit with some distinctions. In particular, the trend toward greater individualisation of bargaining and de-collectivisation of the workforce first appeared in the UK in the 1980s. Yet, it was not until the 1990s, during which both countries witnessed a concomitant shift towards less bargaining coordination, that bargaining decentralisation took hold in New Zealand and Australia (Aidt and Tzannatos 2001).

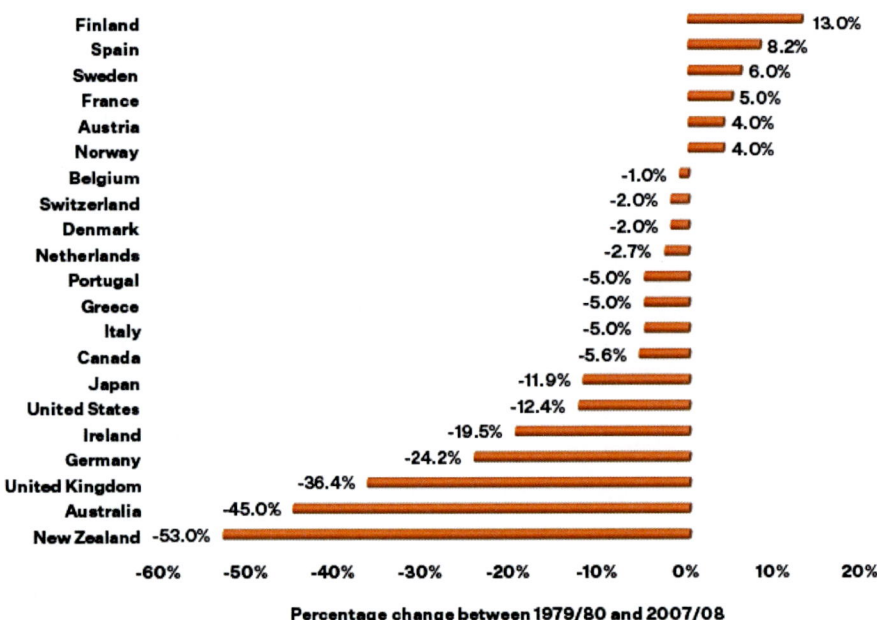

Figure 1: Changes in collective bargaining coverage, selected countries, 1980–2008

Amongst industrialised countries, New Zealand experienced the greatest decline in collective bargaining coverage between the late 1970s and the mid-to-late 2000s – a position that New Zealand held as a consequence of being the only country to have shifted from one of the industrialised world's most regulated labour markets to one of its most deregulated. To that end, the enactment of the ECA transformed industrial relations in New Zealand from the largely interventionist historical arbitration and award model, that was first established almost a century earlier under the Industrial Conciliation and Arbitration (IC&A) Act 1894, to the voluntarist, self-regulatory model that currently exists. Overnight, the ECA extinguished the arbitration system, the effects of which on bargaining coverage have never been reversed. At just over 15 per cent, collective bargaining coverage rates in New Zealand are currently higher than the United States (11.9 per cent) but lower than Japan (17.1 per cent) and Great Britain (29.5 per cent), although the private sector in all of those countries has suffered far greater losses than the public sector in that time.[2] Moreover, as might be expected, given that it is typically the case that trade unions are either the only or the foremost representative of workers at the bargaining table, collective bargaining coverage rates closely mirror union density rates in all of these countries (OECD 2016).

With the enactment of the IRA in 1973, the term 'collective agreement' first appeared in New Zealand's employment legislation, marking a shift away from what were called 'industrial agreements' (Szakats 1976). One consequence of the national awards system, established in 1894 under the IC&A, was that, at the time, none of the social partners had any real experience with collective bargaining (Young, 1976). In addition to this, as with the Labour Relations Act 1997 (LRA) fourteen years later, the IRA retained the three-tier settlement procedure: voluntary settlement, conciliation and arbitration (Harbridge and McCaw 1992). Hence, it was not until the ECA was enacted that the rigid structure of the arbitration and award system was completely dismantled and efforts to affect voluntary collective bargaining took hold (Harbridge and Walsh 1999).

Collective Bargaining Coverage

Collective bargaining coverage reflects the extent to which terms and conditions of employment across establishments, organisations, industries and labour markets are determined by collective agreements. It indicates the relevance of collective self-regulation and, to a certain degree, reflects the power and capacity of unions to influence employment relationships and labour market regulation (Schnabel, Zagelmeyer and Kohaut 2006).

---

2 These coverage rates, as reported to the OECD each year by member countries, are based on total employment, which include wage-and-salary workers as well as self-employed proprietors.

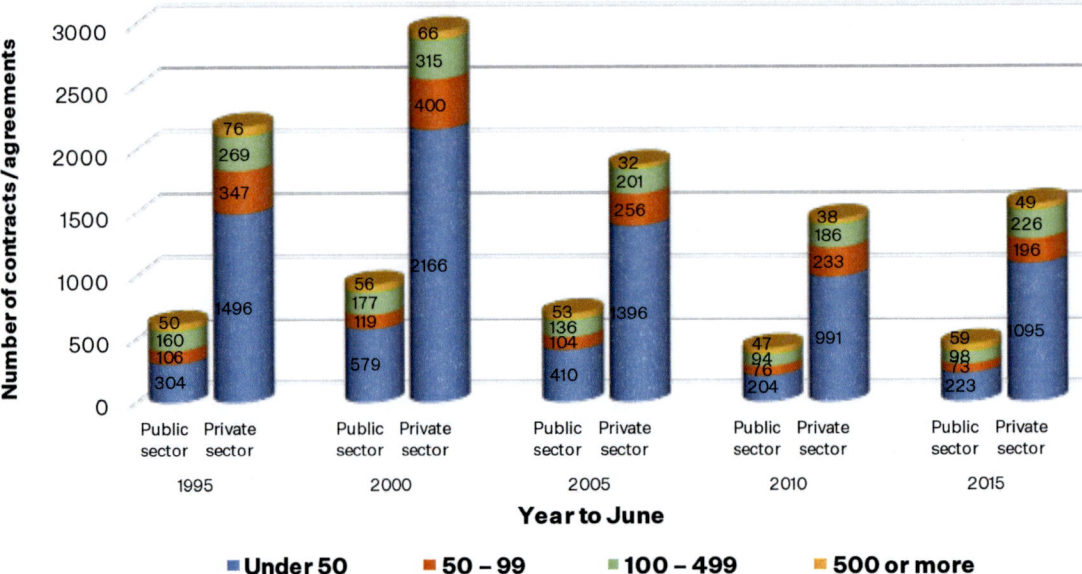

Figure 2: Number of CECs and CEAs by coverage and sector, selected years, 1995–2015

Figure 2 reflects the number of collective agreements, broken down by agreement size and sector, every five years from 1995. In this regard, not much has changed in the previous twenty years. Collective agreements covering 500 or more employees have consistently accounted for around 5 per cent or less of all collectives since 1995. Collective employment contracts (CECs) covering fewer than 50 employees accounted for 64.1 per cent of the total number of CECs in effect in the year to June 1995, while 4.5 per cent of CECs in that year had coverage of 500 or more employees. Despite this, larger coverage collectives – and, where single-employer bargaining is the norm, larger employers – account for the majority of collective bargaining coverage across both private and public sectors, with an increasing share of workers employed on agreements covering 500 or more employees since 1995.

Notwithstanding stability in terms of the breakdown of coverage numbers across CECs and collective employment agreements (CEAs), the total number of collectives present in New Zealand declined by around 28 per cent, from 2808 to 2019, over that twenty-year period from 1995 to 2015. In the last five years of the ECA, though, the number of CECs in any given year grew by nearly 40 per cent – by 50 per cent in the public sector and 35 per cent in the private sector. However, unlike in the private sector, where most CECs were negotiated by trade unions, in the public sector, many of those CECs were settled without a union or unions being party to the agreement, let alone with a union representation in bargaining. Hence, while the number of CEAs in New Zealand has dropped since the end of the ECA era by close to the same extent in both sectors, much of that phenomenon in the private sector – unlike in the public sector – can be attributed to the redefinition of what constitutes a collective – versus an individual – agreement, rather than to any actual decline in the number of collectives settled in that sector. In the five-year period from June 2000 to 2005, the number of agreements fell by a third from 3877 to 2593. Much of the loss occurred in the private sector, where the number of agreements dropped by 36 per cent, while the number of public sector collective agreements fell by just a quarter, bearing in mind that most collectives have always covered workers in the private sector.

With the removal of compulsory unionism in 1991, a process of radical de-collectivisation ensued in the period which immediately followed. In effect, direct bargaining between employers and individual employees was promoted under the ECA. Once the decline of collective bargaining and commensurate shift towards individualised bargaining was triggered by enactment of the ECA, union membership became strictly a matter of individual choice (Foster, Rasmussen, Murrie and Laird 2011). Workers covered by agreements and awards settled prior to the ECA remained under those terms and conditions until their expiry. As a result, the proportion of employees covered by CECs remained relatively high in the first months of the ECA. Nevertheless, collective bargaining coverage soon dwindled. Despite a brief respite, collective representation of bargaining over wages, hours and working conditions declined over a relatively short period of time (Harbridge, Honeybone and Kiely 1994). Between May 1991 and August 1992, the proportion of employees covered by individual employment contracts (IECs) increased from just over a quarter to around half of the waged and salaried workforce (Hector and Hobby 1998). Between mid-1990 and mid-1995 collective bargaining coverage fell by more than 45 per cent, from 721,400 to 394,800, while the total number of jobs increased by 8.5 per cent.

As Figure 3 shows, across the labour force, between 1995 and 2015, the number of workers covered, by CECs under the ECA, and CEAs under the ERA, declined by 15.4 per cent, from 394,800 to 334,100. While the number increased by nearly 20 per cent in the public sector, from 163,100 to 195,000, the number of collectivised workers in the private sector fell by 40 per cent, from 232,000 to 139,100, over this period. Despite this, the number of workers covered by CEAs negotiated has remained relatively static since 2005. For that matter, notwithstanding an upsurge in both sectors at the end of the ECA era, the number of public sector workers covered by a collective agreement has remained relatively steady since 1995, although coverage in the private sector has declined considerably over that time. The number of wage and salary jobs in New Zealand, however, increased by 42.3 per cent, from 1,186,600 to 1,688,300, between 1995 and 2015. Hence, relative collective bargaining coverage – the share of jobs covered by collective bargaining across the overall labour force – declined by 26

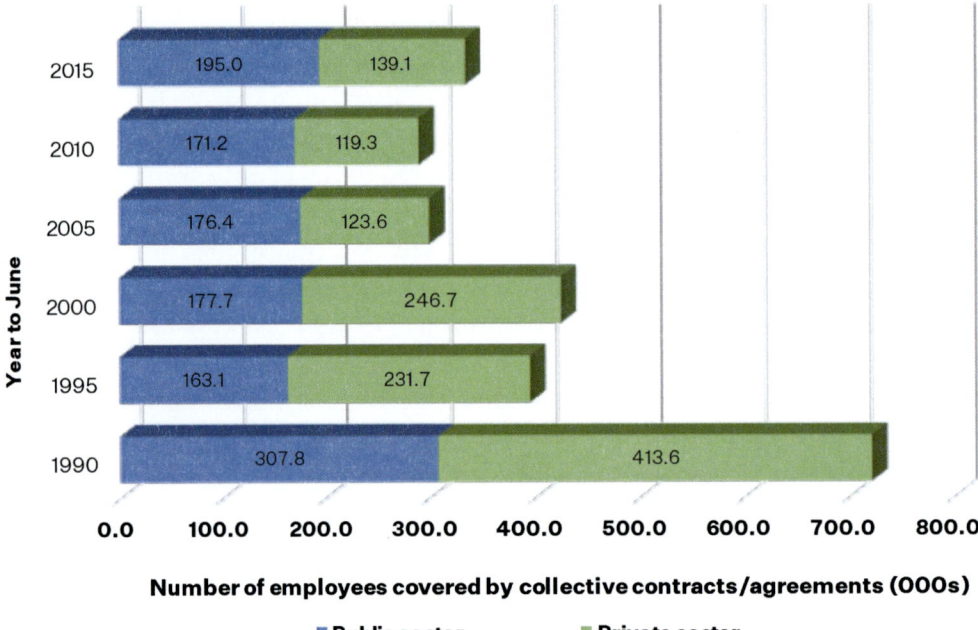

Figure 3: Collective bargaining coverage (000s) by sector, selected years, 1990–2015

per cent over those two decades. Somewhat surprising, though, was the fact that coverage continued to decline throughout the first half of the 2000s, following enactment of the ERA, albeit at a far slower pace than in the first few years of the ECA.

Under the ECA, in both the private and public sectors, the number of workers covered in collective bargaining fell by around half. Significantly, though, the decline in relative collective bargaining coverage since the mid-1990s has occurred almost exclusively in the private sector, where the share of workers covered by a collective agreement fell by 49 per cent in the two decades commencing June 1995. That is, because the number of public sector jobs increased by only 3.8 per cent, from 317,500 to 329,500, the share of the public sector labour force covered by CECs and CEAs actually increased by 5 per cent between 1995 and 2015. Over that same twenty-year period, private sector jobs grew by 56.3 per cent, from 869,100 to 1,358,800. Therefore, despite the fact that a greater number of private sector employees than those in the public sector were covered by CECs during the nine-and-a-half years of the ECA, due to the greater number of private sector employees in the labour force, a larger share of the public sector labour force was covered by collective agreements over that period. It remained the case that, prior to enactment of the ERA in 2000, the majority of those covered by collective agreements were employed in the private sector. This changed, however, by the mid-2000s, when close to three-in-five workers covered by collective agreements were employed in the public sector.

The primary impetus for both this shift, and the decline in collective coverage in the years immediately following the enactment of the ERA, was that a large share of employees covered under private-sector CECs at the end of ECA era, in fact, did not belong to a union. More to the point, under the ECA, a number of what were technically CECs, in that they were signed by more than a single employee, were negotiated by a party other than a union. Nonetheless, while the ECA allowed an employee to choose any organisation or individual to represent them in negotiations for an employment contract, the ERA permitted only registered unions to negotiate collective agreements. Yet, as the data in Figure 4 shows, trade unions continued to be the main representative of employees in collective negotiations throughout the ECA period.[3] A sizeable number of employees (14 per cent overall), though, were unrepresented in contract negotiations at the end of the ECA era. This, nevertheless, was largely a private sector phenomenon, with only 4 per cent of employees in local government and none in central government being unrepresented in contract negotiations in that year (Harbridge, Crawford and Kiely 2000).

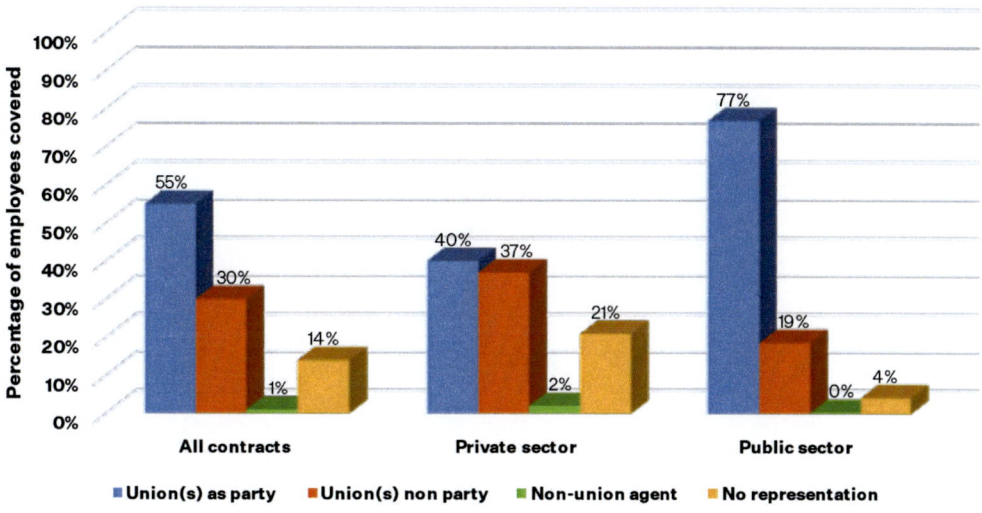

Figure 4: Representation of employees in collective bargaining by sector, year to June 2000

In keeping with developments across most industrialised countries, collective bargaining coverage relative to the size of the labour force declined from the 1990s and, in particular, in the last decade, following the global financial crisis

---

3   Many of those unrepresented employees ultimately became party to an individual employment contract (IEC), hence this data should not be construed as a structural breakdown of collective employment contracts (CECs) settled in the year to June 2000.

(GFC) and subsequent recession. Three years after the introduction of the ECA, the 721,000 workers that were covered by an award or collective in the 1989/90 bargaining round reduced to 370,000 employees, a decline of 49 per cent (Harbridge et al. 1994). Despite this, while most of the decline in bargaining coverage occurred in the first three years of the ERA, the trend from that point onwards was toward less collectivisation of the workforce, after accounting for the concomitant growth in total employment following enactment of the ERA in 2000. Under the ECA, collective bargaining coverage in the private sector slumped from 50 per cent of the workforce in 1990 to under 25 per cent by the time the ECA was repealed (Harbridge, Walsh and Wilkinson 2001).

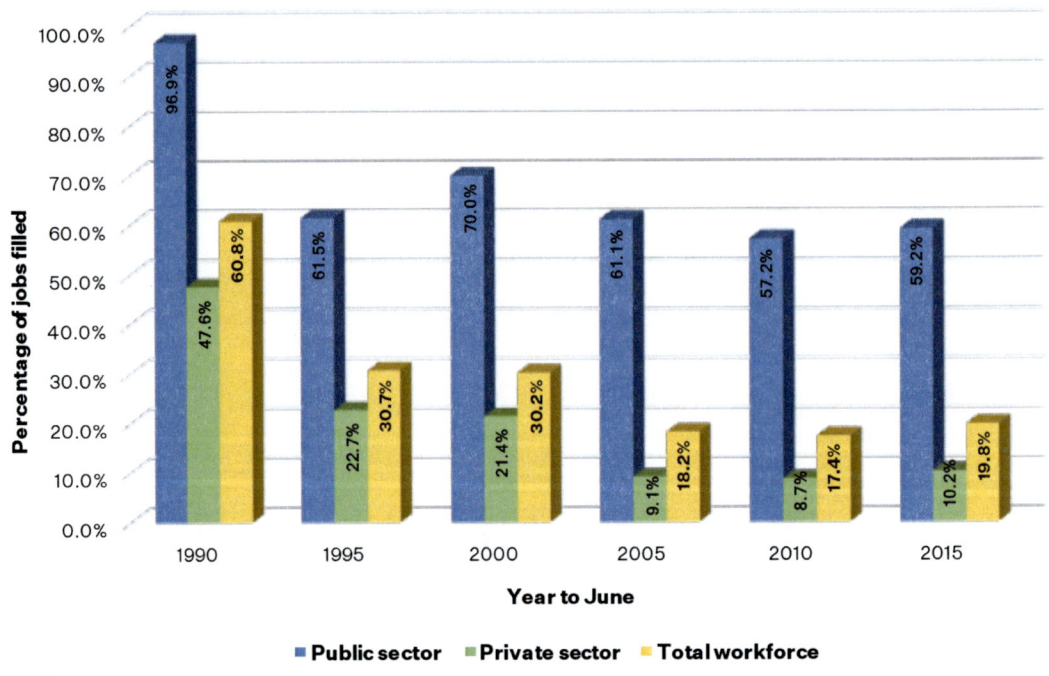

Source: Statistics New Zealand Quarterly Employment Survey, Table: Filled Jobs by Sector by Status in Employment, March quarter, QEX018AA

Figure 5: Share (%) of jobs covered by collective bargaining, selected years, 1990–2015

As can be seen in Figure 5, the share of the workforce covered by collective agreements – regardless of union membership status – dropped from more than three-in-five to just over three-in-ten during the first four years of the ECA. Nonetheless, although the public sector experienced some gains, overall collective bargaining coverage levelled off 30 per cent during the second half of the 1990s.

Finally, the deregulatory environment of the 1990s also produced a growing disparity between public and private sector coverage in New Zealand. That is, at least since the enactment of the ERA, collective bargaining has become effectively a public sector phenomenon. Interesting, though, is the fact that, notwithstanding the ECA, throughout the 1990s, more employees were covered by CEAs in the private sector than in the public sector. The situation changed following the enactment of the ERA – from 2004 onwards more employees in the public sector were covered by CEAs than in the private sector. By 2005, two main features of collective bargaining coverage were discernible: first, most employees were covered by collective agreements of 500 or more employees, within a small number of organisations; and there was a marked difference between the collective bargaining coverage rates in public and private sectors. While unionisation and collective bargaining remained strong across the public sector, coverage and union density in the private sector had dwindled (Blackwood, Feinberg-Danieli, Lafferty and Kiely 2005).

Recent coverage rates point towards, on average, around 30 per cent more collectivised workers located in the public sector than in the private sector. At the same time, only around one in five of the labour force has been employed in the public sector. This points to the conclusion that, notwithstanding the great promise the ERA held for trade unionism and collective bargaining in New Zealand, the share of the workforce whose wages, hours and working conditions were determined through collective bargaining has actually declined from where it stood at the time of its enactment. Yet, despite a dip in the immediate aftermath of the GFC and domestic recession, the proportion of wage and salary jobs held by workers covered by collective agreements has remained relatively constant at just under 20 per cent since the mid-2000s.

To a large extent, the significant drop in private sector coverage by CEAs in the first year following enactment of the ERA in October 2000 is a consequence of large numbers of non-union employees included in CEA coverage under the ECA. Furthermore, one factor explaining the shift in collective bargaining to the public sector and away from the private sector is the relative decline of the manufacturing sector. That is, in terms of its share of both the labour market and overall collective bargaining coverage, manufacturing has greatly declined over the past quarter century. Only one of every six collectivised employees now works in manufacturing.

Among the more noteworthy trends that CLEW has identified since enactment of the ERA, though, is a significant increase in bargaining coverage within some industries. To this end, the total coverage figure of 328,700 employees for the year to June 2016 reflects an increase in collective bargaining coverage of 2.9 per cent in the that year. That shift is due more to the successes of unions in collective bargaining than to the numerous legislative changes aimed at limiting the collective rights of workers enacted by the National-led Government first elected in November 2008. For instance, contributing to increases in bargaining coverage over the past few years is a number of supermarkets who have agreed to the establishment of CEAs, extending both union access and coverage. This, of course, has affected an increase in coverage in the food retail industry, in particular. Nonetheless, overall, there has been a relative stabilisation in both coverage and, for the most part, the content of CEAs in that time. Importantly, although around only one-in-five workers are in the public sector, the majority of workers on CEAs are employed in the public sector. More than half of all employees on CEAs work in three sectors: education and training, health and social services, and government administration and security services. This has been the case for more than a decade now. So too has the fact that the vast majority of workers on multi-employer CEAs are in the public sector, primarily in education and health.

Extension of Coverage

During the 1990s, under the ECA, employers began excluding employees from existing contracts by not providing for the extension of existing contracts to new employees. In response, unions began to negotiate the inclusion of a 'new employees' clause requiring employers to offer new employees the right to join existing contracts. A more common form of discretionary provision was, where parties agree, new employees were added to the contract, whereas other provisions required consent of the employer. This led to a two-tiered employment system as organisations began to hire new employees on lower pay and conditions of employment with many employers refusing to extend contracts to new hires (Harbridge et al. 1994).

From October 2000 new legislative requirements under the ERA required employees on collective agreements to belong to a union. As a result, employees on non-union collectives moved to join existing unions or to form new unions (by 2002 over 140 organisations registered as unions), while some agreements extended their coverage to *all* employees, not just union members. One year after the ERA came into effect, representation of those previously unrepresented was found to fall into two groups: those who joined existing unions, and, those who joined small enterprise-based unions in single sites (Barry and May 2004). The increasing stability of bargaining arrangements led to a growth in contracts providing for automatic extension of terms to new employees. Correspondingly, there was a drop in the proportion of employees covered by settlements without a discretionary extension provision (from 27 per cent to 16 per cent), and an increase in the share of employees on settlements with automatic extension to new employees (Harbridge et al. 2001). The percentage of employees covered by collective settlements where the union was a party to the settlement rose from 55 to 68 per cent by the end of 2002 (Harbridge, Walsh and Thickett 2002).

Under the ERA, the legal enforceability of a CEA extends only to the parties named in its coverage clause. The primary reason why a union member would not be covered by a CEA is that there is no CEA covering the work they perform in their workplace. It is also the case, though, that an increasing proportion of union members are not covered by a CEA. This underscores union concerns that, notwithstanding their members' irritation at the inherent unfairness of collectively negotiated gains benefiting non-dues paying co-workers, 'passing on' these gains is not as significant a barrier to increasing collective bargaining as the substantial number of workplaces where work is simply not covered by any union-negotiated CEA (Department of Labour 2009).

Currently, a collective agreement specifically allows employees who are not members of the union which negotiated that agreement to be covered under the terms and conditions of the collective. Otherwise, new employees and other employees who are not union members are employed under the terms of an independent employment agreement (IEA) negotiated with the employer. The Employment Relations Amendment Act 2014 (entered into force 6 March 2015) removed the requirement first put into effect with enactment of the ERA in 2000 that employers offer new employees at least the same terms and conditions for 30 days as employees doing the same work as those covered by a union, even if the new employee does not belong to a union. Also, when a collective agreement expires or is no longer in force, each existing employee will automatically have an IEA based on the expired CEA. Those employees will also be covered by any additional terms and conditions agreed previously, although the employer and employee can agree to change this IEA.

Bargaining Structure

Under the longstanding arbitration and award system, an industrial agreement was binding on the parties and on every member of any union or association which was a party to that agreement. Accordingly, most bargaining over wages, hours and terms and conditions of employment in New Zealand was conducted, in effect, on a multi-employer basis (Dannin 1995). Following enactment of the IRA, multi-employer bargaining continued to play a significant role in determining wages, hours and working conditions. 'Composite agreements', voluntary multi-union, single plant agreements covering members of more than one union employed in a single establishment or workplace, were also prevalent at that time. In the first two years of that legislation, close to 60 per cent of collective agreements were voluntary, with the remainder being conciliated agreements, typically covering an entire industry or industries in the district in which the application for conciliation was filed. Additionally, while most voluntary collective agreements were determined at the plant or worksite level, the rest covered an entire industry or at least several employers in a district (Szakats 1976).[4]

Because the arbitration and award system was designed to ensure standardised pay and working conditions across the labour market, it operated at a level far removed from most employers and employees, and effectively ignored differences between workplaces. Faced with increasing global competition due to the reduction or removal of trade barriers in a growing number of product markets, government and business interests came to perceive the longstanding system of industrial relations in New Zealand to be incompatible with their goal of enhancing productive efficiency. Those in the Fourth Labour Government who advocated labour market deregulation and scrapping the arbitration system argued that long-established relativities hindered employers' ability to adjust to rapidly changing market conditions (Franks 1994). This resulted in the enactment of the LRA, which was intended to decentralise the structure or the level at which bargaining occurs and remove legal restrictions on the scope or the range of subjects negotiated in collective bargaining. Nonetheless, concerned with the implications of conceding plant-level decision-making power to unions, employers were generally reluctant to expand the subject matter of bargaining following enactment of the LRA (McAndrew 1989). Hence, multi-employer bargaining still accounted for 77 per cent of all employees covered by awards or collective agreements in 1989/90 (Harbridge 1991).

Passage of the ECA marked radical changes to bargaining structures (Harbridge and Crawford 2000). With the enactment of the ECA, multi-employer bargaining was discouraged and strike action in support of multi-employer settlements legally prohibited. In the three years that followed the enactment of the ECA, multi-employer bargaining was effectively replaced by single-employer, enterprise bargaining (McAndrew 1993; Boxall 1993). Multi-employer bargaining declined from 94 per cent of collectives in the private sector to just 2 per cent of all collective contracts, with 60,000 workers covered by multi-employer contracts (Harbridge et al, 1994). Harbridge et al. (2002) suggest, to this end, that the dramatic decline in collective bargaining coverage in the first few years of the ECA was mainly a result of the failure of trade unions to achieve industry-wide, multi-employer bargaining agreements.

By the end of 1994, just over 85 per cent of employees were covered by collective arrangements, with a small number of contracts negotiated by enterprise-based bargaining units. At the end of a decade under the ECA, though, single employer employment contracts (SECAs) accounted for 74 per cent of the share of workers

---

4 Geare (1983) estimates the share of voluntary settlements as a proportion of total settlements between 1975 and 1981 to range from a low of 44 per cent in 1975 to a high of 64 per cent in 1980.

covered by a collective, while multi-employer employment contracts (MECAs) accounted for just 18 per cent of the collectivised workforce. Collective bargaining in the private sector resulted in primarily single-employer collective agreements, with multi-employer bargaining confined to a small number of cases. In contrast, collective bargaining in the public sector had a very different set of defining features with multi-employer collective bargaining more commonly found in particular sectors (such as education) and single union collective contracts more common than in the private sector. Yet, in spite of the dramatic decline in multi-employer bargaining, unions continued to be the preferred choice of bargaining agent for employees across the workplace (Harbridge and Crawford 2000).

The data in Figure 6, which describes collective bargaining structure over the past two decades, indicate that very little change occurred in the distribution of collective bargaining coverage across the various types of agreements over that time. For the most part, they are only established in the public sector where a central authority often negotiates for the employer parties. This has been the pattern going back to even before the enactment of the ERA. To establish a MECA under the ERA, it is necessary for unions to line up the expiry dates of the various CEAs to be amalgamated within a six-month period. This frequently takes several rounds of bargaining to accomplish, which explains why it was not until 2004 that we witnessed an increase in the number and coverage of MECAs.

Also relevant is the fact that union members have typically not been willing to strike over bargaining structure alone, even prior to March 2015, when the right to strike in pursuit of a MECA was repealed. For that matter, many unions – particularly in the public sector – appear to have grown disillusioned with the purported benefits of multi-employer bargaining. Despite this, a majority of employees on CEAs in both education and training and health care and social assistance have remained on MECAs, even after the right to strike in pursuit of MECAs was abolished. Nevertheless, even under the ERA, which ostensibly encourages multi-employer bargaining, collective agreements covering more than one employer can be difficult to negotiate. Therefore, since 2000, the only MECAs negotiated have been where both parties have acquiesced to bargaining on a multi-employer basis in the bargaining process agreement (BPA) reached prior to the commencement of bargaining. It would appear, therefore, that the right to strike in pursuit of MECAs had little or no effect on the prevalence of such agreements in the private sector.

Nearly 40 per cent of employees currently covered by CEAs are on MECAs rather than SECAs. Prior to 2008/09, there was a trend away from SECAs and towards MECAs. That trend appeared to have abated for several years thereafter, although coverage by MECAs did increase somewhat in the year to June 2013, and it has remained at that level since then. At present, around three-in-five central government employees are covered by a MECA, with just over half of

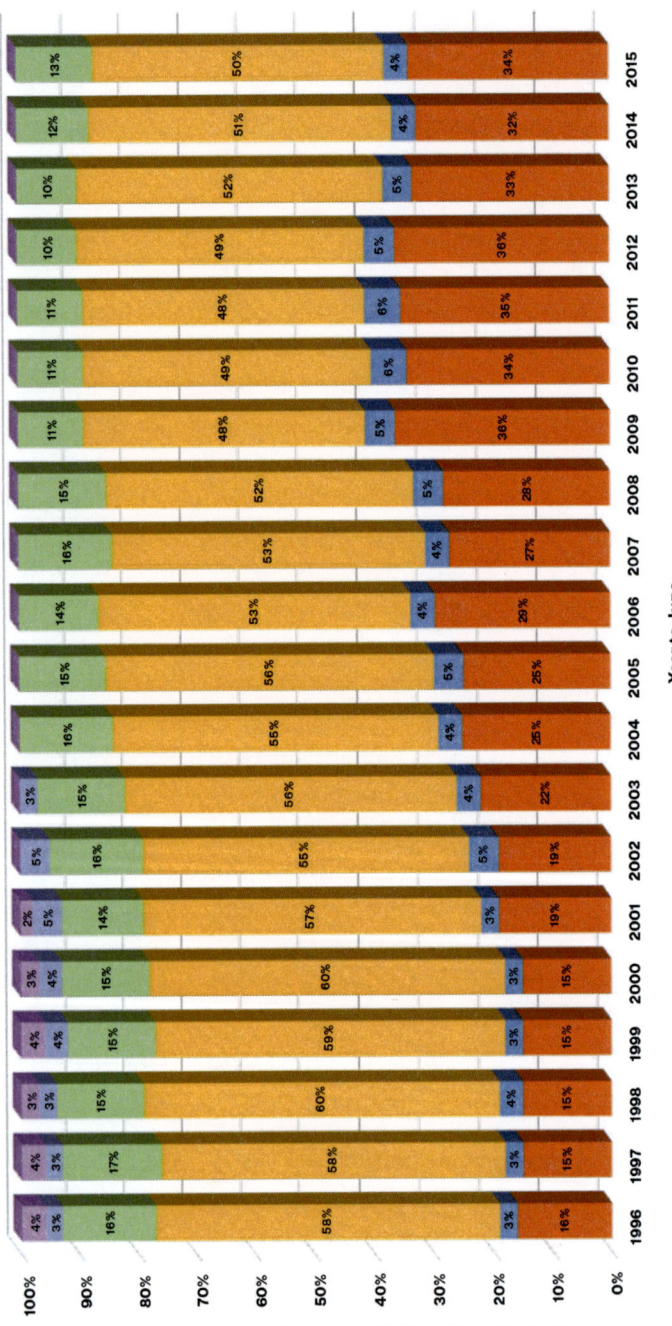

Figure 6: Share (%) of jobs covered by collective bargaining, selected years, 1990–2015

those on CEAs being covered by a single-union MECA and only 5 per cent covered by a multi-union MECA. Parallel shifts in primary and secondary education and the health sector have significantly contributed to the identifiable shift from SECAs to MECAs within the public sector over the past decade. Despite that trend, as has been the case across the labour market as a whole, effectively no change has taken place in the share of public sector workers on MECAs over the previous four years.

In the private sector, where both single and multi-party CEAs cover a much smaller share of the workforce, there was a trend toward coverage under SECAs rather than MECAs which began with the LRA in 1987 and was reinforced by the ECA in 1991. Since that time, and notwithstanding the ERA's support for more centralised bargaining structures by allowing strikes over the issue of bargaining structure, multi-employer collective bargaining has been for the most part a public-sector phenomenon in New Zealand. The main exceptions to this are in the mining industry and in property, administration, science and technology, in which close to 40 per cent of collectivised employees are currently on MECAs.

Finally, under changes in effect from early 2015 under the Employment Relations Amendment Act 2014, employers can opt out of MECA bargaining. Opponents argued the change would undermine the sort of bargaining that sets industry standards. Previously, if a workforce voted to be covered under a MECA, the employer was required to join the negotiations. Clearly, the government's amendment was aimed at negotiations with its own employees, as the vast majority of employees on MECAs are in the central government sector, particularly health and education. Nevertheless, notwithstanding that the share of collectivised central government employees on a MECA has fallen slightly since that time, there is little other evidence at this point to suggest that this legislative change has had any significant effect on multi-employer bargaining.

Terms and Conditions

Although this ostensibly broad scope was limited in a number of ways by subsequent judicial interpretations, the IRA essentially retained the IC&A's range of matters negotiable within the centralised award system, including those affecting or relating to work to be performed and the rights and duties of employees and employers in any industry (McAndrew 1989). Furthermore, notwithstanding the emergence of decentralised plant-level bargaining at this time, variations to the basic pattern existed – in general, the same issues were covered in settlements reached in first few years of the IRA, regardless of whether those agreements resulted from voluntary or 'free' collective bargaining or conciliation (Szakats 1976).

Typical clauses set out in collective agreements settled under the IRA included the industry or parties to which the agreement applied, term of agreement, wages, allowances, hours of work, types of employment (casual, temporary, part-time), shift-work, overtime, holidays, breaks and sick pay, safety and health, redundancy, personal grievances and disputes, preference in hiring, and union access. Depending on the industry, a collective agreement might include provision for shift allowances, incentive bonuses, call-back pay, or long-service leave, to name a few. In-plant agreements, although rarely deviating from the standard clauses, might include provisions related to matters specific to the workplace covered (Szakats 1976).

Early collective agreements between unions, employers or employer associations contained minimal detail, reflecting both their novelty and the fact that, theretofore, legislation offered what was considered to be adequate protection. In these areas, there was a tendency for the parties to replicate or merely refer to statutory provisions in their collective agreements. On the other hand, notwithstanding statutory protections against unjustified dismissal and the presence of redundancy provisions in some agreements, job security was typically not covered in the provision of the earliest collective agreements (Szakats 1976).

As in other countries, workload and work-life balance along with pay and job security have become increasingly important to employees. Over recent decades, New Zealand has emerged as one of the countries in the OECD with the longest working hours, with a 20 per cent increase in average hours worked since the 1970s – a period in which working hours across other countries (for example, France, Germany and Japan) have declined by around the same amount (OECD 2004). Despite trending downward in the past year, the typical work week stipulated in CEAs still remains at 40 hours, and employee access to more flexible working arrangements, such as rostering employees across a seven-day period or no specific detailing of the days of the week, is a growing phenomenon. There has been an increase in the share of private-sector employees covered by CEAs who have their ordinary days of the week stipulated as Monday to Sunday, typically with flexible arrangements, such as four-by-ten-hour shifts.

New flexible working hours provisions, giving employees the 'right to ask' or to make choices about what hours they work, though, mark somewhat of an improvement in this area. Moreover, a law change passed on 10 March 2015 will prevent employers from requiring workers to be available for shifts with no guarantee of work and no compensation. The elimination of 'zero-hours contracts' is an attempt to pull back on the worst excesses of hours-of-work provision. Also, despite extension of statutory annual-leave entitlements eight years ago to a minimum of four weeks, New Zealand still lags behind a number of OECD countries in terms of both statutory and average collectively-agreed entitlement to paid annual leave.

Almost all employees on CEAs also enjoy entitlement to both domestic leave, which is generally drawn from unused sick leave, and bereavement leave, for which the number of days is at the discretion of the employer for half of the collectivised workforce. Additionally, more than seven out of 10 employees on CEAs are entitled to long-service leave, with more than two-thirds having access to this entitlement after 10 years' service. More than three in five employees in the public sector have collectively agreed entitlement to paid parental leave above the statutory entitlement, while a mere 5 per cent of private sector employees receive more than the state-funded payment for parental leave.

Further to this, nearly all employees on CEAs are entitled to a period of notice in the event of redundancy, typically four weeks. Most of these employees receive compensation of between six and 10 weeks' wages for their first year of service, and two weeks' wages for each subsequent year of service. Time-and-a-half remains the most common rate for overtime payments for work beyond ordinary working hours on Monday to Friday, and most employees on CEAs below any overtime bar are entitled to a premium for overtime work on either a Saturday or a Sunday. More than a third of employees on CEAs now have entitlement to shift leave.

As the vast majority of collective bargaining currently takes place at the workplace level, unions in New Zealand are effectively compelled to organise at individual workplaces. The change to decentralised bargaining suggests that unions, accustomed to negotiating industry- or occupation-wide awards or agreements, were ill-prepared for dealing with nuances that existed at the workplace. Two decades on, there is evidence that some unions in the private sector may still lack the necessary resources to organise effectively and may be unable to muster the support necessary to initiate collective bargaining. It may also be the case that some employers actively resist unionisation and therefore collective bargaining. Very few non-union employees, however, appear to feel threatened by reprisals from employers if they were to join a union. Many employers, in fact, articulate a preference for collective bargaining (Department of Labour 2009).

Conclusion

Publication of the first issue of the *New Zealand Journal of Industrial Relations* in 1976 coincided with a tipping point in New Zealand industrial relations. To this end, it was in the shadows of the 1968 'nil wage order' that the factors, which ultimately proved to drive change in the labour market for several decades, took shape. Significant amongst these changes was enactment of the IRA, which heralded the shift away from the long-standing system of compulsory arbitration to de facto collective bargaining and, along with the Equal Pay Act 1972 and the Human Rights Commission Act 1977, marked the beginnings of a process of restructuring which continued for the next three decades. Although trade unions, arbitration and industrial awards remained formidable components of that system for most of the next two decades, the 1970s stand out, in retrospect, as a period in which serious challenges to those institutions began to emerge.

The 1990s, though, were characterised by negotiation of non-union collective contracts and the loss of automatic and exclusive rights for unions within workplaces, which swiftly led to decentralisation of collective bargaining, the demise of multi-employer bargaining, and the retrenchment of employment conditions (Harbridge et al. 1994). This was achieved by replacing, effectively overnight, the country's long-standing highly-centralised industrial relations system with a system based on individual employment contracting (Harbridge and Walsh 2002). Hence, collective bargaining shifted to the level of the enterprise, and pattern bargaining was abandoned. Enactment of the ECA in 1991 was, in this sense, a watershed event that would forever change relationships between employers and employees and transform the country's industrial relations landscape. Its introduction represented a radical ideological shift which, by the mid-1990s, had irrevocably altered the nature of industrial relations in New Zealand.

The ERA brought together a set of legislative requirements and institutional arrangements for employers and employees that would ostensibly create a more favourable environment for unions and collective bargaining. Yet, after more than a decade and a half under legislation which purports to support the negotiation of collective agreements to regulate pay and working conditions, the share of the workforce covered by them has continued to fall. It is now apparent that, although the ERA established a legislative framework that promoted and facilitated the negotiation of wages, hours and working conditions by trade unions, collective bargaining was unlikely to recover fully within a labour market that was permanently transformed a decade earlier. In particular, despite the encouragement to return to multi-employer bargaining, movement towards MECAs did not occur in the manner it was anticipated. Consequently, while the number of workers in New Zealand covered by collective agreements increased, the share of the workforce covered by collective bargaining has remained largely static under the ERA.

The last few years, nonetheless, have been something of a truce period, notwithstanding changes implemented by the National-led Government in recent employment relations reform legislation. A number of those changes affect union security and collective bargaining, in particular, new regulations relating to strikes and lockouts and 'good faith' requirements for bargaining. Also, under recently enacted legislative changes, the Employment Relations Authority can now, in 'certain circumstances', declare that collective bargaining has ended, effectively allowing employers to use the threat of contracting out the jobs of striking workers to compel agreement on their terms. Another of the Government's recent legislative reforms allows employers to opt out of multi-employer collective bargaining before bargaining actually commences. With those reforms, the Government has underscored its belief that many employment law obligations impose unnecessary constraints on employers.

In this sense, it is noteworthy that while National-led has initiated a few sorties at the ERA, it has held off on launching a full-on offensive. Importantly, the ERA's key objectives to promote collective and 'good faith' bargaining have not changed. The parties are still required to bargain in good faith with the intention of reaching an agreement. In addition, there are continual rumblings from the Labour Party and its allies for change, which would ultimately benefit unions and collective bargaining. For instance, the debate over inequality has gathered traction in recent years, particularly with unions bringing the pay equity issue before the courts on behalf of vulnerable workers. The Government has accepted the Joint Working Group on Pay Equity's recommendation that a bargaining process based on the ERA framework be used to address pay equity. Finally, the Labour Party's recently announced election policy to introduce Fair Pay Agreements that set fair, basic employment conditions across an industry based on the employment standards that apply in that industry is likely to reignite debate on industry-wide pay setting and fairer work arrangements. Taken as a whole, these policy proposals suggest there is still a role in New Zealand workplaces for collective bargaining.

References

Aidt, T. and Tzannatos, Z. 2001. *The Costs and Benefits of Collective Bargaining: A Survey*. Social Protection discussion paper, no. SP 0120. Washington, DC: The World Bank.

Barry, M. and May, R. 2004. "New Employee Representation." *Employee Relations* 26 (2): 203.

Blackwood, L., Feinberg-Danieli, G., Lafferty, G. and Kiely, P. 2005. *Employment Agreements: Bargaining Trends & Employment Law Update 2004/2005*. Wellington, New Zealand: Industrial Relations Centre, Victoria University of Wellington.

Boxall, P. 1993. "Management Strategy and the Employment Contracts Act 1991." In *Employment Contracts: New Zealand Experiences*, ed. R. Harbridge, 148–164. Wellington, New Zealand: Victoria University Press.

Dannin, E. 1995. "We Can't Overcome? A Case Study of Freedom of Contract and Labour Law Reform." *Berkeley Journal of Employment and Labour Law* 16 (1): 1–168.

Department of Labour. 2009. *The Effect of the Employment Relations Act 2000 on Collective Bargaining*. Wellington, New Zealand: Department of Labour.

Foster, B., Rasmussen, E., Murrie, J. and Laird, I. 2011. "Supportive Legislation, Unsupportive Employers and Collective Bargaining in New Zealand." *Relations Industrielles* 66 (2): 192–212.

Franks, P. 1994. "The Employment Contracts Act and the Demise of the New Zealand Clerical Workers Union." *NZ Journal of History* 28 (2): 194–210.

Geare, A. J. 1983. "Formal Collective Agreements in New Zealand Private Sector Industrial Relations." *New Zealand Journal of Industrial Relations* 8 (1): 23–29.

Harbridge, R. 1991. "Collective Bargaining Coverage in New Zealand: The Impact of the Employment

Contracts Bill." *Australian Bulletin of Labour* 17 (4): 310–24.
Harbridge, R. and Crawford, A. 2000 *The Employment Contracts Act and Collective Bargaining Patterns: A Review of the 1999/2000 Year*. In Harbridge, R., Crawford, A. and Kiely, P. (eds) *Employment Contracts: Bargaining Trends and Employment Law Update 1999/2000*. Wellington, New Zealand: Industrial Relations Centre, Victoria University of Wellington.
Harbridge R., Crawford, A. and Kiely, P. 2000. *Employment Contracts: Bargaining Trends and Employment Law Update 1999/2000*. Wellington, New Zealand: Industrial Relations Centre, Victoria University of Wellington.
Harbridge, R., Honeybone, A. and Kiely, P. 1994. *Employment Contracts: Bargaining Trends & Employment Law Update 1993/1994*. Wellington, New Zealand: Industrial Relations Centre, Victoria University of Wellington.
Harbridge, R. and McCaw, S. 1992. "Award, Agreement or Nothing? A Review of the Impact of S. 132a of the Labour Relations Act 1987 on Collective Bargaining." *New Zealand Journal of Industrial Relations* 17 (1): 175–183.
Harbridge, R. and Walsh, P. 1999. *The Evolution of Enterprise Bargaining in New Zealand*. Working Paper 1/99. Wellington, New Zealand: Industrial Relations Centre, Victoria University of Wellington.
Harbridge, R. and Walsh, P. 2002. "Globalisation and Labour Market Deregulation in Australia and New Zealand: Different Approaches, Similar Outcomes." *Employee Relations* 24 (4): 423–436.
Harbridge. R., Walsh, P. and Thickett, G. 2002. *The Employment Relations Act and Collective Bargaining Patterns: A Review of the 2001/2002 Year*. Wellington, New Zealand: Industrial Relations Centre, Victoria University of Wellington.
Harbridge, R., Walsh, P. and Wilkinson, D. 2001. "Free Riding: Trends in Collective Bargaining Coverage and Union Membership Levels in New Zealand." *Labor Studies Journal* 26 (3): 51–72.
Hector, J. and Hobby, M. 1998. "Labour Market Adjustment under the Employment Contracts Act: 1996." *New Zealand Journal of Industrial Relations* 22: 311–322.
McAndrew, I. 1989. "Bargaining Structure and Bargaining Scope in New Zealand: The Climate of Employer Opinion." *New Zealand Journal of Industrial Relations* 14 (2): 133–148.
McAndrew, I. 1993. "The Process of Developing Employment Contracts: A Management Perspective." In *Employment Contracts: New Zealand Experiences*, ed. R. Harbridge, 165–184. Wellington, New Zealand: Victoria University Press.
Organisation for Economic Co-operation and Development. 2004. *Employment Outlook 2004*. Paris, France: OECD.
Organisation for Economic Co-operation and Development. 2016. *Economic Policy Reforms 2016: Going for Growth Interim Report*. Paris, France: OECD.
Schmitt J. and Mitukiewicz, A. 2011. *Politics Matter: Changes in Unionization Rates in Rich Countries, 1960–2010*. Washington, DC: Center for Economic Policy and Research.
Schnabel, C., Zagelmeyer, S. and Kohaut, S. 2006. "Collective Bargaining Structure and its Determinants: An Empirical Analysis with British and German Establishment Data." *European Journal of Industrial Relations* 12 (2): 165–188.
Szakats, A. 1976. "Industrial Relations in New Zealand: New Vista for Collective Bargaining: Extension or Restriction?" *New Zealand Journal of Industrial Relations* 11 (3): 50–5.
Woods, N. S. 1963. *Industrial Conciliation and Arbitration in New Zealand*. Wellington, New Zealand: Government Printer.
Young, F. J. L. 1976. "Retrospect and Prospect." *New Zealand Journal of Industrial Relations* 1 (1): 3–7.

Areas of Transformation

Reforming Workplace Health and Safety Regulation: Second Time Lucky?

Viktoriya Pashorina-Nichols, Felicity Lamm and Gordon Anderson

Introduction

Prior to the enactment of the Health and Safety at Work Act 2015 (HSW Act), it had been apparent that New Zealand's work-related fatality, injury and illness rates were high when compared with countries such as Australia and the United Kingdom. This was in spite of the fact that there had been major revisions of New Zealand's health and safety law in 1992 and a decade later in 2002. Although previous governments had taken initial steps to address the weakness in the occupational health and safety (OHS) law, it took a major disaster, the Pike River Coal Mine explosion in 2010 that killed 29 men[1] to force a comprehensive revision of the health and safety law. The Royal Commission Report on the Pike River Coal Mine Tragedy (2012) and the subsequent Independent Taskforce Report on Workplace Health and Safety (2013) provided a comprehensive analysis of New Zealand's health and safety law, policy and practice, identifying deep and systemic failures with the existing regulatory model. Both reports recommended major legislative changes. The legislative response was to create a new independent regulator, WorkSafe New Zealand, and pass a new principal Act, the HSW Act.

The historical record of health and safety reform in New Zealand does not, however, inspire confidence. New Zealand has had legislation regulating OHS since the 19th century[2] including the Health and Safety in Employment Act 1992

---

1   J Ryan Lamare and others "Independent, dependent, and employee: Contractors and New Zealand's Pike River Coal Mine disaster" (2015) 57(1) JIR 72 at 82; and see generally Simon Mitchell and Penny Swarbrick "Health and Safety Reforms" (paper presented to New Zealand Law Society Seminar, June 2014) 1 at 6–7.
2   Glyn Jeffrey "The Industrial Relations Context of Workplace Health and Safety" in Carol Slappendel (ed) *Health and Safety in New Zealand Workplaces* (Dunmore Press, Palmerston North, 1995) 157 at 159–168; Felicity Lamm "Participative and productive employment relations: the role of health and safety committees and worker representation" in Erling

(HSE Act). The HSE Act itself was the result of a major review of the structure of health and safety law in the late 1980s and was based on the United Kingdom's Robens' model of one Act, administered by one regulator, covering all workers and joint participation. The HSE Act was also significantly amended in 2002, as it failed to cover all workers and did not include joint participation, among other things. Despite these reforms, however, New Zealand's health and safety record remained abysmal.[3] In 2014–2015, it was estimated that there were 600–900 deaths from work-related diseases and 50–60 deaths from work-related injuries.[4] The Report by the Independent Taskforce on Workplace Health and Safety,[5] two decades after the enactment of the HSE Act, stated:[6]

> When the Taskforce was established, the best available data on New Zealand's workplace injury, health and fatality rates were Statistics New Zealand's Serious Injury Outcome Indicators (SIOIs). These showed that on average there were 102 fatal work-related deaths a year between 2008 and 2010, and New Zealand had a workplace fatality rate of around four deaths per 100,000 workers a year. On the basis of international comparisons using historical SIOIs and data from other jurisdictions, New Zealand was identified as having a high rate of deaths compared with many Organisation for Economic Co-operation and Development (OECD) countries.

In its Report, the Taskforce described New Zealand's health and safety culture as having inadequate leadership in the workplace, including a general lack of capacity among managers; poor and ineffective worker engagement; and a risk-tolerant culture making workplaces liable to develop, accept and defend low standards, dangerous practices and inadequate systems. Among the factors identified as contributing to this situation were a weak regulator, which had failed to deliver on core responsibilities, and the lack of incentives and deterrents needed to drive compliance with minimum health and safety standards or to

---

Rasmussen (ed) *Employment Relationships: Workers, Unions And Employers In New Zealand* (2nd ed, Auckland University Press, Auckland, 2010) 168 at 169; see generally Noel S Woods *Industrial Conciliation And Arbitration In New Zealand* (RE Owen, Government Printer, Wellington, 1963); and see also Michael Quinlan, Philip Bohle and Felicity Lamm "Law and prevention" in *Managing Occupational Health and Safety: A Multidisciplinary Approach* (3rd ed, Palgrave Macmillan, South Yarra (Victoria), 2010) 312 at 322–327.

3   Philip Gunby "How Bad is the State of Occupational Fatalities in New Zealand?" (2011) 36(1) NZJER 35 at 39–40; and WorkSafe New Zealand *Our Performance Story 2015* (January 2016) at 8.
4   WorkSafe New Zealand *Annual Report 2014–2015* (November 2015) at 11.
5   *Executive Report of the Independent Taskforce on Workplace Health and Safety* (2013); and *Main Report of the Independent Taskforce on Workplace Health and Safety* (2013).
6   *Executive Report of the Independent Taskforce on Workplace Health and Safety*, above n 5, at 9, and see also *Main Report of the Independent Taskforce on Workplace Health and Safety*, above n 5, at [14–15].

foster behaviours that lead to continual improvement.[7] The Taskforce also noted further failures of the HSE Act:[8]

> ... weaknesses across the system are the direct result of a fundamental failure to implement properly the Robens health and safety model in New Zealand ... The plethora of issues arising from this factor alone are, across the system, multiple, persistent and compounding.

This chapter provides a detailed account of the development of OHS regulation in New Zealand over the last 40 years and considers whether the most recent reforms are likely to overcome the problems identified by the Royal Commission of Inquiry and the Independent Taskforce and are likely to result in a substantial improvement in the country's OHS statistics. In particular, we ask whether the latest reforms will address the lack of workers' voice in matters concerning their own health and safety. Finally, we provide a commentary on the different roles of employers, employees and the state under the new HSW Act.

The Robens' Model

The underlying model for contemporary health and safety legislation in a number of countries, including New Zealand, originated from the 1972 Report of the United Kingdom Committee on Safety and Health at Work chaired by Lord Robens (known as the Robens' Report), which was "asked to look at the subject as a whole in all of its aspects".[9] The Report recommended a number of changes to existing health and safety law based on two principal objectives.[10] The first objective was to streamline the state's role in the traditional regulatory system by unifying health and safety legislation into an umbrella statute containing broad general duties covering a range of parties and seeking to address all health and safety risks. The general duties were to be supplemented with regulations and codes of practice. It also recommended a single regulatory body with inspectors empowered to issue administrative sanctions and to prosecute for contraventions.

Second, it recommended greater self-regulation involving systematic management approaches to eliminate or reduce work-related risks with workers and management working together to implement and improve upon the health and safety standards set by the state. That is, the primary responsibility for managing safety and health risks should fall on those who create the risks and work with them.

---

7   *Main Report of the Independent Taskforce on Workplace Health and Safety*, above n 5, at 20.
8   At [61].
9   Great Britain *Safety and Health at Work: Report of the Committee 1970–72* (Committee on Safety and Health at Work, 1970–1972) at 2 [Robens' Report].
10 At 12.

Finally, the Robens' Report highlighted the role of workers in OHS by emphasising that "real progress is impossible without the full co-operation and commitment of all employees".[11] In particular, the Report encouraged the use of health and safety representatives and joint safety committees as methods of worker involvement,[12] but it also advised that there be a statutory requirement of a general nature for employers *to consult* with their workers on OHS matters.[13]

Although the Robens' Report has been highly influential, it has not been without criticism,[14] for example as one commentator noted:[15]

> ... while excellent in its survey of the problems, and in its diagnosis of the present weaknesses of the system of accident prevention, it is less persuasive in its suggested remedies for the failings that it has identified.

Even in its United Kingdom context, the Robens' model does not provide more than a broad approach to regulating health and safety at work. To be effective, the model requires a proper balance to be struck between the state as legislator/regulator, employers and workers. At its simplest there must be a sufficient legal base on which the other parties can rely in order to determine their actions and with sufficient incentives to ensure compliance with legislative obligations, particularly those that are based on self-regulation. The self-regulatory approach inherent in the Robens' model is also its weakest point, as it requires both a commitment to properly prioritise health and safety and to have the capacity to do so. Self-regulation is dependent upon the notion of voluntary compliance by the employer. However, the ambiguity of 'performance standards' and, in particular, the self-regulatory approach are particularly difficult to implement, especially in the small business sector, and have done little to reduce the incidence of occupational injury and disease.[16]

There is also the key issue of worker involvement under the Robens' model. The treatment of workers under a Robens' model is at best paternalistic. Instead of being an integral part of the joint consultation process, they are often required to operate on the side lines within a primarily state-employer constructed regime.

The Robens' model, therefore, provides a structural starting point for health and safety regimes but, as with many models, the devil is in the detail of the domestic environment in which it must operate.

---

11 At 18.
12 At 18–19 and 22.
13 At 21–23.
14 Alison Broadhurst "Robens: A missed opportunity?" (1972) Industrial and Commercial Training 4(12) 595; and Adrian Brooks "Rethinking Occupational Health and Safety Legislation" (1988) 30(3) JIR 347.
15 RWL Howells "The Robens Report" (1972) 1 ILJ 185 at 196.
16 Felicity Lamm "Occupational safety and health" in Erling Rasmussen *Employment Relations in New Zealand* (2nd ed, Pearson New Zealand, North Shore (Auckland), 2009) at 168.

Development of OHS in New Zealand

New Zealand was relatively slow to adopt the Robens' model. The Walker Report of 1981, which led to the Factory and Commercial Premises Act 1981, was New Zealand's first attempt at adopting the Report's recommendations.[17] The 1981 Act amalgamated some of the previous health and safety legislation, set out the duties of employers and employees, provided for training of workers, suggested a move away towards less prescriptive codes of practice, and provided for the possibility of health and safety representatives and committees.[18] Notwithstanding these changes, the Factory and Commercial Premises Act 1981 still did not cover all workers (for example, it omitted public sector workers). The responsibility for enforcing that Act was also divided among five government agencies[19] and there remained approximately 31 Acts and over 50 regulations dealing with OHS matters.[20] In 1984 Sir Geoffrey Palmer (the then Deputy Prime Minister) called the OHS arrangement the 'Balkanisation of control' because:[21]

> ... the system was limited in its coverage, rigid in its *modus operandi*, paternalistic in its provisions against the employment of women and young people, and provided overly prescriptive technical specifications for the control of hazards.

The mid-1980s saw the first emergence of tripartism of OHS in New Zealand with the creation of the Advisory Council on Occupational Safety and Health (ACOSH) in 1985.[22] The Council's creation led to a number of changes in New Zealand's health and safety law,[23] but, more significantly, in 1988, it produced a discussion paper, *Occupational Safety and Health Reform*, which set out proposals for a new framework for legislation and the administration of health and safety law.[24]

Because New Zealand was suffering from many of the same problems that affected the United Kingdom – too many pieces of legislation, overly complex and outdated law, fragmentation of administrative jurisdictions, different treatment of similar hazards, and gaps in coverage – the proposals broadly reflected the

---

17 John Wren "From The 'Balkanisation Of Control' To Employer Management Systems: OHS Policy And Politics In New Zealand 1981–1992" in Michael Lloyd (ed) *Occupational Health And Safety In New Zealand: Contemporary Social Research* (Dunmore Press, Palmerston North, 2002) 43 at 44.
18 At 44.
19 At 45.
20 At 44.
21 At 45 (emphasis in original).
22 At 46.
23 See at 46.
24 Advisory Council for Occupational Safety and Health *A Public Discussion Paper: Occupational Safety And Health Reform* (June 1988).

recommendations of the Robens' Report.[25] The ACOSH Report placed some stress on the need for a tripartite approach to health and safety:[26]

> Because occupational health and safety is an issue affecting employers, workers and the Government, the establishment of policy and the determination of the basic standards of safety and health secured by law should involve a statutory tripartite process at national level. In addition, it is through these tripartite structures that any conflicts which may arise between employers and unions over health and safety issues can be resolved.

As a result of the ACOSH Report, the Labour Government introduced the Occupational Safety and Health Bill 1990, which was intended to replace all previous legislation and proposed to extend protection to all workers.[27] The Bill had three main features. First, most existing statutes relating to OHS were to be repealed and replaced by the one statute containing a series of general provisions about OHS, supported by more specialised codes of practice and regulations. Second, the Bill provided for the establishment of a Health and Safety Commission separate from the Department of Labour. Third, the Bill contained provision for the election and establishment of workplace safety representatives and committees. Wren suggested that if this Bill had been passed there would have been an OHS tripartite management system with joint oversight by government, union and employer and "responsibility that placed greater emphasis on employer and employee self-help".[28]

While the Bill was broadly welcomed by unions, it was heavily criticised by employers, who argued that it was still overly "prescriptive" and, in particular, that it gave too much power to unions and union representatives in the workplace.[29] This first major attempt to introduce a modern Robens-based health and safety system in New Zealand failed when the Bill was allowed to lapse by the National Government elected in 1990.

The Health and Safety In Employment Act 1992

The in-coming National Government conducted a review of Labour's Occupational Safety and Health Bill 1990 by a subcommittee of the Caucus Labour Committee, and released a discussion paper, *Management of Health and Safety in Employment*. Following this review the National Government introduced its own, much diluted, Health and Safety in Employment Bill. This Bill retained the

---

25 At 3–4.
26 At 2.
27 Wren, above n 17, at 46.
28 At 46.
29 For several comments on the reforms, see "Symposium: Occupational Safety and Health" (1989) 14 NZJIR.

previous emphasis on a single piece of legislation, and increased the emphasis on hazard-control procedures, although many of the prescribed standards in the Occupational Safety and Health Bill were either abandoned or diluted.

The tripartite character of the Bill in particular was anathema to a Government determined to deregulate and deunionise New Zealand workplaces. Any enforceable right for employees or their unions to be involved in matters involving their health and safety in the workplace, whether by way of consultation or otherwise, was abandoned. Likewise, the statutory right of employees to refuse to do dangerous work, and the right of their representatives to order a cessation of dangerous work, were removed. Health and safety was to be a matter for management alone.

The Department of Labour, in a summary of the new law, stated that, unlike earlier legislation where "[e]mphasis was placed on compliance with legislation and [e]mployers generally saw [the Department of Labour] as responsible for ensuring workplaces were complying with safety and health standards, and therefore took little ownership of workplace health and safety matters":[30]

> In contrast, the new HSE Act provides a framework for the employer to take responsibility for managing risks in the workplace. The framework is based on a set of incentives and sanctions. It is less prescriptive than previous legislation and thus consistent with the Government's wider industrial relations reform ... Increased emphasis on self-regulation and less reliance on Government workplace Inspectors, is an important facet of employers taking ownership of managing workplace risks. Self-regulation in a framework of incentives and sanctions, is the cornerstone of the HSE Act.

The Department of Labour was also to state:[31]

> The changes contained in the Health and Safety in Employment Act 1992 [were] consistent with those contained in the Employment Contracts Act 1991, Accident Rehabilitation and Compensation Insurance Act 1992 and the Industry Training Act 1992. In particular, the Health and Safety in Employment Act has put increasing emphasis on enterprise level decision making, where employers and employees determine the best solution to meet the performance requirements of the Act.

The Department neglected to explain how, in the absence of any requirement for employee involvement, this optimistic outcome could be met under the labour law regime of the Employment Contracts Act 1991 and the general deregulatory environment of the 1990s.

As Wren rightly notes, the HSE Act rejected tripartism "in favour of minimalist government involvement and a system emphasising the rights and

---

30 Department of Labour *An Introduction to the Department of Labour* (November 1993) at 89.
31 At 88.

responsibilities of employers to manage their affairs".[32] This approach could only be tested over time – and time was to provide a very negative verdict.

Nevertheless, leaving aside the provisions for worker involvement, when originally enacted, the HSE Act represented a major departure from previous OHS legislation. The Act replaced a significant body of highly detailed and overlapping legislation with a less prescriptive framework based on the underlying precept that employers in particular should take all practicable steps to minimise harm to health and safety arising from the workplace. Under that Act, the emphasis was changed from the detailed control of specific hazards to 'managing risks' in relation to work activities, in respect of which the Act purported to create a coherent framework. As stated at the time, "the principal object of the Act [was] to provide for the prevention of harm to employees".[33] The Act covered, and still covers, employees, employers, principals, contractors and subcontractors. The approach under the Act had four key components:

(a) place of work – the Act covers people in a workplace and in its vicinity, with responsibilities largely allocated to those with control of hazards in the workplace;

(b) "all practicable steps" – the Act imposes a standard of care that requires steps to be taken that are practicable in the circumstances, bearing in mind the current state of knowledge, the benefits of reducing risk and the cost;

(c) systematic management of hazards – the Act establishes a process for assessment and control of hazards in a place of work as opposed to simply requiring compliance with standards relating to particular workplaces, so that employers must manage hazards through identification and elimination, isolation or minimisation; and

(d) enforcement – the Occupational Safety and Health Service (OSH Service) enforces the Act through warnings and notices requiring improvements, and ultimately through criminal prosecution.

The 2002 Amendment Act

The newly elected Labour Government's promise for better workplace health and safety[34] resulted in a comprehensive review of OHS legislation undertaken

---

32 Wren, above n 17, at 47; and see also Gordon Anderson and John Hughes "Occupational Health and Safety" in *Employment Law in New Zealand* (LexisNexis, Wellington, 2014) 691 at 695.

33 *Health and Safety in Employment Bill:* Report of the Department of Labour to the Labour Select Committee (July 1992) at 6.

34 See generally (31 October 2001) 596 NZPD 12709; and see generally (3 December 2002) 604 NZPD 2441.

as part of the Government's wider labour market legislation reforms, which led to the Employment Relations Act 2000 and the Injury Prevention, Rehabilitation and Compensation Act 2001.[35] The review concluded that the framework of the HSE Act was fundamentally sound, but did not encourage a workplace culture where development of positive health and safety processes and behaviours were a real priority.[36] In the Parliamentary debates, emphasis was laid on ensuring New Zealand's laws were comparable to those of other countries in order "to match the highest international standards",[37] especially given the very poor statistics of New Zealand's workplace fatalities and injuries.[38]

The review resulted in the Health and Safety in Employment Amendment Act 2002 designed to address the gaps in the HSE Act that were seen to impede its effectiveness. In parallel to the policy approach behind the original HSE Act, the Amendment Act was seen as complementing the Government's legislative initiatives in employment relations and accident compensation. According to the briefing paper, the common thread throughout the strategy for reform of the Act was the notion of partnership: joint employer, management, trade union and employee responsibility for improving health and safety performance. The substantive changes in the Amendment Act fell into five broad areas:

(a) more comprehensive coverage – the maritime, air and rail industries were included, coverage of mobile workers was confirmed, and protection was extended to some volunteers, persons receiving on-the-job training or work experience and 'loaned employees'. Court decisions establishing that the concept of 'harm' under the HSE Act covered work-related stress, and that a person's behaviour could be a 'hazard' under the Act, were confirmed;

(b) employee participation – provision was made for good faith co-operation to ensure employee participation in decision-making affecting health and safety;

(c) enforcement – more effective enforcement measures, including the imposition of infringement fees and hazard notices, were introduced;

(d) penalties – penalties for offences were increased significantly; and

(v) indemnities – indemnification against the costs of fines and infringement fees was prohibited.

---

35 Office of the Minister of Labour *Discussion Paper on the Review of the Health and Safety in Employment Act 1992* (2000); and Department of Labour *Report on Submissions* (2001).
36 Department of Labour *Health and Safety in Amendment Bill 2001, Briefing Paper Presented to the Chair, Transport and Industrial Relations Select Committee.*
37 (5 December 2001) 597 NZPD 13470.
38 (5 December 2001) 597 NZPD 13469; and see (3 December 2002) 604 NZPD 2448.

These measures were also intended to comply with the International Labour Organisation's conventions on health and safety, with particular reference to Convention 155, which requires governments to adopt coherent national OHS policy and law with the purpose of improving OHS in the workplace.[39]

The HSW Act 2015

The Pike River mine explosion[40] had the effect of forcing a comprehensive review of New Zealand's OHS law[41] the result of which was the National Government's sweeping reforms contained in the HSW Act 2015. The Taskforce Report was clear in that the Robens' performance-based model was appropriate for OHS regulation, but argued that its implementation in New Zealand had been weak.[42] In order to remedy the situation, the Taskforce Report recommended that New Zealand align its law with that of Australia by adopting the Australian Model Health and Safety Act 2011. This recommendation was based on the fact that the Model Law, the most recent expression of the Robens' approach, had been the culmination of a long period of investigation and consultation, domestically and internationally and, as Australia has been through an extensive modernisation process, including the development of regulations and information, on which New Zealand could capitalise.[43]

As we have argued, to be effective the Robens' model requires a proper balance to be struck between the three parties, namely the state, as legislator/regulator, employers and workers. In the following sections we look at whether the objects of the HSW Act have been achieved, as well as the evidence that the tripartite balance is working.

---

39 Health and Safety in Employment Amendment Act 2002, s 3; see also Anderson and Hughes, above n 32, at 695–696; and ILO Convention No 155 Occupational Safety and Health Convention (adopted 22 June 1981).
40 See also Lamare and others, above n 1, at 82; and see generally Mitchell and Swarbrick, above n 1, at 6–7.
41 Royal Commission on the Pike River Coal Mine Tragedy: Volume 1, Overview and Volume 2 (October 2012); *Main Report of the Independent Taskforce on Workplace Health and Safety*, above n 5; and see also Anderson and Hughes, above n 32, at 701–703.
42 *Main Report of the Independent Taskforce on Workplace Health and Safety*, above n 5, at [62]–[67].
43 Richard Rudman "Health and Safety" in *New Zealand Employment Law Guide* (2015 ed, CCH New Zealand, Auckland, 2015) 391 at 425; and see *Main Report of the Independent Taskforce on Workplace Health and Safety*, above n 5, at [215].

The State

Development of the role of state

In 1990s the Government had at its avail three tools, which would "establish a more optimal level of investment in occupational injury and illness prevention": (1) creation of financial incentives to encourage the desired outcomes; (2) provision and enforcement of minimum standards via legislation; and (3) provision of information with the aim of increasing knowledge about hazards, best practice and other relevant matters.[44] In order to help the Government in its task, the HSE Act was meant to be administered by the OSH Service of the Department of Labour.[45] This was an appropriate response to the Robens' Report's criticism of fragmentation of administrative jurisdictions, which was certainly evident in the 1980s in New Zealand with five governmental departments charged with the task of administering OHS enforcement. Nevertheless, there was still some overlap evident between the OSH Service and the Accident Compensation Corporation (ACC), despite the focus of the OSH Service being on the *prevention* of injuries and illnesses at work, and the focus of ACC being on the *compensation* of accidental injury.[46]

Inspectors,[47] on behalf of the OSH Service, were "appointed to see that the principles of the Act are applied in places of work".[48] Despite the much more "comprehensive coverage of almost all places of work" by the HSE Act, suggesting that inspectors that had been previously employed by other government departments would now enforce the HSE Act, "much of ... [inspectors'] powers ... [was] a continuation or slight variation of the status quo".[49]

The main functions of inspectors under the HSE Act were (and still are): (a) to help people in improving safety at places of work by providing information and education; (b) determining if the HSE Act was being complied with; and (c) taking all reasonable steps to ensure HSE Act was complied with.[50] If an inspector were to find incompliance, they could issue improvement or prohibition notices,[51] and only an inspector could take prosecutions under HSE Act.[52] Other officers

---

44 Department of Labour, above n 30, at 86.
45 See Occupational Safety and Health Service *A Guide to the Health and Safety in Employment Act 1992: Outlining the Law Affecting People at Work from 1 April 1993* (Department of Labour, October 1992) at 18.
46 Department of Labour, above n 30, at 91.
47 On the role of the inspectorate and enforcement see generally Quinlan, Bohle and Lamm, above n 2, at 354–371.
48 Occupational Safety and Health Service, above n 45, at 18.
49 At 18.
50 Health and Safety in Employment Act 1992, s 30; and see generally Rudman, above n 43, at 419–420.
51 Health and Safety in Employment Act, ss 39–45.
52 Section 54.

working for the OSH Service were the departmental medical practitioners whose main task was to issue suspension notices[53] to those employees who were detrimentally affected by the hazardous work processes,[54] but essentially they "have almost the same powers as an inspector".[55]

The 2002 Amendment to HSE Act aimed "to provide a greater range of tools for enforcing the Act and to increase the effectiveness of the existing enforcement tools".[56] The following changes in particular were significant: (a) permissible private prosecutions, which meant that people other than just the inspectors could bring prosecutions under the Act under certain circumstances; (b) introduction of infringement notices, which would be issued for straightforward breaches of the Act (less serious breaches of general duties);[57] and (c) higher penalties, about a five-fold increase.[58]

The HSW Act introduced significant changes to the administration of enforcement and policy. In particular, it made clear that, for the time being, policy will be undertaken by the Ministry of Business, Innovation and Employment while WorkSafe New Zealand (WorkSafe) becomes the regulator of workplace health and safety.[59] The crown entity, WorkSafe[60] was established in December 2013, with its primary objective being "to promote and contribute to securing the health and safety of workers and workplaces".[61] The previous roles of the inspectorate and health and safety medical practitioners were largely rolled over under the new Act. The types of notices that inspectors can issue include improvement notices, prohibition notices and non-disturbance notices.[62]

As with previous statutes, HSW Act has substantially increased the maximum penalties for offences, which has also meant that New Zealand penalties are comparable to those of Australia.[63] The new feature, however, is the ability of a person to give WorkSafe a voluntary written enforceable undertaking,[64] which

53   See Rudman, above n 43, at 420.
54   Health and Safety in Employment Act, s 37.
55   Occupational Safety and Health Service, above n 45, at 20.
56   Shona Carr and Alastair Sheriff "Health and Safety in Employment Amendment Act 2002" (paper presented to New Zealand Law Society Seminar, Wellington, April–May 2003) 1 at 68.
57   See generally Rudman, above n 43, at 421.
58   Carr and Sheriff, above n 56, at 68–71; and see generally Paul Gordon and Alan Woodfield "Incentives and the Changing Structure of Penalties in New Zealand's Health and Safety in Employment Act" (Working Paper No 03/2006, University of Canterbury, 2006).
59   Health and Safety at Work Act 2015, s 189.
60   See also Rudman, above n 43, at 417–418; and Anderson and Hughes, above n 32, at 704–706.
61   WorkSafe New Zealand Act 2013, s 9(1); and see s 10 for the list of its functions.
62   Health and Safety at Work Act, pt 4 sub-pt 1.
63   Mitchell and Swarbrick, above n 1, at 27–28.
64   See generally Richard Johnstone and Michelle King "A Responsive Sanction to Promote Systematic Compliance? Enforceable Undertakings in Occupational Health and Safety Regulation" (2008) 21 AJLL 280; and see generally Richard Johnstone and Christine Parker

does not amount to an admission of guilt, for an alleged contravention of the Act.[65]

Commentary on the role of state

When it comes to assessing the role of the state within the tripartism framework, the work of the regulator becomes key. As Neil Gunningham writes, "[t]he history of ... [work health and safety] disasters provides compelling evidence that even the best legislation may not deliver its intended outcomes, if it is not effectively implemented."[66]

The disestablishment of the Department of Labour OSH Service and its replacement by WorkSafe in itself is evidence of a very problematic regulator. The issues within the Department of Labour began in the period of 1980s and 1990s when the Department took on "a more passive, consultant-like role, dispensing advice via a centralised call centre and often without the necessary expertise or staff to effectively undertake their statutory duties of enforcement".[67] Alternatively explained "the Department saw itself as being a systemic risk based regulator" focused on encouraging industries "to put in place risk management systems which are then scrutinised", instead of inspecting for compliance with the OHS laws.[68]

Moreover, as the Department's resources began to decline from the late 1980s onwards, the number of inspectors employed reduced dramatically from 320 in 1988 to barely 120 in 2008, while the number of businesses grew exponentially.[69] Decades of continuous under-funding of the OSH Service created a significantly over-stretched inspectorate unable to carry out its job adequately.[70] In addition, the level of training given to the OSH inspectors also suffered during this time. As Gunningham commented, when reflecting upon the role of the OSH inspectors in the Pike River Coal Mine disaster, the Department of Labour provided little or no training and as a result many of the inspectors lacked the essential capabilities required.[71] Moreover, it noted that at the time of the Pike River Coal Mine disaster in 2010, there was just one mine inspector (who admitted they had

"Enforceable Undertakings in Action: Report of a Roundtable Discussion with Australian Regulators" (Legal Studies Research Paper No 464, Melbourne Law School, February 2010).
65   Health and Safety at Work Act, pt 4 sub-pt 4.
66   Neil Gunningham "Lessons from Pike River: Regulation, Safety and Neoliberalism" (2015) Social Science Research Network <www.ssrn.com> at 5.
67   Felicity Lamm, Erling Rasmussen and Danaë Anderson "The Case of the Disappearing Department of Labour: Whither goes state protection for vulnerable workers?" in Malcolm Sargeant and Martina Ori (eds) *Vulnerable Workers and Precarious Working* (Cambridge Scholars Publishing, Newcastle upon Tyne, 2013) 184 at 202.
68   Gunningham, above n 66, at 6.
69   Lamm, Rasmussen and Anderson, above n 67, at 203.
70   At 203.
71   Gunningham, above n 66, at 6–7.

little training), overseeing almost 1000 mines. The lesson, then for successive governments is that an adequately resourced and competent inspectorate is essential in OHS. In short, the growing number of work-related fatalities since 2002, particularly in the primary sector,[72] highlighted the inadequacy of New Zealand's OSH inspectorate and legislative framework.[73]

The Employer

Development of the role of employer

As noted above, self-regulation had become the dominant philosophy of HSE Act whereby the role of the employer in managing health and safety at the workplace was increased. As the Department of Labour in 1993 succinctly stated:[74]

> Increased emphasis on self-regulation and less reliance on Government workplace inspectors, is an important facet of employers taking ownership of managing workplace risks. Self-regulation in a framework of incentives and sanctions, is the corner-stone of the HSE Act.

A general duty was also placed on the employer to take "all practicable steps" to ensure the safety of its employees while at work.[75] Subsequently, case law established that the employer had to become *proactive* in managing health and safety in the workplace.[76] Moreover, "[e]mployers … [were] also under a number of particular duties in relation to the working environment", relating to workplace facilities and machinery.[77]

In line with its other employment law reforms, the 2000 Labour Government introduced the concept of good faith co-operation between employers and employees in the 2002 amendment to the HSE Act. Specifically, the reform indicated the need for the employer to involve their employees in health and safety matters via employee participation practices. However, it was only later that a more comprehensive worker participation requirement was introduced under the HSW Act, the details of which will be discussed later in the context of the role of workers.

Suffice to say that the new HSW Act replaced 'employer' with the wider term

---

72 See for example *Independent Forestry Safety Review: An agenda for change in the forestry sector* (October 2014).
73 See generally WorkSafe New Zealand "Workplace fatalities Summary 2013–2015" <www.business.govt.nz>.
74 Department of Labour, above n 30, at 89.
75 Health and Safety in Employment Act, s 6; and see generally Rudman, above n 43, at 415–416.
76 *Mair v Regina Ltd* DC Dunedin CRN3045004405, 4 March 1994 at 18–19; see *Mair v Frasers Bacon Ltd* DC Dunedin CRN3012009612, 24 February 1994 at 14; and see also Rudman, above n 43, at 401–404.
77 Anderson and Hughes, above n 32, at 697.

'person conducting a business or undertaking', or PCBU for short,[78] in order to better reflect and accommodate the complexities of current labour market where networks of supply chains and the practice of subcontracting are common.[79] As well as changing the terminology, the HSW Act stipulates that PCBUs have the *primary* duty of care for the health and safety of workers and other persons.[80] Moreover, a new feature of the HSW Act is the creation of a due diligence duty for officers of PCBUs – persons who would typically hold a governance role, such as a company director, or who "exercises significant influence over the management of the business or undertaking".[81] The liability of an officer is separate from the liability of a PCBU and, furthermore, "an officer may be charged with an offence whether or not the PCBU has been convicted or found guilty of an offence".[82]

Commentary on the role of employer

There are two new features that may make a difference in terms of attempting to improve New Zealand's OHS statistics: the primary duty of care of PCBUs and the due diligence duty of PCBUs' officers.

The change from taking 'all practicable steps' to ensure health and safety to imposing the primary duty of care on PCBUs could go somewhat in changing the behaviour of those in control. The standard applied to the primary duty of care is 'so far as is reasonably practicable'. Given that the provision is pretty much word-for-word comparable to the section found in the Australian Model Act, the Australian guidelines state that there are two elements to what is reasonably practical:[83]

(a) A duty-holder must first consider *what can be done* — that is, what is possible in the circumstances for ensuring health and safety. They must then consider whether it is *reasonable, in the circumstances* to do all that is possible.
(b) This means that what can be done should be done unless it is reasonable in the circumstances for the duty-holder to do something less.

With regard to officers, the HSE Act prescribed that: "officers, directors or agents who directed, authorised, assented to, acquiesced in, or participated in" a corporate health and safety offence were personally liable for the same offence

---

78 Health and Safety at Work Act, s 17.
79 See also Anderson and Hughes, above n 32, at 706–708.
80 At 709; and Rudman, above n 43, at 427–428.
81 Health and Safety at Work Act, s 18(b).
82 Anderson and Hughes, above n 32, at 710.
83 Safe Work Australia Interpretive Guidelines – Model Work Health and Safety Act: The Meaning of 'Reasonably Practicable' (2011) as quoted in Richard Johnstone and Michael Tooma "The General Duties" in *Work Health & Safety Regulation in Australia: The Model Act* (The Federation Press, Sydney, 2012) 39 at 75.

as the company (whether or not the latter has been prosecuted or convicted).[84] Hence, this type of liability was accessorial based on the poor conduct or performance of the company. The due diligence duty introduced by the HSW Act is novel in the sense that the Act imposes a *positive and proactive* duty on officers to make sure that their PCBU complies with its duties and obligations.[85]

The Workers

Development of the role of workers

The main duty of an employee,[86] as prescribed in HSE Act, is to look after his or her own health and safety and to ensure that others are not harmed by his or her actions or inactions while at work.[87] The only extra amendment to this duty in 2002 was to include reference to using suitable protective clothing or equipment in the course of ensuring own health and safety.[88] The more significant change brought about by the 2002 amendment, as alluded to previously, was the enactment of employee participation provisions. Before dealing with this particular change, a brief background on the subject of worker participation in New Zealand is necessary.

As with other inquiries into New Zealand working conditions, such as the Sweating Commission of 1890,[89] the authors of the ACOSH Report in 1988 argued the benefits of giving workers a more participative role in OHS.[90] Among the OHS community such a view was welcomed as it was generally agreed that "real progress is impossible without the full co-operation and commitment of all employees".[91] The ACOSH Report's conclusions were primarily based on the Robens' Report, whereby the two documents advocated for the need to impose:[92]

> ... a statutory duty on every employer to consult with his employees or their representatives at the workplace on measures for promoting safety and health at work, and to provide arrangements for the participation of employees in the development of such measures.

---

84 Health and Safety in Employment Act, s 56.
85 Richard Johnstone and Michael Tooma "The Duty of Officers" in *Work Health & Safety Regulation in Australia: The Model Act* (The Federation Press, Sydney, 2012) 98 at 108.
86 For employees' rights generally see Joanna Cullinane, Michael Pye and Mark Harcourt "The Rights and Obligations of Employees in Occupational Health and Safety Law in New Zealand" in Michael Lloyd (ed) *Occupational Health and Safety in New Zealand: Contemporary Social Research* (Dunmore Press, Palmerston North, 2002) at 119.
87 Health and Safety in Employment Act, s 19.
88 Health and Safety in Employment Amendment Act, s 12.
89 Report of the Sweating Commission, AJHR, 1890, H-5.
90 Advisory Council for Occupational Safety and Health, above n 24; and see generally Wren, above n 17, at 43–47.
91 Robens' Report, above n 9, at 18–19.
92 At 22; and see also Advisory Council for Occupational Safety and Health, above n 24, at 11.

Reforming Workplace Health and Safety Regulation

As stated earlier, despite the ACOSH Report's recommendations in 1988, the HSE Act did not give workers a statutory right of participation. Nevertheless in 2002 (approximately 20 years later behind United Kingdom and Australia) when speaking in Parliament, Margaret Wilson – then Minister of Labour – showed her support for inserting statutory rights for the participation of workers: "[t]he [Health and Safety in Employment Amendment Bill] . . . recognises that health and safety issues are fundamentally employment relations issues. A good culture of health and safety practices requires the participation of everyone."[93]

As a consequence, the 2002 Amendment Act introduced a general duty to involve employees in OHS matters: "[e]very employer must provide reasonable opportunities for the employer's employees to participate effectively in ongoing processes for improvement of health and safety in the employees' places of work".[94] The purpose of this new duty was to ensure that all those with relevant knowledge and expertise were involved in OHS, thereby resulting in better decision making by the employers on health and safety matters at the workplaces.[95] The employee participation provisions were to be enforced via compliance orders set out in the Employment Relations Act 2000, meaning that it would "be dealt with in the same way as any other employment relationship problem".[96]

The 2002 amendment also stated that an agreed employee participation system was required if (a) an employer employs 30 or more employees, or (b) an employer employs fewer than 30 employees, but at least one employee or a union representing them requires the development of such a system.[97] To set up a system, the employers, employees and unions were to "co-operate in good faith to seek to develop, agree, implement, and maintain a system that sets out the ways in which the employer must seek to comply".[98] The only necessary ingredient of the system was to specify a process by which the system must be reviewed. Otherwise, the Act left it up to the parties to arrange what would work best for the particular workplace.[99] If such a system were not agreed upon within the six months, the Act provided for a 'default' employee participation system.[100]

The HSE Act also suggested the use of health and safety representatives (who would be entitled to paid leave for training)[101] – whether acting independently or as part of a health and safety committee – and having processes for ensuring

---

93 (3 December 2002) 604 NZPD 2442.
94 Health and Safety in Employment Amendment Act, s 13; and see generally Rudman, above n 43, at 410–414.
95 Health and Safety in Employment Amendment Act, s 13.
96 Carr and Sheriff, above n 56, at 67.
97 Health and Safety in Employment Act, s 19C(1).
98 Section 19C(2).
99 Section 19C(3).
100 Section 19D.
101 Section 19E and sch 1, pt 1.

the regular and co-operative interaction between the employers' and employees' representatives.[102] The health and safety representatives were given the power to issue hazard notices, which would act as the required prior warning before an inspector were to issue an infringement notice against an employer.[103]

With regard to worker participation, the HSW Act in 2015 also introduced two new statutory duties on PCBUs and prescribed for two particular practices in certain circumstances, as outlined below.

(a) Opportunities for engagement

The HSW Act places a duty on a PCBU to engage with workers whenever engagement is required.[104] A PCBU and its workers may agree on adequate procedures for engagement, but the procedures must not be inconsistent with section 59, which prescribes what engagement with workers must involve.[105] The Act also places another duty on a PCBU to have worker participation practices, which should "provide reasonable opportunities for workers ... to participate effectively in improving work health and safety in the business or undertaking on an ongoing basis".[106] In essence, the change from the HSE Act is that, instead of having a general duty to provide reasonable opportunities for employee participation, there must now be practices implemented to ensure the provision of such opportunities.

(b) Health and safety representatives and committees

The HSW Act prescribes two practices of worker participation: health and safety representatives and committees.[107] A health and safety representative may be elected if either a worker notifies the PCBU that he or she wishes to have a representative or if PCBU wishes do so on its own initiative.[108] If elected, workers may be divided into work groups with different representatives.[109] A health and safety committee may be established if there is a request made and directed at PCBU by a health and safety representative or by five or more workers at that workplace.[110]

The controversy surrounding the HSW Bill on these two types of practices arose because there was a significant change between the Bill's original wording

---

102 Section 19C(5); and see generally Rudman, above n 43, at 412–413.
103 At 413–414.
104 Health and Safety at Work Act, s 58(1).
105 Sections 58(2) and 58(3).
106 Health and Safety at Work Act, s 61(1).
107 Health and Safety at Work Act, pt 3, sub-pt 2.
108 Sections 62(1) and 62(3).
109 Section 64(1).
110 Section 66(1).

and its post-Select Committee version, which has been adopted in the Act.[111] In essence, a PCBU may decline to respond affirmatively to a worker's request for a health and safety representative if a PCBU runs a small business with fewer than 20 workers in a low-risk sector, which controversially included dairy farming and sheep and cattle farming, sectors that are responsible for a large proportion of workplace deaths and serious injuries.[112] Moreover, the same kind of business may also reject a request for a health and safety committee.[113]

Commentary on the role of workers

The recently passed HSW Act is meant to improve the OHS legislative framework in New Zealand, especially because it repeals, *inter alia*, the HSE Act.[114] It is true that the recent reform is a step in the right direction, because, as is explained next, worker participation is instrumental in creating healthier and safer working environments and the HSW Act places statutory duties of participation on every PCBU. However, the exceptions to the twin duties could in practice reduce the potential significance of the recent OHS reform because they would *effectively* deprive workers of smaller businesses of the right to have health and safety representatives or committees.

Arguably, the permissible exclusion in HSW Act is not appropriate because many businesses in New Zealand may fall into that category: "small business sectors ... represent approximately 90 per cent of the business population and [employ] 60 per cent of the business population".[115] In short, many workplaces around New Zealand might not take advantage of the two practices, which empirically are shown to be the most useful in dealing with OHS. There is irrefutable evidence that health and safety representatives and committees are effective in improving OHS.[116] The Robens' Report was also of the view that the role of health and safety representatives is key to any success in OHS and,[117] thus, health and safety representatives "should have strong channels of communication

---

111 WorkSafe New Zealand "Health and Safety Reform Bill – key changes" <www.business.govt.nz>.
112 Health and Safety at Work Act, s 62(4).
113 Section 66(3).
114 Section 231.
115 Raymond Markey and others "Exploring employee participation and work environment in hotels: Case studies from Denmark and New Zealand" (2014) 39(1) NZJER 2 at 7.
116 Lamm, above n 2; see generally Felicity Lamm and David Walters "Regulating Occupational Health and Safety in Small Businesses" in Elizabeth Bluff, Neil Gunningham and Richard Johnstone (eds) *OHS Regulation for a Changing World of Work* (The Federation Press, Sydney, 2004) 94 at 109–110; and David Walters and Theo Nichols "Effectiveness of Representative Worker Participation" in *Worker Representation and Workplace Health and Safety* (Palgrave Macmillan, Hampshire, 2007) at 24.
117 Robens' Report, above n 9, at 21.

with government work health and safety inspectors".[118] In the period 2011–2012, just after the Australian Model Act was passed, the injury incidence rate fell by 26 per cent and fatalities' incidence rate fell by 41 per cent.[119] Moreover, Australia has reported the lowest number of work-related deaths in 11 years[120] and the lowest compensated fatality rate in a decade.[121] It sounds somewhat nonsensical, therefore, that a New Zealand Act modelled on that of Australia introduced such an exception where none exists in the Model Act.

Conclusion

The overall conclusion is that recent health and safety reforms starting 2013 with the establishment of WorkSafe are certainly a step in the right direction, but no doubt improvements are needed. It is hoped for that WorkSafe learns from the lessons of its predecessor to ensure its role as the OSH inspectorate is carried out adequately. The role of the employer in tripartism can never be understated and, thus, the enactment of PCBU's *primary* duty of care and the due diligence duty on officers are likely to change the behaviour of those responsible, but only time will show if there is any change in practice. Lastly, worker participation is a topic that has finally been given proper attention in New Zealand and it is optimistic to see positive duties imposed on PCBUs to engage with workers and to have worker participation practices established. But the biggest failure of the HSW Act is the exemption given to those businesses that are not high risk with fewer than 20 employees from having health and safety representatives or committees: there might be too many workers in New Zealand still left without adequate representation and voice on their own health and safety.

---

118 See generally Richard Johnstone and Michael Tooma "Worker Representation and Participation" in *Work Health and Safety Regulation in Australia: The Model Act* (The Federation Press, Sydney, 2012) at 136; David Walters "Workplace Arrangements for Worker Participation in OHS" in Elizabeth Bluff, Neil Gunningham and Richard Johnstone (eds) *OHS Regulation for a Changing World of Work* (The Federation Press, Sydney, 2004) at 68; and Richard Johnstone, Michael Quinlan and David Walters "Statutory Occupational Health and Safety Workplace Arrangements for the Modern Labour Market" (2005) 47(1) JIR 93.
119 Safe Work Australia Comparative Performance Monitoring Report: Comparison of work health and safety and workers' compensation schemes in Australia and New Zealand (October 2014) at vii.
120 Safe Work Australia "Lowest number of work-related deaths in 11 years" (media release, 15 July 2014).
121 Safe Work Australia "Lowest compensated fatality rate in a decade" (media release, 9 October 2014).

Women in the Workforce: Still Unequal after all these Years?

Amanda Reilly and Annick Masselot

In 1893, women in New Zealand were the first in the world to get the vote and in more recent times women have had a run as Prime Minister, Opposition Leader, Chief Justice and Governor General. Even the Queen is a woman. The country's most famous pop singer, best known opera star, most famous short story writer, greatest novelist and most consistent world champion athlete are all women. They're not allowed in the All Blacks as yet, but don't be fooled. It's just a matter of time...[1]

Introduction

The John Clarke quote above paints a picture of New Zealand women inexorably striding forward in terms of gender equality. It is true that women in New Zealand have a low gender pay gap at 'only' 11.8 per cent in 2015.[2] This is consistently one of the lowest in the world when comparing full-time workers.[3] New Zealand women's employment rate is one of the highest in the OECD (Organisation for

---

1   John Clarke "New Zealand: A User's Guide" (2014) *Briefing Papers* <http://briefingpapers.co.nz/new-zealand-a-users-guide/>. Clarke was a well-known social commentator and comedian.
2   Ministry for Women "Empirical evidence of the gender pay gap in New Zealand" (1 March 2017) <http://women.govt.nz/our-work/utilising-womens-skills/income/gender-pay-gap>; Statistics New Zealand "Measuring the gender pay gap" (19 January 2016) <http://www.stats.govt.nz/browse_for_stats/income-and-work/Income/gender-pay-gap.aspx>.
3   Ministry for Women "New Zealand Women" <http://women.govt.nz/new-zealand-women#sthash.2o5JqUey.dpuf>.

Economic Co-operation and Development)[4] at 64.7 per cent in 2015.[5] New Zealand also frequently tops various international gender equality indexes and reports.[6] New Zealand women have made considerable progress in terms of equality. There are more women working in the labour market and in professions now than 40 years ago, which represents a formidable structural transformation.[7] Nevertheless, female labour force participation here is still lower than their male counterparts (12 per cent difference between the sexes in 2011).[8] Worse yet, there is backsliding: the number of women in senior positions[9] is declining and the gender pay gap is increasing.[10] While workforce transformation has been dramatic for New Zealand women, there is still some way to go to reach gender equality here.

To understand how far we have come and to understand the drivers of workplace transformation for women, we need to understand where we started from. This chapter draws on articles published over 40 years in the *New Zealand Journal of Employment Relations* (NZJER) (formerly the *New Zealand Journal of Industrial Relations* (NZJIR)) to summarise progress and setbacks over the decades. It then

---

4   Reports on the rate of women in the NZ labour force varies from 62.5 per cent in the Household Labour Force Survey to 72 per cent in the World Economic Forum Report. Department of Labour *Labour Force Participation in New Zealand: Recent Trends, Future Scenarios and the Impact on Economic Growth* (Department of Labour, Wellington, 2009); Department of Labour and World Economic Forum "Global Gender Gap Report 2014" (January 2014) <http://www3.weforum.org/docs/GGGR14/GGGR_CompleteReport_2014.pdf >.
5   Ministry for Women "New Zealand Women" (March 2015) <http://women.govt.nz/new-zealand-women#sthash.2o5JqUey.dpuf>.
6   World Economic Forum "Global Gender Gap Report 2013" (2013) <http://www3.weforum.org/docs/WEF_GenderGap_Report_2013.pdf>.
7   Since 1986 the female labour force has increased by more than 50 per cent. In 2016 women's labour force participation was 64.5 per cent, above the OECD average. Ministry for Women "Labour Force Participation" <http://women.govt.nz/work-skills/paid-and-unpaid-work/labour-force-participation>.
8   Families Commission *Families and Whanau Status Report 2013* (Families Commission, Wellington, 2013) at 62.
9   Ministry for Women "Women in Leadership" <http://women.govt.nz/our-work/women-leadership>. Only 14.75 per cent of the NZSX 100 directorships in 2012 were women and this number decreased with only 12 per cent of female directors disclosed by 109 NZSX companies in 2013. Judy McGregor "New Zealand Census of Women's Participation 2012" (2012) <www.hrc.co.nz>; and New Zealand Stock Exchange "Gender Diversity Annual Statistics Memorandum" <www.nzx.com>. For a general oversight of the situation of female board members on large listed private companies in New Zealand, see Annick Masselot and Timothy Brand "Diversity, quotas and compromise in the boardroom: Can New Zealand adopt a legislation to tackle gender imbalance in economic decision making?" (2015) 26 NZULR 23.
10 Since the late 1990s the gender pay gap has been steadily reducing from 16.3 per cent in 1998 to 9.1 per cent in 2012, but since then the gap is increasing. In 2016, the gender pay gap was 12 per cent. Ministry for Women "Gender Pay Gap" <http://women.govt.nz/work-skills/income/gender-pay-gap>.

identifies the continuities with the past as well as areas of progress to determine where New Zealand women are currently at and to pinpoint changes that will need to be made if there is to be further progress.

The Third National Government (1975–1984)

Certainly in comparison to what had gone before, the 1970s heralded a progressive period for women's employment. Female labour market participation was at 32.5 per cent in 1976 compared to 20 per cent in 1926.[11] The 1970s witnessed the adoption of some serious legislative support for women's participation in the workforce. In the 1950s the Public Service Commission set different levels for salary progression for men and women; the Government Service Equal Pay Act 1960 put an end to this practice and the Equal Pay Act 1972 extended the principle of equal pay to the private sector.[12] The Human Rights Commission Act 1977[13] also provided that it was illegal to discriminate on the grounds of sex in terms of employment, conditions of work, fringe benefits and opportunities for training, promotion, and transfers to people with the same or substantially similar qualifications.[14] On the international scene, New Zealand ratified the United Nations Convention on the Elimination of all Forms of Discrimination against Women (CEDAW) in 1979.

Despite these normative improvements, the legal framework reflected a social setting which would be unimaginable nowadays.[15] For instance, the Factories Amendment Act 1972 set limits on the hours that women could work at night in factories, with no comparable restriction for men, effectively depriving women of the opportunity to earn overtime. There were restrictions on the weights women were permitted to lift and Sharp notes the practice which then existed of some firms giving women workers one half day off work each month to go shopping.[16] Women were also treated in law as dependents: under Regulation 56(2) of the Public Service Regulations 1964, a government department would meet transfer expenses for an employee and his family, but transfer expenses for married women employees would have to be referred to the State Services Commission.[17] While these restrictions are now gone, some of the most structural issues have remained the same. For example, then as now, there is a gender pay gap.

---

11 Audrey Sharp "Towards equal employment opportunity for women" (1978) 3 NZJIR 121.
12 Equal Pay Act 1972, s 2A.
13 Now repealed under the Human Rights Act 1993.
14 Human Rights Commission Act 1977, s 15(1)(b), also extending to cases of dismissal, s 15(1)(c).
15 Above n 11 at 125.
16 At 125.
17 At 126. Similarly, under the Education (Staff and Salaries) Regulation, the education manual allowed for the removal expenses for a married woman only if her husband was shown to be totally dependent on her.

Gender Pay Gap

According to Hyman, in May 1980 women's gross weekly earnings were 62.3 per cent of those of a man.[18] Hyman notes some narrowing of the differences between men and women's earnings between 1973 and 1977 following the period of implementation of the equal pay legislation. The Equal Pay Act certainly helped reduce gender pay discrimination through its elimination of separate male and female rates in awards, agreements, scales and other collective agreements.[19]

Female Dominated Occupations and Job Segregation

Then, as now, women clustered in female dominated occupations. Hyman observes that occupational segregation between the sexes was extreme and diminished only very slowly.[20] Women formed just over one third of the labour force, yet over half of all women workers were engaged in occupations which were over 70 per cent female or more.[21]

In the 1970s New Zealand women were not represented in all job areas but were concentrated mainly in three industrial groups: (1) community, social and personal health services (that is, teaching and health); (2) manufacturing; and (3) wholesale and retail, restaurants and hotels.

Women and Unions

As highlighted by Butterworth, the particular industries women were clustered in were characterised by widely dispersed small units, subject to cyclical and seasonal fluctuations and shifts. Butterworth notes this posed particular problems for union organisation.[22] This lack of female trade union involvement and activism was also echoed by Paterson,[23] who applauds researchers who connect women's low participation in unions with their disadvantaged marginal and segregated labour market status. Indeed, the absence and inaction of unions with regards to women workers left women vulnerable to the grossest

---

18   Prue Hyman "Women and pay" (1978) 6 NZJIR 79 at 80. Over the years Prue Hyman has been a strong advocate for recognition of the need for further action to address the status of women in New Zealand and a consistent presence in the pages of the *New Zealand Journal of Employment Relations*. Her most recent book, *Hopes Dashed? The Economics of Gender Inequality* (Bridget Williams Books, Wellington, 2017), continues this work.
19   Prue Hyman "Equal pay for women after the Employment Contracts Act: Legislation and practice – The emperor with no clothes?" (1993) 18 NZJIR 44 at 47.
20   Prue Hyman "Review Article: Women and Pay" (1981) 6 NZJIR 79 at 83.
21   Above n 11 at 122.
22   Ruth Butterworth "Women in the workforce" (1978) 3 NZJIR 11 at 11.
23   Karen Paterson "Review of – Geare Alan, Joyce Herd, and John Howells, *Women in trade unions: A case study of participation in New Zealand*'. Victoria University of Wellington, Industrial Relations Centre, 1979" (1979) 4 NZJIR 43.

exploitation and the "plight and plaints of women workers have too often been ignored by male dominated unions".[24]

The Distinctive Position of Māori and Pasifika Women

Butterworth also comments on the particular disadvantage of Māori and Pasifika women who were often hampered by family responsibility, needing a wage but limited in hours and ability to travel compounded by other challenges including language and lack of contact with formal agencies.[25] Revell and Brosnan further comment in a later article that there are substantially different participation rates for different ethnic groups.[26] New Zealand's non-Māori female workforce has been increasing almost continuously since 1891[27] while Māori female participation has been lower than non-Māori female participation at every census since comparable data first became available.

Lack of Work-Family Reconciliation Mechanisms

Finally, the 1970s were characterised by a lack of work-family reconciliation mechanisms. Sharp comments on a reluctance on the part of employers "to concede variations in working hours"[28] and also explains that 86 per cent of awards in 1976 made no provision for maternity leave at all. However, in 1980, the Maternity Leave and Employment Protection Act 1981 was introduced, which allowed women to take unpaid maternity leave for up to 26 weeks and prohibited dismissal due to pregnancy or maternity leave. The protection applied under two conditions. First, women had to have been employed by the same employer for the immediately preceding 18 months for at least 15 hours a week. Second, their position would be presumed to be kept open unless the employer proved that it could not be kept open.

Whilst this new Act was definitely a step in the right direction, it was only a small step. The legislation was subject to sharp criticism by Szakats[29] who noted the complete lack of pay during the leave – either in the form of a welfare payment or the continuation of wages – which made it stingy compared to the relative generosity of overseas provisions. In comparing the British and German systems, he concluded that this legislation offered the least protection.[30] He also

---

24 Above n 22, at 12.
25 Above n 22, at 14.
26 Phillipa Revell and Peter Brosnan "New Zealand labour force participation: The ninety years to 1981" (1986) 11 NZJIR 88.
27 At 79.
28 Above n 11, at 121.
29 Alexander Szakats "Maternity leave legislation: The timidity of the New Zealand approach" (1981) 6 NZJIR 11 at 19.
30 At 18.

criticised the lack of paternity leave provision for fathers who might have to stay at home to look after older children. Moreover, he argued that the employment protection provision "amounts to a mere possibility – not a probability let alone a firm right to be re-employed after 26 weeks if the job or a similar job is available".[31] He finally concluded that the protection offered was misleading: "the statute appears to grant a protection which might prove to be illusory, like the fairy tale gift which the hero was commanded to give, and not to give to the king. He solves this impossible demand by presenting a bird which immediately flew away".[32]

In the final years of the Muldoon government, at least two other legislative developments are noteworthy: (1) the Minimum Wage Act 1982 entitled women over 20 to the same minimum wage as men; and (2) the International Labour Organisation (ILO) Convention on Equal Remuneration was ratified in 1983.

The Fourth Labour Government (1984–1990)

In 1984, a Labour government took power and the years of 'Rogernomics' began.[33] Although women suffered alongside men due to the effects of deregulation, legislatively a number of measures aimed at furthering the position of women in the workplace were put in place. A feature of the 1980s was that the trade union movement – historically male dominated – became more responsive to women's concerns as women achieved positions of power within the unions and with a growth of women unionists representing occupational groups with large female memberships.[34] Politically, as well, women organised politically and their "assaults on the citadels of political power" produced various law changes.[35]

The Ministry of Women's Affairs was established and recognised as a separate department in 1984. The Parental Leave and Employment Act 1987 strengthened rights of mothers to return to their employment at the end of their leave. The 1987 Act extended the period of unpaid maternity leave from 26 to 52 weeks and extended the protection to both parents. The Act also introduced two

---

31   At 19.
32   At 19.
33   The term *Rogernomics* – a portmanteau of *Roger* and *economics* – was coined by journalists at the *New Zealand Listener* by analogy with Reaganomics to describe the economic policies followed by Roger Douglas after his appointment in 1984 as Minister of Finance in the Fourth Labour Government of New Zealand. Such politics were characterised by market-led restructuring and deregulation.
34   Linda Hill and Rosemary Du Plessis "Tracing the similarities, identifying the differences: Women and the Employment Contracts Act" (1993) 18 NZJIR 31 at 43; Margaret Wilson "Contractualism and the Employment Contracts Act 1991: Can they deliver equality for women?" (1994) 19 NZJIR 256 at 274.
35   At 274.

weeks' unpaid leave for fathers.[36] The eligibility requirements were reduced to 12 months' service of 10 hours or more per week.[37] Sexual harassment provisions were introduced in 1987 in the Labour Relations Act. The State Sector Act adopted in 1988 set requirements for policies on equal employment opportunities in the state sector. Public Service and the public health and public education sectors were required to be good employers and to create Equal Employment Opportunities (EEO) plans and practices to deal with discrimination.

Pay equity – that is, the issue of whether men and women get the same or a similar wage for doing a comparable job – became a focus of concern in 1986. A group of working and union women established the 'Coalition for Equal Value Equal Pay'. As discussed by Hyman[38] this grew out of a dissatisfaction with the Equal Pay Act 1972, which apparently failed to clearly incorporate the principle of equal pay for work of equal value. Presciently, she notes that "the Act appears to extend well beyond equal pay for identical work to allow comparisons on the basis of skills, effort, responsibility and conditions."[39] There was "considerable doubt that it was ever applied in this way and the Arbitration court judgment in the 1986 Clerical Workers Case means that for all practical purposes this is now impossible".[40]

The Coalition for Equal Value Equal Pay produced a report, 'Towards Employment Equity', which recommended new legislation covering equal opportunity and equal pay for work of equal value. The recommendations hinged on comparisons of work between female and male occupational classes. The Employment Equity Act 1990, was the culmination of this concerted activism. In 1989, the Employment Equity Bill had its first reading and was passed by Labour in 1990. It provided a way in which national award negotiations "could address systematic gender inequality in access to earnings using pay equity assessments provided by the Employment Equity Commission".[41]

---

36 Pheroze Jagose "Babies and bosses: An examination of section 41 of the Parental Leave and Employment Protection Act 1987" (1994) 19 NZJIR 131 at 150.
37 Paul Callister and Judith Galtry "Paid parental leave in New Zealand: A short history and future policy options" (2006) 2 *Policy Quarterly*, 38 at 46.
38 Prue Hyman "Equal pay for work of equal value – Job evaluation issues" (1988) 13 NZJIR 237 at 237.
39 Much later, in *Bartlett v TerraNova* in 2015, the New Zealand Courts accepted that the Equal Pay Act could be interpreted to mean that equal pay for work of equal value did not simply mean the same pay for the same work. However, prior to this decision, the Act had been effectively neutered in 1986 when the Clerical Workers Union took a case to the Arbitration Court seeking a ruling that employers should be directed to negotiate a claim for equal pay for work of equal value and the Court dismissed the case.
40 Hyman above n 38 at 237 referring to *New Zealand Clerical Administrative etc IUOW v Farmers Trading Co Ltd* [1986] ACJ 203 (AC).
41 Linda Hill and Rosemary Du Plessis "Tracing the similarities, identifying the differences: Women and the Employment Contracts Act" (1993) 18 NZJIR 31 at 33.

Fourth National Government (1990–1999)

A change of government in 1990 heralded the era of the Employment Contracts Act, which was passed in 1991. Characterised by an ideology that was anti-union and anti-market intervention, it moved New Zealand's labour relations system away from the historical tradition of conciliation and arbitrations to settle wages and conditions of employment, to a system centred on the negotiation of individual and collective contracts. The Employment Equity Act 1990 was antithetical to this and was deeply embedded in the previous system of wage fixing. It was repealed after only a month and thus, as commented by Margaret Wilson, who was a key architect of the legislation, it "must have had one of the shortest legislative lives on record".[42]

It would not be true to say that the then National Government evinced no concern with regards to the disadvantaged position of women in the workplace. However, the National Working Party on Equity in Employment considered that "progress towards an equal employment opportunities environment will be most effectively achieved where employers are closely involved in the voluntary promotion of progressive EEO management practices".[43] Equal employment opportunities were defined as being where "all employment and promotion decisions are made on the basis of merit".[44] An Equal Employment Opportunities approach is not concerned with measuring equality outcomes, but rather with inputs in the sense of the introduction of bureaucratic measures aimed at reducing indirect barriers by developing and implementing policies and programmes which promote objective criteria and offer management training for women. Accordingly, in 1992 the EEO Trust was established to promote EEO programmes and practices in private sector workplaces. Described by Hyman as "small and toothless, but acceptable [and] at least working for positive change", the EEO (now known as Diversity Works) has largely and to this day focused on the business case for diversity.[45]

Another change which could be seen as seeking to protect women and other groups from discrimination was the adoption of the Human Rights Act 1993, which replaced the Human Rights Commission Act 1977. The protection against discrimination provided by this legislation mirrored that of the Employment Contracts Act providing alternative routes for the aggrieved employee:[46]

---

42 Margaret Wilson "Contractualism and the Employment Contracts Act 1991: Can they deliver equality for women?" (1994) 19 NZJIR 256 at 266.
43 At 270.
44 Rose Ryan "Collection: Women at work – Issues for the 1990s" (1993) 18 NZJIR 1.
45 Prue Hyman "Equal pay for women after the Employment Contracts Act: Legislation and practice – The emperor with no clothes?" (1993) 18 NZJIR 44 at 55.
46 Peter Kiely "Discrimination and human rights: An overview of remedies" (1993) 18 NZJIR 375.

There is no doubt that the passing of the Human Rights Act has indicated a new commitment to the prevention of discrimination in New Zealand. The Act sends a clear message to both employers and the Courts that discrimination in the workplace is unacceptable and will be punished. The raising of the maximum amount of damages from $2000 to $200000 for humiliation, loss of dignity and injury feelings certainly gives the Courts the power to be more severe in their orders.

The Conciliation system had its faults and it is questionable how much it ever would have furthered equality even if the Employment Equity Act had managed to be fully implemented.[47] Proponents of the Employment Contracts Act argued that it would be good for women:[48]

> Some advocates of the Employment Contracts Act argued that that it would strip away the institutional forms which, in a variety of ways, perpetuated women's unequal access to earnings. It was presented as offering women just what they wanted "flexibility" and the "freedom" to determine their own wages and conditions of employment in direct negotiations with their employers.

However, there were many that expressed doubt about the Employment Contracts Act, pointing to the weak bargaining position of women[49] and the inequality that employers and employees bring to negotiations.[50] That inequality was most pronounced in low-wage jobs. Those who predicted the Employment Contracts Act did not have any advantages for women were soon proven correct[51] as the pay gap between men and women started to stagnate and widen. In 1994, the ILO Application of Standards Committee heard evidence regarding the Convention 100 on Equal Remuneration that after decades of slow but steady progress, the introduction of the ECA had resulted in a steady widening of the gap between men's and women's wages as well as effectively rendering inoperative the Equal Pay legislation.[52]

---

47 Rosemary Du Plessis Novitz, and Nabila Jabert "Pay equity, the 'free' market and state intervention" (1990) 15 NZJIR 251 at 256; see also Prue Hyman "Equal pay for women after the Employment Contracts Act: Legislation and practice – The emperor with no clothes?" (1993) 18 NZJIR 44 at 46.
48 Linda Hill and Rosemary Du Plessis "Tracing the similarities, Identifying the Differences: Women and the Employment Contracts Act" (1993) 18 NZJIR 31 at 33.
49 Janet Sayers "Women, the Employment Contracts Act and bargaining: a discussion paper" (1991) 16 NZJIR 159.
50 Margaret Wilson "Contractualism and the Employment Contracts Act 1991. Can they deliver equality for women?" (1994) 19 NZJIR 256.
51 Suzanne Hammond and Raymond Harbridge "The impact of the Employment Contract Act on women at work" (1993) 18 NZJIR 15; Suzanne Hammond and Raymond Harbridge "Women and enterprise bargaining: The New Zealand experience of labour market deregulation" (1995) 20 NZJIR 359; and Raymond Harbridge and Maryan Street "Labour market adjustment and women in the service industry: A survey" (1995) 20 NZJIR 1.
52 Robert Wilson "The decade of non-compliance: The NZ government record of non-compliance

The Fifth Labour Government (1999–2008)

In 2000 a Labour-led government took power again and the Employment Contracts Act was replaced by the Employment Relations Act. The Clark government demonstrated more commitment to furthering equality for women in the workplace than previous governments. There was progress on a number of fronts and particularly in relation to the issue of work-life balance. Such steps were underpinned by the idea of social development, social inclusion and social investment, but they were also realised as a way to increase and strengthen female labour force participation.[53]

Work–Family Balance Mechanisms

Three pieces of employment legislation were adopted as the back bones of the New Zealand work-family balance architecture. First, the Parental Leave and Employment Protection Act 1987 was amended in 2002[54] to introduce for the first time in New Zealand the right to paid parental leave. (Qualifying) parents,[55] employed in minimum employment, could take up to 12 weeks of government-funded paid parental leave as well as up to 52 weeks of job-protected unpaid parental leave. The leave could be transferred to the qualifying father but was conditional upon the mother qualifying first. In December 2004, the paid parental leave was increased to 14 weeks and the eligibility criteria were extended to employees who had six months or more continuous service with the same employer. In July 2006, the entitlement to paid parental leave was extended to the self-employed.

Although the adoption of the legislation introducing paid parental leave has been positively evaluated by families who have been entitled to the payment,[56] the

---

with international labour standards, 1990–1998" (2000) 25 NZJIR 84.

53 See, in particular, "Prime Minister's Opening Statement to Parliament" (2004) <www.beehive.govt.nz/Print/PrintDocument.aspx?DocumentID=18877> and (2005) <www.beehive.govt.nz/Print/PrintDocument.aspx?DocumentID=22087>.

54 Parental Leave and Employment Protection Amendments Acts 2002.

55 In order to qualify, parents must have continuously been employed or self-employed for an average of 10 hours a week *and* no less than one hour in every week or 40 hours in every month, for the twelve months immediately before the expected date of birth or adoption: Parental Leave and Employment Protection Amendments Acts 2002, s 7. The entitlement varies according to the length of the continuous period of employment. Employees who meet the minimum hour test but only over six months of continuous period of employment qualify for the 14 weeks paid leave but not for the extended unpaid leave. The Act also covers self-employed individuals who have worked for an average of 10 hours a week over 12 months immediately before the birth or the adoption. Similar restrictions are imposed on self-employed persons who meet the minimum hour test but for only six months of continuous self-employment.

56 Katherine Forbes "Paid parental leave under (new) labour" (2009) 34 SPJNZ 12.

Act fails to respond to work-family conflict for many families.[57] The qualifying requirement meant that a large number of women – especially those in precarious employment – have not been able to benefit from the legislation.[58] Moreover, paid parental leave has always been limited in New Zealand and capped to 50 per cent of the average weekly earnings, lower than the minimum wage, inferring that production is more valued than reproduction.[59] In addition, the "raison d'etre of the paid parental leave . . . has been to contribute to economic growth rather than the wellbeing of families".[60]

Second, the Employment Relations (Breaks, Infant Feeding, and Other Matters) Amendment Act 2008 created a right for employees who are breastfeeding and wish to breastfeed to request adequate (but unpaid) breaks and appropriate facilities. The Act was introduced to reflect New Zealand's international obligations under the United Nations Committee on the Elimination of All Forms of Discrimination against Women (CEDAW 2003). To help employers understand their obligations, the Minister of Labour must under the Act publish a Code of Employment Practice. Although the code of practice should aim to provide useful guidance on the range of factors an employer can consider when negotiating a breastfeeding arrangement and gives practical ideas on the factors to consider, such as health and safety, facilities, resources and space for breastfeeding employees, the first advice given is that "there is no absolute obligation on employers to provide breaks and/or facilities".[61] This gives a frivolous tone to the Act, which limits the employers' obligation to reasonable and practical circumstances relating to the employer's operational environment and resources. The Act, far from being concerned with infants' wellbeing or gender equity, is considered as an instrument to enhance the functioning of the labour market.[62]

Finally, the main tool for the work-family balance mechanism in this period was developed though the Employment Relations (Flexible Working Arrangements) Amendments Act 2007, which created a statutory right for employees who have care responsibilities for any person to request a variation in their time and place

---

57 Families Commission *The Kiwi Nest: Sixty Years of Change in New Zealand Families* (Families Commission, Wellington, 2008).
58 Sarah Crichton *Work Patterns after Paid Parental Leave* (Department of Labour and Statistics, New Zealand, 2008).
59 Annick Masselot "The right and reality of flexible working arrangements in New Zealand" in Grace James and Nicole Busby (eds) *Families, Care-Giving and Paid Work* (Edward Elgar, Cheltenham, 2011) at 69–85.
60 Katherine Forbes (2009) "Paid Parental Leave under (New) Labour" 34 Social Policy Journal of New Zealand 12, at 20.
61 Kate Wilkinson "Information for mothers who are returning to work" (2010) avaiable at <https://www.employment.govt.nz/hours-and-wages/breaks/breastfeeding-at-work/>
62 Paul Callister and Judith Galtry "'Baby bonus' or paid parental leave: Which one is better?" (2009) 34 SPJNZ 1.

of work. The right to request operated under three conditions of application: (1) the request had to be linked to the existence of a care commitment for the employee; (2) the employee had to have at least six months continuous service with the same employer; and (3) the request could only be made once every 12 months by the same employee. The request process was relatively heavy and complex. It had to be made in writing, explain what variations were required and how the said variations would enable the provision of better care for the dependent. Employers were obligated to consider the request seriously and in a timely fashion (within three months of receipt of the request) but could refuse on the grounds that the variations were not compatible with the business operation.

The Act provided a grievance mechanism, a right of appeal and a penalty of up to $2,000 in compensation to the aggrieved employee. However the difficulty of accessing justice and the relatively low level of compensation has left the Act without the necessary teeth to truly enact change. The right to request was, in the main, not actually used formally. Most employees have the right to ask for changes in their terms and conditions of employment. The right to request only represented a symbolic yet powerful acknowledgment of employees' care commitment.[63]

Overall, this period shows a great deal of activity related to work-life balance and some significant policy developments. There is no doubt that those laws contributed to transforming the work place as well as supporting women's ability to participate in the labour market. However, Ravenswood rightly pointed out that these work-family balance mechanisms were still primarily motivated by the business case within a liberal paradigm and they did not go far enough in recognising the value of care work.[64] Indeed, the New Zealand work-life balance policy, as developed in the 2000–2009 period, lags behind many post-industrial countries.[65]

Access to Childcare

Moreover, work-life balance policy cannot be considered in isolation from the strategy on care and specifically on childcare. Although childcare is not placed within the realm of employment law, the impact of the organisation of care on the labour market participation of women in particular is significant.[66] Childcare

---

63 Annick Masselot "Gender implications of the right to request flexible working arrangements: Raising pigs and children in New Zealand" (2015) 39 NZJER 59.
64 Katherine Ravenswood "The role of the State in family-friendly policy: An analysis of Labour-led government policy" (2008) 33 NZJER 34.
65 Annick Masselot "The right and reality of flexible working arrangements in New Zealand" (2011); and Katherine Forbes "Paid parental leave under (new) labour" (2009) 34 SPJNZ 12.
66 OECD *Teachers Matter: Attracting, Developing and Retaining Effective Teachers* (OECD, Paris, 2005).

has been a private issue for a long time with women doing the bulk of the work for free but at a cost. In the 1980s and 1990s, the substantial increase of female workforce participation precipitated the debate over childcare in many developed countries. Early childcare in New Zealand had been skewed almost exclusively towards private organisations. This has resulted in a booming private sector with high prices and large inequality of access. In 2004, the Working for Families scheme was introduced to provide incentives for people to work, especially solo parents. The weighing up of care versus work dilemma faced by many women meant that the government had to intervene in the area of childcare. However, such intervention has remained limited. In 2000, a requirement for early childcare qualification was introduced. In 2005, the government established financial structures designed to encourage the employment of qualified staff in order to boost quality. In 2007, a scheme was introduced to provide 20 hours per week free in qualified teacher-led childcare services for three and four year olds with an aim to increase both the quality and affordability of childcare. However, privately provided childcare remains low in terms of quality and is particularly expensive, thus pricing out a large number of women (especially Māori and Pasifika women). Kesting and Fargher argue that the comparatively low female labour-force participation rate of mothers with dependent children in New Zealand can be explained at least in part by how childcare is organised.[67] Watane and Gibson note that labour-force survey evidence shows that the barriers to training that are felt with relatively greatest frequency by Māori and Pasifika but also by others in precarious employment relate to family circumstances and access to childcare.[68]

Other Developments

The Clark government established the role of EEO Commissioner, the Human Rights Amendment Act and extended new grounds of discrimination to the public sector as well as providing a revised complaints resolution process. The EEO provisions found in the State Sector were also extended to the wider public sector through the Crown Entities Act. Another development was the establishment of a Tripartite Pay and Employment Equity Taskforce and they developed a five-year Pay and Employment Equity Plan of Action. The Pay and Employment Equity Unit was established in the then Department of Labour to support the implementation of the Government's Plan of Action on Pay and Employment Equity. The Tripartite Steering Group was established to lead and monitor the development and implementation of the Plan of Action.

---

67 Stefan Kesting, and Scott Fargher "The effect of early childhood education and care (ECE) costs on the labour force participation of parents in New Zealand" (2008) 33 NZJER 16.
68 Carolyn Watane, and John Gibson "Barriers to employment-related training in New Zealand: Differences across ethnic groups" (2001) 26 NZJIR 227.

Fifth National Government (2008–Present)

In a move reminiscent of the earlier repeal of the Employment Equity Act 1990, one of the first actions of the Key government in 2009 was the discontinuations of pay investigations, the five-year Pay and Employment Equity Plan of Action and the disestablishment of Pay and Employment Equity Unit of the Department of Labour.[69] Subsequently, there has been little further government movement on furthering equality for women in the workplace beyond minor tinkering. The changes to the Employment Relations Amendment Act 2014 came into force. It changes the process and right to request flexible working arrangements by opening the right to request to all employees, not just the ones with care commitments, and paid parental leave was extended from 14 to 16 and eventually to 18 weeks. Arguably, both measures look like a gain for employees, but in fact contribute to the further entrenchment of women into traditional caring roles.[70] Indeed the use of flexible time by employees shows that men choose to work flexibly to do more work, while women choose to work flexibly to meet their care commitments. Thus, opening the right to request to all merely reinforces traditional structural gendered patterns. Providing longer parental leave might be welcomed by many, but without adequate compensation, only women can 'afford' to take such leave. Furthermore the systemic under-resourcing of the Human Rights Commission demonstrates a rather luke-warm commitment to furthering equality.

The Present Day

Forty years of workplace transformation revealed through the pages of the *NZJIR* and *NZJER* reveals a depressing degree of continuity. Concerns raised in the earlier years remain concerns today. In particular, the earliest issues of the *NZJIR* identified as problematic the fact that Māori and Pasifika women fare worse in the workplace than other women. This remains largely unchanged. Writing in 1994, Wilson commented that "women are still ghettoised in the workforce in occupations that are distinguished by their low skill and low pay. The trend of women into positions of authority is painfully slow."[71] Despite progress in education, this remains true today.

---

69 Prue Hyman "Pay equity and equal employment opportunity in New Zealand: Developments 2008/2010 and evaluation" (2011) 36 NZJIR 65.
70 Annick Masselot "Gender implications of the right to request flexible working arrangements: Raising pigs and children in New Zealand" (2015) 39 NZJER 59.
71 Margaret Wilson "Contractualism and the Employment Contracts Act 1991: Can they deliver equality for women?" (1994) 19 NZJIR 256 at 271.

Gender Pay Gap and Union Responsiveness to the Concerns of Women

However, there is some light on the horizon. Although there has been little impetus from government in furthering equality, McGregor discusses how civil society has taken on a more active role.[72] One thing that has changed from the 1970s is that it can no longer be said that unions are non-responsive to the needs of women and that they are male-dominated. Unions have led key campaigns and funded litigation to improve the working lives and financial situations of women.[73] Most significantly, the Equal Pay Act of 1972, which had seemed ineffectual and largely moribund, formed the basis of the *Bartlett v TerraNova* decision.[74] This established that in female-dominated work the Equal Pay Act 1972 requires equal pay for work of equal value (pay equity), not simply the same pay for the same work as had been previously thought. In response to this, the government set up a Joint Working Group on Pay Equity in 2015, including employer, union and government representatives charged with developing and recommending pay equity principles.[75]

The Joint Working Group on Pay Equity Principles presented its report on 24 May 2016.[76] Its recommendations covered both a process and criteria for the resolution of disputes. The recommendations largely build on existing good faith arrangements in the Employment Relations Act and on existing institutions and favour an approach rooted in early resolution. The government indicated on 24 November 2016[77] that it accepted the recommendations although it intends to provide additional guidelines on the determination of suitable comparators. The Government also announced that it intended to introduce a Bill in 2017 which would make the necessary changes to the Equal Pay Act 1972 and the Employment Relations Act 2000 needed to implement the changes. At the time of writing, the Bill had just been introduced into Parliament following a period of public consultation.[78]

---

72 Judy McGregor "The human rights framework and equal pay for low paid female carers in New Zealand" (2013) 38 NZJIR 4.
73 See for example the "Treat her Right Campaign" <http://www.treatherright.co.nz/>.
74 *Bartlett v TerraNova* [2014] NZCA 516.
75 See <www.ssc.govt.nz/pay-equity-working-group-terms-reference>.
76 See <http://www.ssc.govt.nz/sites/all/files/pay-equity-jwg-recommendations.pdf>.
77 See <https://www.beehive.govt.nz/release/govt-accepts-recommendations-pay-equity-0>.
78 Employment (Pay Equity and Equal Pay) Bill 2017, see <http://www.mbie.govt.nz/info-services/employment-skills/legislation-reviews/exposure-draft-employment-pay-equity-and-equal-pay-bill>.

The Failure of Equal Employment Opportunities (EEO) and the Declining Number of Women in Senior Positions

Although it is arguable women today have more likelihood of ascending to senior roles than they would have had in the 1970s, the number of women in senior positions remains low. Shamefully the number of women in senior positions has fallen under the Key government and the gender pay gap in government departments is not only broader in some State sectors than in the private sectors, it also has increased.[79] It seems that women's progress has not only stalled, but that New Zealand women are going backwards in terms of equality.

In the 1990s, as discussed above, the view was formed that EEO were best dealt with under a voluntarist regime. Apart from the requirements not to discriminate (which require an individual to raise a complaint),[80] private sector organisations have no obligations, other than those they may voluntarily choose to assume to ensure EEO. They are not required to disclose any information regarding gender equity or equal employment opportunities.

There are some requirements around EEO in the state sector who must develop and implement EEO policies specifically targeted at women (as well as Māori, ethnic minorities and people with disabilities). Edgar suggests that this obligation has produced some measure of success by increasing the employment opportunities for target group members.[81] Nonetheless, after all these years of EEO in the state sector, women are still unequal here with a recently reported shocking pay gap of 37 per cent.[82]

It seems the voluntarist approach is not working and perhaps it is time for more stringent measures. Mandatory reporting on gender outcomes for both the public and the private sector is one possibility. Brooks, Fenwick and Walker emphasise the importance of monitoring and evaluating progress rather than relying on measures such as the presence of EEO policies.[83] A well-funded regulatory body to oversee this with the power to impose significant penalties on those non-compliant with reporting or found to be acting in ways that are

---

79 See <http://www.radionz.co.nz/news/national/294770/no-progress-on-gender-pay-gap-professor>; and New Zealand Government *Human Resource Capability Survey: In the New Zealand State Sector* <http://www.ssc.govt.nz/sites/all/files/hrc-survey-2015_0.pdf>.

80 For a discussion on the limitations on relying on individually driven complaints to effect systemic change, see Amanda Reilly "Equality and family responsibilities: A critical evaluation of New Zealand law" (2012) 37 NZJER 161.

81 Fiona Edgar "Equal Employment Opportunity: Outcomes in the New Zealand Public Service" (2001) 26 NZJIR 217.

82 New Zealand Government "Human Resource Capability Survey: In the New Zealand State Sector" (2015) <http://www.ssc.govt.nz/sites/all/files/hrc-survey-2015_0.pdf>.

83 Ian Brooks, Graham Fenwick and Bernard Walker "The effect of changing perceptions of EEO on the appointment of women to management and supervisory positions in a public sector organisation" (2003) 28 NZJIR 23.

discriminatory (such as in Australia) would also be desirable. Alternatively, mandatory measures such as quotas for women in senior roles have been proven to work in some countries where they are part of a holistic approach to gender equality.[84] Unfortunately, New Zealand has not shown such a clear, holistic commitment to gender equality and, maybe more importantly, the public has generally been resistant to the introduction of mandatory measures like quotas.[85] The 2012 HRC Census of Women's Participation observes that:[86]

> Quotas appear to cut across one of the nation's most cherished myths, that we are a country where a "fair go" rules, both in aspiration and in practice. Successive administrations have denied any interest in debate about quotas in the belief that it would evoke negative political and business reactions and a "nanny state" backlash.

Work and Family Mechanisms are Still Unsatisfactory

In the 1970s there was a total absence of work-family reconciliation mechanisms. The first maternity leave provisions did not come into effect till 1981 and paid leave was only introduced in 2002, but take-up remains painfully low. The range of mechanisms supporting work-life balance is broad and relatively well articulated. However, it remains weak overall in comparison to other post-industrial countries, with low penalties for breaches and difficult access to justice for many in vulnerable positions. Moreover, although the work-life balance legal framework is drafted as gender neutral, it heavily impacts on women who continue to be seen as primary carers. For instance, the lack of adequate paid leave combined with the gender pay gap does not encourage fathers to be involved in childrearing nor a better sharing of unpaid domestic tasks. The amendments to the right to request flexible working arrangements (which extended the right to request for all workers) effectively treated the concept of care as irrelevant. Care giving, far from being considered a necessity, is treated as a lifestyle choice akin to gardening or golf playing. Arguably, a state-owned universal childcare model should be considered urgently, given the need to address the poor employment outcomes of Māori and Pasifika women. The emphasis on a business case and productivity arguments, as well as the failure to value care underpinning these mechanisms in New Zealand, is fundamentally flawed and counterproductive to any attempt to secure gender equality. Finally, there is a gap between the letter

---

84 Annick Masselot, and Timothy Brand "Diversity, quotas and compromise in the boardroom: Can New Zealand adopt a legislation to tackle gender imbalance in economic decision making?" (2015) 26 NZJULR 1.
85 Prue Hyman "Pay equity and Equal Employment Opportunity in New Zealand: Developments 2006/2008 and evaluation" (2008) 33 NZJER 1.
86 Judy McGregor "New Zealand Census of Women's Participation 2012" (2012) <www.hrc.co.nz>.

of the law and its application. The lack of strong enforcement gives the message that gender equality and work-family reconciliation are issues for women only and, as such, are not serious issues in themselves.

Sexual Harassment

The poor record of employment institutions in dealing with sexual harassment has been raised in the pages of the *NZJER* over the years.[87] Whether sexual harassment is being satisfactorily dealt with by New Zealand law remains an unanswered question. In one controversial Employment Relations Authority Decision,[88] the view was expressed that a "fun slap" to the bottom can be seen in context as acceptable in the workplace. The high-profile Roger Sutton incident,[89] and the Prime Minister repeatedly pulling a waitress's hair[90] suggest some unacceptable attitudes towards sexual harassment are still prevalent and this may be seen as reflective of New Zealand's high domestic violence rates.[91] Conversely, though the recent case where a sex worker was able to succeed against her employer for sexual harassment in the Human Rights Commission jurisdiction demonstrates the presence of more enlightened attitudes to sexual harassment.[92]

The different approaches between jurisdiction is also apparent in the variance in the awards for humiliation, loss of dignity and injury to feeling in the Employment Relations Authority and the Human Rights Review Tribunals, with

---

87 Colin Hicks "Does the sexual harassment procedure work?" (1988) 13 NZJIR 291; William Davis *A Feminist Perspective on Sexual harassment in Employment Law in New Zealand Monograph* (New Zealand Institute of Industrial Relation Research, Wellington, 1994); Julie Debono "Sexual Harassment in Employment: An Examination of Decisions Looking for Evidence of a Sexist Jurisprudence" (2001) 26 NZJIR 329.
88 The Authority stated that "While inappropriate and which should not be repeated by Mr Sanson, [it] must be seen in context . . . It was a one-off slap which I accept was a 'fun slap'". Ms Newman was not only unsuccessful in her allegation of sexual harassment but was ordered to pay $5,000.00 damages: *Newman v Taxi Lease Ltd t/a The Plant Place* [2014] NZERA 481 and [2014] NZERA 525. The determination was challenged but settled before a hearing.
89 <http://www.stuff.co.nz/national/politics/63891913/roger-sutton-and-his-dramatic-downfall>.
90 <http://www.stuff.co.nz/national/68235578/John-Key-Ponytail-pull-not-sexist>.
91 Family Violence Death Review Committee *Fourth Annual Report: January 2013 to December 2013* (Health Quality and Safety Commission, Wellington, 2014) <http://www.hqsc.govt.nz/our-programmes/mrc/fvdrc/publications-and-resources/publication/1600/>; Statistics New Zealand "New Zealand Police recorded crime and apprehension tables" (2015) <http://nzdotstat.stats.govt.nz/wbos/Index.aspx?DataSetCode=TABLECODE7407>; See also the debacle over the Roast Busters, <http://www.stuff.co.nz/national/crime/10674764/Roast-Busters-case-No-charges-to-be-laid>.
92 *DML v Montgomery* [2014] NZHRRT 6.

much higher awards being made in HRRT[93] compared to the Authority.[94] It may be this is an area where further improvement is possible.

Conclusion

Although New Zealand women have come a long way since the 1970s, women are still unequal in the workplace and they will not be equal, in terms of parity with men in the labour market, until adequate provisions are adopted with a view to providing the following:

(i) A pay equity system must be put in place to guarantee women equal pay for doing the same work and female-dominated professions need to be revalued so they receive better pay. Although it must be viewed as positive that subsequent to *Bartlett v Terranova* all parties concerned are in agreement that women should not be paid less because their work is undervalued due to structural gender based differentiation, time alone will tell whether the Recommendations of the Joint Working Group on Pay Equity Principle are fit for the purpose of addressing this or, indeed, whether or in what form they will be implemented. Barriers to women entering male-dominated fields must also be addressed;

(ii) Effective mechanisms must be put in place to prevent discrimination and to address gender bias (both conscious and unconscious). In particular, sexual harassment should not be tolerated in the workplace and equal employment opportunity policies should not be voluntary. Outcomes should be measured and transparent and failures to comply should be penalised. Quotas could be another interim possibility to get more women into senior roles; and

(iii) Suitable mechanisms must be put in place to ensure work and family can be managed and the unpaid work evenly distributed. Access to child care must be improved.

Transformations for women at work do not occur in a vacuum and changes in the wider environment also impact on women (as they do on men). Pike River was a particularly egregious outcome of systemic under-enforcement of New Zealand's occupational health and safety law. However, this theme of under-enforcement of the law pertaining to equalising women in the workplace has been recurrent in the NZJER[95] and there is little sign of improvement, with cuts to the Human Rights Commission and general under-resourcing of the institutions charged with enforcement as well as the increasing cost linked to individual access to justice.

---

93 *MacGregor v Craig* [2016] NZHRRT 6.
94 However, see Judge Inglis's comments in *Hall v Dionex PTY Ltd* [2015] NZEmpC 29 at 87.
95 Prue Hyman "Review Article: Women and Pay" (1981) 6 NZJIR 79.

Not all transformations in the workplace are positive. Unions are associated with better working conditions for women, but the decline of unions, the growing precariousness of work, the emergence of new ways of working and the decline of the standard employment contract all may operate to undermine ongoing further improvement in women's working lives. It may be that the future evolution of work will require new ways of thinking about work and an emphasis, as feminists have continuously called for, on valuing care work.[96]

As noted by McGregor, "women's progress in closing the gender pay gap in New Zealand at a governmental level is marked by the ebbs and flows of political will".[97] Prue Hyman further explains that "since the 1980s Labour led governments have been somewhat more proactive in pursuing measures to further women's equality but both are nervous of any major interventions in the market".[98] It is quite apparent that equal employment policies are not a priority in the current government's eyes, as is evidenced by the lack of progress and the continuing pay gap in the public sector. Coming up to an election year in 2017, if there is a change to a Labour-led government, perhaps there is hope that the current environment of backsliding and complacency towards women's inequality will change. This remains to be seen.

---

96   Amanda Reilly "Time, Work, and Law: A New Zealand perspective" (2012) 37 NZJER 152.
97   Judy McGregor "The human rights framework and equal pay for low paid female carers in New Zealand" (2013) 38 NZJIR 4.
98   Prue Hyman "Pay Equity and Equal Employment Opportunity in New Zealand: Developments 2008/2010 and Evaluation" (2011) 36 NZJER 65 at 66.

Waves of interest in employee participation in New Zealand

Erling Rasmussen and Ronny Tedestedt

Introduction

When the *New Zealand Journal of Industrial Relations* started in 1976 there was a strong interest in worker participation and industrial democracy in several OECD countries. This international interest facilitated new legislative backed participation schemes and structures as well as stronger union-employer collaborations and discussions (Rasmussen 2009, 506–508). European examples included works councils, workplace committees in occupational health and safety, and employee directors on boards of private sectors firms (Rasmussen and Lind 2003; Streeck 1992). There was also considerable interest in New Zealand, where a Private Members' Bill introduced to Parliament in 1974 advocated that workplaces with at least 100 employees had a works council. However, there was already then considerable variation in the interest in employee participation amongst New Zealand employers, unions and employees, and these diverse opinions have continued throughout the post 1976 period.

Since 1976, there has been considerable change in employment relations worldwide as well as its wider political, economic and social context. The mid-1970s is now being considered the final stage of the 'Golden Weather' of post-war economic prosperity, with many OECD countries still having extensive collective bargaining coverage and strong unions (Marglin and Schor 1990). The frontal attack on collective bargaining and unions, spearheaded by Margaret Thatcher and Ronald Reagan in the 1980s, shifted the fundamentals, debates and thinking about employment relations. This also influenced the debates and implementation of participation schemes in New Zealand in the post 1970 period.

Our section on historical trends in employee participation in New Zealand highlights that employee participation or workplace 'voice' is contested terrain: unions and employers have always had diverse mind-sets about what constitute appropriate 'voice' and participation mechanisms. It is only on the union side that these mind-sets appear to have changed considerably over time while employers have maintained their emphasis on voluntary employer initiated approaches. These attitudinal positions will also be highlighted in our discussion of two major attempts to introduce voluntary employee participation schemes – workplace reform and workplace partnership – where the rather limited traction of these voluntary workplace approaches is linked to ambivalent union attitudes as well as mainstream employers having limited interest in being actively involved.

Employer interest in avoiding comprehensive legislatively based schemes and employer preference for 'softer' forms of employee 'voice' has a long history and has meant that these forms of employee 'voice' have dominated recent New Zealand debates and practices. There has been less progress on legislatively backed participation structures and we focus, therefore, on the only legislative stipulated participation structures: the health and safety committees as prescribed originally in the 2002 Health and Safety in Employment Amendment Act. Again, the controversial nature of legislative prescribed participation schemes is highlighted in our discussion of 'turning points' in the journey towards more comprehensive employee involvement in occupational health and safety.

Employee Participation: Waves of Interest and Definitional Confusion

In New Zealand, the interest in employee participation schemes has waxed and waned in the decades since the early 1970s, as shown below. This fluctuation was captured by Ramsey (1977) in his famous article on 'cycles' of employee participation. Ramsey's article challenged the view that employee participation is a result of "gradual and ongoing humanisation of capitalism" (Harley, Hyman and Thompson 2005, 2). Instead, Ramsay (1977) argued that the interest in participation emerged in cycles whenever the authority of management was threatened or challenged. According to him, the participatory schemes could be seen as a response by management to regain control. However, as time goes by, the interest in employee participation decreases and the earlier schemes put in place weaken or fade away.

However, Ramsey's article was written as OECD countries moved towards a post-industrial society and as collective bargaining and union density started their long-term decline in many countries. Thus, the 'cycles' explanation has been criticised for not taking into account the decline in collectivism and, particularly, the increase in non-union forms of participation (Townsend, Wilkinson and Burgess 2012). Rather than explaining the interest for participation in terms of 'cycles', Marchington (2005) has suggested that a 'waves' concept might be more constructive. In the 'waves' theory the increased interest for participation can be understood through changes in internal managerial relations. The 'waves' explanation contemplates why, at certain points in time, there seem to be more schemes put in place for employee participation. This fluctuation in implemented participation schemes may stem from young managers being more interested in implementing new strategies when first entering the role.

While there are distinct differences between the 'cycles' and 'waves' explanations of a fluctuating interest in employee participation, they are also talking about different types of participation. This different understanding of employee participation is at the heart of a conceptual confusion which has bedeviled the employee participation debates. This has prompted different understandings, forms and ranges of employee participation (for an overview of possible forms, ranges and understandings see Budd 2014; Caraker, Jørgensen, Madsen and Baadsgaard 2016; Rasmussen 2009, 495–497; Wilkinson, Gollan, Marchington and Lewin 2010).

In this chapter, we are particularly interested in the distinctions between legally based forms, collectively negotiated forms and managerially implemented forms of employee participation. As will be discussed below, collectively negotiated forms of employee participation were often the preferred options amongst New Zealand unions, while managerially implemented forms – 'soft', direct forms of employee involvement – were the preferred options amongst New Zealand employers. However, it has taken some time before a New Zealand government introduced legally prescribed employee participation. This did not happen until 2002, with health and safety committees becoming mandatory for large workplaces.

Based on Table 1, the major changes in employee participation and the associated diverse opinions will be discussed below.

Year	Waves of participation	Focus
1974	Eric Holland's Private Member's Bill	A Private Member's Bill was introduced in Parliament in 1974 that sought to implement works councils in workplaces with more than 100 employees. The Labour Government referred the discussion of the Bill to the tripartite Industrial Relations Council. However, neither the Government nor the unions made a concerted effort to establish works councils before the 1975 election and, when the National Government took office in 1975, plans to introduce works councils were abandoned.
1976	Tax incentives support employee share ownership plans (ESOPs)	A particular form of worker participation is through employee share ownership plans (ESOPs). The first New Zealand legislation supporting such arrangements can be found in the Companies Empowering Act 1924. However, it was revised and extended in the Income Tax Act 1976, whereby employees would have a tax incentive to become part-owners of their employing firm. Research showed that, ten years later, less than a quarter of the listed companies had implemented ESOP schemes and many eligible employees had not participated in ESOPs.
1987	The Voluntary Code of Practice for health and safety representatives and committees	Seen as a critical part of the major reforms of New Zealand's occupational health and safety (OHS), the Voluntary Code of Practice was introduced in 1987 by the Labour Government. Based on similar UK and Australian OHS regulations, its importance lay in the fact that it was based on joint consultation and shared responsibilities for OHS between managers and workers.
1989	Committee of Enquiry into Industrial Democracy	The Fourth Labour government set up a Committee of Enquiry into Industrial Democracy in 1989 to "identify the extent to which industrial democracy would help employers, workers and their organisations work to the benefit of the economy". The Committee proposed Joint Consultative Committees in enterprises with 40 or more employees. However, these recommendations were never implemented, as they were not given high priority in union–government discussions and employers were against legislative prescription.

Year	Waves of participation	Focus
1990s	Workplace Reform	Workplace reform was a popular concept from the late 1980s to mid-1990s. It was described in the Workplace Reform Conference 1992, as: "... working smarter ... achieving real and sustainable improvements in productivity and competitiveness". Worker participation was part of the Workplace Reform, although in a different, voluntary form. Generally, mainstream employers' and unions' interest was difficult to mobilise.
2000s	Workplace Partnership	Workplace Partnership aimed to encourage a high road to workplace change. The Workplace Partnership advocated a partnership approach in public-sector bargaining and in employer–union relationships. It aligned with other changes under the Fifth Labour government and its interest in a collaborative approach. The Partnership Resource Centre was established in 2004 and it promoted employer-union collaboration in both private and public sectors. The post-2008 National Government was not interested in pursuing the Partnership approach and disestablished the Partnership Resource Centre in 2011.
2002	Health and Safety in Employment Amendment Act	The Health and Safety in Employment Amendment Act 2002 gave employees in New Zealand a legal right to elect health and safety representatives. This covered employers with 30 employees or more. The Act also gave elected representatives the right to access information about OHS systems and issues, make recommendations about OHS matters, and be allowed two days' paid leave to attend training.
2015	Health and Safety at Work Act 2015	As part of the management of OHS, worker participation was mandated. This covered employers with 20 or more employees. However, there are some exceptions where an employer can refuse the election of health and safety representatives, notably in businesses not listed on a so-called high-risk list (for example, agriculture is exempt as it is only considered medium risk).

Table 1. Waves of interest in employee participation in New Zealand

Sources: Firth, Keef and Mear 1987; Lamm 2010; Pashorina-Nichols 2016; Rasmussen 2009; Sisson 2016.

The Shifting Attitudes of Trade Unions, Employers and Governments

Traditionally, *trade unions* have promoted collective bargaining and union workplace representatives as the preferred employee participation mechanism. During the conciliation and arbitration era (1894–1991), this was also the choice of mainstream New Zealand trade unions. This was also associated with stronger unions being able to have considerable influence on workplace arrangements, including the ability to secure 'over-award' pay and conditions in the full employment period before the mid 1980s.

However, this reliance on collective bargaining and workplace representation had two major weaknesses. First, there was often a very narrow bargaining agenda, which seldom allowed a discussion of employee participation mechanisms. Second, the conciliation and arbitration system was crucial for the ability of many trade unions to bolster their membership and achieve broadly based awards or agreements. These weaknesses started to surface in the late 1980s and were fully exposed by the Employment Contracts Act 1991 (ECA).

While the ECA was a revolutionary change, the trade unions' bargaining strategies and their approach to employee participation had already been tested in the 1980s. As Williamson (2017) has shown, pay and employment conditions started to slip for hotel workers well before the ECA. Likewise, many awards had difficulty in improving or even maintaining real wages in a high inflation period (Deeks 1990; Harbridge and McCaw 1989).

As discussed below, the Committee of Enquiry into Industrial Democracy established in 1989 could have been a major step forward, but instead it exposed the limited union interest and a diversity of union strategies. Besides the Engineers Union, there was very little tangible support amongst trade unions. The interest of the Engineers Union fitted with its promotion of 'strategic unionism', which sought more development of and participation in tripartite bodies and a strengthening of workplace organisation (Deeks and Rasmussen 2002). This strategy also facilitated a strong support of the subsequent workplace reform (see below).

However, the limited union interest must also be viewed in respect of the particular historical context where the Labour Government's radical policies had undermined many union strongholds. Many unions were preoccupied with prevention of further collective bargaining decentralisation and membership decline, as major private and public sector restructuring was occurring (Boston, Martin, Pallot and Walsh 1991). Additionally, unemployment was gathering pace in wake of the economic fallout of the 1987 share market (Deeks and Perry 1992). Our discussion of workplace reform and workplace partnership (below) also stresses the limited interest of many unions. In fact, some unions were so against some of these initiatives that they launched protests and wildcat strikes.

On that background, it may be surprising that we suggest that union interest in employee participation has grown since the late 1980s. This position can be explained through several changes. Following the decline in union membership (see Table 2 below and McAndrew, Geare and Edgar in this book), it has become less likely that collective bargaining would be sufficient to deliver broadly based employee participation. Another factor could be the influence of British trade unions that have had similar membership declines, but have also had new experiences with European forms of employee participation and consultation. These changes have moved British trade unions away from their traditional voluntarist approach. Yet another factor could be a stronger influence of larger unions – for example E tū and the Public Service Association (PSA) – traditionally being in favour of collaborative approaches. As shown in Table 2, the largest 10 unions now account for over 80 per cent of all union members. Unions are also now aware – following workplace reform and workplace partnership (as discussed below) – that voluntary arrangements can be difficult to mainstream and sustain. Finally, the attempt to relaunch collectivism and collaborative employment relationships through the Employment Relations Act 2000 (ERA) has partly failed, but there has been a breakthrough with legislative employee participation being implemented in the new millennium (as discussed below).

The approach of *employers* to employee participation has been remarkably stable over the years. There has been constant criticism of attempts to legislate. This was the employer position during the Enquiry into Industrial Democracy in the late 1980s, where a separate employer part of the Report recommended a voluntary, cautious and workplace-based approach (Department of Labour 1989). Similarly, employers were critical of enhancing statutory minima and attacked the plans to support collective bargaining, good faith and union involvement in the Employment Relations Bill (Burton 2004; Rasmussen and Ross 2004). The introduction of statutory health and safety committees was also frowned upon (Lamm 2010) and, as shown below, there is still employer resistance in respect of coverage and influence of health and safety committees.

Employers have often argued that workplace level initiatives provide more suitable and varied forms of employee participation. In respect of participation forms acceptable to and/or driven by employers, there is some support for this position, as voluntary practices have prevailed over legislatively prescribed or collectively agreed practices. Survey information indicates that many employers have initiated consultative and communication arrangements. Rasmussen (1996) found a stronger employer focus on communication, as did Waldegrave, Anderson and Wong (2003) under the ERA 2000. Gilson, Wagar and Brown (2002) found many joint participation programmes in larger organisations and a high level of survival rate over time. Likewise, Boxall, Haynes and Macky (2007) found that many employees had some form of consultative committees at their

Membership range	Dec 1991			Dec 1999			Dec 2005			Dec 2014			Dec 2015		
	#	Members	%	#	Members	%	#	Members	%	#	Members	%	#	Members	%
Under 1000	4	2750	1	48	12703	4	140	19436	5	84	15658	4	89	14803	4
1000–4999	39	87119	17	22	43709	14	23	56801	15	21	48117	13	21	48319	13
5000–9999	9	76489	15	3	19669	7	4	30050	8	3	23981	7	3	23888	7
10000+	14	347967	68	9	226324	75	8	271061	72	9	272887	76	8	271623	76

Table 2: Membership by union size 1991–2015, selected years

Sources: *Industrial Relations Centre Surveys 1991, 1999 and 2005; Centre for Labour Employment and Work Survey 2015.*

workplace, had a high level of employer–employee communications and were generally satisfied with their influence on workplace decisions and changes. The recent strong emphasis on employee engagement and workplace climate surveys follows a similar involvement pattern (Ruck, Welch and Menara 2017).

However, it can also be argued that mainstream employers have become less tolerant of sharing decision-making power. Research by Geare, Edgar and McAndrew (2006 and 2009) indicates that employers have a unitarist view of how to conduct employment relations in their *own* workplaces. Research by Foster, Rasmussen, Murrie and Laird (2011) has also shown that employer attitudes to collective bargaining have become less accommodating and that most employers regard collective bargaining as an unwanted interference with their direct employer–employee relationships. The employer animosity towards legislative interventions has surfaced in recent survey research, with most employers supporting 'more flexibility' in conducting their employment relations (Foster, Rasmussen and Coetzee 2013; Rasmussen, Foster and Farr 2016).

Finally, there has been a noticeable left–right political divide amongst *governments'* interest in employee participation. As discussed below, this can be seen in a number of major public-policy changes. Labour-led governments established the Committee of Enquiry into Industrial Democracy in the late 1980s and supported collectivism, good faith and collaborative employment relationships under the ERA 2000. National-led governments gave little support to collective collaborative efforts during the 1990s and, in the post-2008 period, there has been a piecemeal erosion of collectivism (with changes to health and safety legislation being the key exception, see below).

The Committee of Enquiry into Industrial Democracy was a clear attempt to foster more "meaningful participation of workers in decisions affecting their working lives" (Department of Labour 1989, 1). However, it revealed the differences of opinions regarding the understanding of participatory practices, the suitable structures and practices and, in particular, whether legislative participatory mechanisms should be implemented. While these differences were highlighted in the Committee Report by the inclusion of a separate section of a dissenting employer position, there were also references to diverse trade union opinions. "Some unions felt that existing channels of collective bargaining were sufficient for industrial democracy" (Department of Labour 1989, 5). There are few traces of strong public union support and practical planning of legislative intervention. It was also unclear how much the Council of Trade Unions (CTU) tried to force mandatory employee structures on the government's agenda. This is despite the CTU's (at least in principle) strong support: "The government back away from the conclusions of the inquiry into industrial democracy, despite their being seen by the CTU as vitally linked to union participation in decision-making at a workplace and sector level" (Harvey 1992, 71).

It is noticeable how little attention the Enquiry into Industrial Democracy attracted in the *New Zealand Journal of Industrial Relations*. The Journal has no articles or commentaries and, besides a few lines in the Chronicle (*NZJIR* 14, 103 and 216; *NZJIR* 15, 83), the Enquiry is not covered. It was clearly not a major issue at a time when New Zealand employment relations were in a state of flux. One can only agree with subsequent evaluations that this was more political window-dressing (honouring promises in the 1984 Labour Party election manifesto) than a serious broadly based attempt to further meaningful employee participation (Deeks 1990).

The (ERA) 2000 was heralded as an attempt to overcome conflictual, market-based employment relationships through support of collectivism, good faith and positive employment relationships (Wilson 2010). While the ERA 2000 did lead to some major changes, it is also clear that it fell short of a fundamental shift towards collectivism and in establishing stronger employee participation in the workplace. While a growth in collective bargaining and union density may have enhanced employee participation, there were no legislative participation schemes included in the ERA 2000 and it did not feature in the public policy discussions. Interestingly, this was already commented on during the conception of the ERA 2000 in the early 1990s: "However, it is evident that Labour does not intend to bring New Zealand into line with most other OECD countries by providing some statutory base to a wider system of industrial democracy" (Anderson and Walsh 1993, 165).

Voluntary Workplace Participation: Workplace Reform and Workplace Partnership

The *workplace reform* initiative started in the late 1980s and was based on European ideas and approaches (also the cornerstone of 'strategic unionism', as mentioned above). However, this tripartite, industry-enhancing approach was very different from the decentralised, free-market approach dominating in New Zealand employment relations in the 1990s. Workplace reform also heralded a subtle shift in the philosophical basis of workplace reform with US, Australian and Japanese work practices becoming more dominant influences (Parry, Davidson and Hill 1995; Rasmussen 1997).

Other important characteristics cut across previous attempts to enhance employee participation. Workplace reform was a voluntary workplace initiative that was spearheaded by a member-driven interest organisation – Workplace Reform New Zealand. The focus was firmly on the workplace and work changes; there were no centralised tripartite collaboration or legally based interventions. Fundamentally, it was based on developing closer employer–union collaborations by attempting to create a win-win situation through more employee engagement and involvement. Some of the changes were inspired by Japanese production methods and could be found in concepts such as 'Toyotaism', the 'Nissan Way', and lean production (Parry et al. 1995). This also meant that most organisations involved in workplace reform were in manufacturing.

In terms of developing comprehensive forms of employee participation, there were *three major problems*. First, the workplace reform initiatives did not establish widespread union and employee support. There were only a few unions actively involved, while many unions were focusing on their daily struggle to maintain their collective bargaining position. The latter was understandable, as union membership was plummeting in the early 1990s. In fact, some unions were directly opposed to workplace reform and this prompted wildcat strikes at the Nissan and NZ Steel workplaces and union protesters targeted the 1992 Workplace Reform Conference in Rotorua (Rasmussen 1997). While these unions advocated more traditional, adversarial collective bargaining, they also raised doubts about the potential long-term benefits to workers of the workplace reform.

Second, the employer interest was sporadic and often linked to the enthusiasm and support of individual managers. There was limited or no buy-in from employer associations and, outside the limited number of high-profile organisations participating in workplace reform, the employment relations reality tended to be rather more grim, with an emphasis on cost-cutting and employer-determined 'flexibility' (Gilson and Wagar 1997; McAndrew 1993; McLaughlin 2000).

Third, the comprehensiveness of employee participation was also limited when the extent and depth of practices were considered. Even amongst those organisations involved in Workplace Reform New Zealand the employee participation mechanisms were very mixed. Only a handful of organisations developed effective employee participation through consultative committees and a few organisations also allowed their work teams to have wider decision-making powers (see Appendix 1 in Rasmussen 1997, 405). In most cases, the concerns were mainly about introducing new forms of work organisation and having more collaborative employer-union relationships. This raised two types of questions. What was the real extent of employee participation in managerial decision-making and how interested were employees in actually participating in such decision-making? The first question has yet to be answered conclusively but it appears that employee participation in managerial decision-making was of a more consultative and informative nature and several of the workplace reform organisations moved subsequently to more traditional management approaches or disappeared totally. The second question was partly answered by survey research conducted by Chong (1997), who found that employees working for workplace reform organisations ". . . were mainly interested in influencing their own work situation and less interested in having policy-related types of participation. However, even these modest expectations about more employee influence were not fulfilled" (Deeks and Rasmussen 2002, 219).

As it was generally difficult to obtain broad-based union and employer support in a rather hostile employment-relations environment it was decided in early 1998 to discontinue Workplace Reform New Zealand and its various activities.

Workplace partnership was the second major attempt to establish collaborative and innovative employment relationships in a voluntary fashion at workplace level. Workplace partnership was promoted by the PSA from the late 1990s onwards as a way of overcoming the managerialism of New Public Management (Boston, Martin, Pallot and Walsh 1996) and create more harmonious and effective employment relations across the public sector.

While the approach and key components of workplace partnerships were quite similar to those of workplace reform there were a couple of major differences. There was a major difference in context, which turned out to be more conducive for implementing workplace partnership approaches in the new millennium. With the change to a Labour-led government in 1999 there was an emphasis on growth strategies, and enhancing human capability. There was an alignment with the core notions of the ERA 2000, especially the support of collectivism and 'building productive employment relationships'. There were also growing concerns about the processes and outcomes associated with the public-sector reforms started in the mid-1980s (Boston 1999). The Labour-led government was seeking adjustments to overcome short-termism, conflictual employment relations and staff churn in many parts of the public sector.

There was considerably more government support for workplace partnerships than there ever was for workplace reform. A Partnership Resource Centre was established within the Department of Labour in 2004 and this provided more stability, financial support and consultancy and research resources (Scoping a Partnership Resource 2004). This allowed the Partnership Resource Centre to undertake a number of activities, including supporting workplace partnership initiatives, facilitating information and consultancy about workplace partnerships and developing research projects about partnership projects and approaches (Ballard and McAndrew 2006; McAndrew 2006). ". . . the Partnership Resource Centre has become the depository for information and experiences with employer–union collaboration at workplace level and its efforts have in many ways paralleled and supported the workplace productivity efforts of Department of Labour" (Rasmussen 2009, 483).

Although several successful workplace partnerships were recorded and supported by the Partnership Resource Centre (see 2008 Report) it was downgraded under the National-led government and finally abolished in 2011. Several years later, the concept of workplace partnerships has more-or-less vanished and there is little trace of employee participation being embedded in organisational practices. Consider the amount of resources spent, this places serious question marks over the workplace partnership approach. Why were the partnership initiatives so quickly erased and why were the participative processes not embedded in mainstream employment relations?

There can be several plausible answers to these questions. In hindsight, it is apparent that the support of collectivism and 'productive employment relationships' has failed to shift the employment relations landscape fundamentally. Again, there appears to have been limited support amongst mainstream unions and employers. This may be explained through the focus on unionised and large workplaces that bypassed many smaller and medium-sized private sector organisations. It may also be explained through the negative impacts of the Global Financial Crisis from 2008 onwards and the election of a less supportive government. It may also point to the vulnerable nature of voluntary approaches (the mandatory approach discussed appears to have become embedded).

Turning Points: Employee Participation in Occupational Health and Safety

Parallel to the waves of interest in general employer participation schemes there have been discussions of employee participation in occupational health and safety (OHS) in New Zealand for several decades. Compared to many other OECD countries, New Zealand was late to introduce such legal rights. However, participation in OHS is crucial for any discussion of employee participation, since, at the moment, OHS legislation provides the only legislative stipulated right for New Zealand employees to receive information, be part of OHS discussions and to have input in OHS decision-making processes in the workplace.

This section will focus on three 'turning points' concerning the introduction and coverage of employee participation in OHS. These 'turning points' highlight the controversial nature of legally based participation rights, though they also indicate that these rights have become embedded and the main debate is now over their coverage (what size of workplaces and in which sectors). As New Zealand has recently undergone major changes in its OHS legislation, this has prompted lively policial debate and more academic research, and raised questions about the effectiveness of employee participation schemes in OHS.

The first 'turning point' relates to the transition away from traditional types of OHS regulations in the 1980s and 1990s. By 1980, OHS regulations had become "piecemeal, complex and unwieldy" (Lamm 1994, 59). Instead, the proposal of the Committee on Safety and Health at Work in the United Kingdom, the so-called 'Robens' Report' as the Committee was chaired by Lord Robens, became influential. The 'Robens Report' recommended a joint, self-regulatory approach with OHS being a joint employer–employee responsibility and with employee participation being formalised through workplace OHS committees. Aligned with this, the Department of Labour issued in 1987 a Code of Practice for Health and Safety Representatives and Health and Safety Committees to cover all workplaces employing 10 or more employees (Mullen 1990). However, the Occupational Safety and Health Bill 1990 initiated by the Labour government never made it past the 1990 general election. Instead, the National government introduced the Health and Safety in Employment Act 1992 (HSE). The HSE Act 1992 reflected the dominant ideology of self-regulation and economic liberalisation, "and enshrined managerial prerogative on decision making on health and safety issues" (Harris 2004, 2). There were no stipulated rights for worker participation and election of health and safety representatives to OHS committees.

The second 'turning point' came with the election of the Labour-led government in late 1999. This government made several changes in the area of employment relations, with one of the key changes being the Health and Safety in Employment Amendment Act 2002. This Act introduced a general duty to "provide reasonable opportunities for the employer's employees to participate effectively in ongoing processes for improvement of health and safety in the employees' places of work" (HSE Amendment Act 2002, Part 2A, s 19B). Further, every employer was required to develop an employee participation system if the employer employed 30 or more employees. If there were fewer than 30 employees, then one or more employees (or a union representing them) could require a workplace employee participation system to be implemented. The HSE Amendment Act 2002 gave employees for the first time a legal right to elect health and safety representatives (Harris 2011).

The aim of both the HSE Amendment Act 2002 and ERA 2000 was to promote collective action and joint workplace regulation. However, as union density did not increase much after the introduction of the ERA 2000 and started to decline in several private industries, the effectiveness of the HSE Amendment Act 2002 and its OHS employee participation can rightly be questioned. It was of particular concern that New Zealand's poor OHS record continued, with Lilley, Samaranayaka and Weiss (2013) finding that New Zealand ranked last for overall occupational safety performance in comparison with some other OECD countries (Australia, Canada, Finland, France, Norway, Spain, Sweden and the United Kingdom).

When the explosion in the Pike River Coal Mine in November 2010 killed 29 men, the New Zealand government was forced to take action. The Royal Commission on the Pike River Coal Mine Tragedy (2012) as well as the Independent Taskforce on Workplace Health and Safety (2013) clearly pointed to a need to strengthen health and safety legislation, including worker participation. In April 2016, the Health and Safety at Work Act 2015 replaced the previous HSE 1992 and its amendments.

The Health and Safety at Work Act 2015 constitutes the third 'turning point'. Under this Act (Part 3, s 58), a person conducting a business or undertaking (typically an employer) has a duty to, "so far as is reasonably practicable, engage with workers - (a) who carry out work for the business or undertaking; and (b) who are, or are likely to be, directly affected by a matter relating to work health or safety". The Act has reduced the threshold to employers with 20 or more employees (compared to 30 or more employees, under the HSE Amendment Act 2002). It has also extended employer responsibilities and the associated penalties, which has propelled OHS to the forefront of current employment relations debate and practices.

However, there has been extensive criticism of the Act (see for example Sissons 2016; Pashorina-Nichols 2016; Tipples 2015), as it has been suggested that the Act constitutes a watered-down version of the recommendations from the Independent Taskforce (Edwards 2015; Small 2015). In particular, an employer, with fewer than 20 employees and not listed on the so-called 'high risk list', is exempt from the requirement of health and safety representatives and health and safety committees (Health and Safety at Work Act 2015, Subpart 2, 62, para: 4). Additionally, agriculture is not on the 'high risk list', although many fatalities have occurred in the agriculture sector (Tipples 2015).

Thus, employee participation in OHS has had a tortuous and controversial development. It appears that, over time, New Zealand has aligned more and more with other OECD countries (though the many decades of embedding such schemes in other OECD countries constitutes a major difference). However, the OHS participatory practices are still under scrutiny. This relates partly to the coverage of workplaces which questions the appropriate size of the workplace – is the cut-off point of 20 or more employees too high or too low? – and whether the 'high risk list' captures the appropriate jobs and sectors. The latter has raised questions of whether worm farming or flower growing really are more dangerous than agriculture.

The continuous debate of participatory practices is also partly related to the relatively little research that has evaluated the extent and effectiveness of OHS representatives and OHS committees. It is a well-known theme in international literature that employee participation is a cornerstone of effective OHS management systems (Frick, Jensen, Quinlan and Wilthagen 2000), since the practical experience and understanding of workplace processes amongst employees is regarded as a key factor in identifying and managing OHS hazards in the workplace (Walters and Frick 2000). This theme needs to be explored and may be confirmed in New Zealand through detailed, rigorous analyses of the impact of employee participation in OHS matters.

In light of the fact that legal requirements for employee participation have been in place since 2002 and that OHS committees are the only legally based employee participation schemes in New Zealand, one can only wonder why the various governments and academic researchers have yet to put major efforts into evaluating employee participation in OHS. It is also interesting to note that some of the preliminary research findings show an uneven pattern across employers and their willingness to implement participatory process. Thus, Foster and Farr (2016) found that some smaller employers were willing to engage in participatory practices, and Markey, Harris, Ravenswood, Simpkin and Williamson (2015) found that their research contradicted European notions of a complementary role of direct and representative participation (including union representation). These are only tentative and preliminary findings and there is clearly room for more evaluative research of the effects of employee participation in OHS.

Conclusion

Since the start of the *New Zealand Journal of Industrial/Employment Relations* the notion of employee participation has regularly featured in in employment relations debates. The international concepts of 'cycles' and 'waves' can be used to describe the fluctuations in interests and debates over time, but there has also been something very New Zealand specific about the debates. In particular, the specific New Zealand context has played a major role and the employment relations 'landscape' has been transformed dramatically since the early 1970s.

The shift from collectivism to workplace and individualised employment relationships, which started in the 1980s and really gathered steam under the Employment Contracts Act 1991, has clearly influenced how the key actors 'see' employee participation. The major unions have become more positive about playing a role in workplace relationships and they have also been supportive of legally prescribed employee participation in OHS. This may be a result of the current weakness of collective bargaining and narrow bargaining agenda, but it could also have been influenced by changing union attitudes overseas (for example, in the UK). Nevertheless, trade unions will have probably be faced with stronger employer resistance than ever. Mainstream employers have continued to advocate 'softer', more direct forms of employee participation, though this has taken on a more unitarist tone which entols the virtue of managerial prerogatives.

While employee participation in OHS matters has been controversial, this also appears to be an area where there are some common employer–union–employee interests. The breakthrough for legally prescribed employee participation in 2002 has now become embedded in New Zealand workplaces, though there are still obvious disagreements over its coverage and its effectiveness. There is ample room for evaluative research of the effectiveness and processes associated with employee participation in OHS and this could be lead to another 'wave' of research, including articles in the *New Zealand Journal of Employment Relations*.

It also raises the question of whether this could lead to renewed public-policy debates about legally prescribed employee participation schemes in areas such as information and consultation rights, works councils and employee directors.

References

Anderson, G. and Walsh, P. 1993. "Labour's New Deal: A Bargaining Framework for a New Century?" *New Zealand Journal of Industrial Relations* 18 (2): 163–176.

Ballard, M. and McAndrew, I. 2006. *Illustrated Report and Stocktake on Workplace Partnership in New Zealand*. Wellington, New Zealand: Partnership Resource Centre.

Boston, J. 1999. "New Models of Public Management: The New Zealand Case." *Samfundsøkonomen* 5: 5–13.

Boston, J., Martin, J., Pallot, J. and Walsh, P. 1991. *Reshaping the State*. Auckland, New Zealand: Oxford University Press.

Boston, J., Martin, J., Pallot, J. and Walsh, P. 1996. *Public Management*. Auckland, New Zealand: Oxford University Press.

Boxall, P., Haynes, P. and Macky, K. 2007. "Employee Voice and Voicelessness in New Zealand." In *What Workers Say: Employee Voice in the Anglo-American Workplace*, ed. Freeman, R., Boxall, P. and Haynes, P., 145–165. Ithaca, NY: Cornell University Press.

Budd, J. 2014. "The Future of Employee Voice." In *The Handbook of Research on Employee Voice*, ed. Wilkinson, A., Donaghey, J., Dundon, T. and Freeman, R., 447–487. Cheltenham, United Kingdom: Edward Elgar.

Burton, B. 2004. "The Employment Relations Act according to Business New Zealand." In *Employment Relationships: Workers, Unions and Employers in New Zealand*, ed. Rasmussen, E., 134–144. Auckland, New Zealand: Auckland University Press.

Caraker, E., Jørgensen, H., Madsen, M. O. and Baadsgaard, K. 2016. "Representation without Co-determination?" *Economic and Industrial Democracy* 37 (2): 269–295.

Chong, K. P. 1997. "Giving Voice to the Employee: Employee Perspectives on Workplace Reform in New Zealand." Masters Thesis, University of Auckland, Auckland, New Zealand.

Deeks, J. S. 1990. "New Tracks, Old Maps: Continuity and Change in New Zealand Labour Relations 1984–1990." *New Zealand Journal of Industrial Relations* 15 (2): 99–116.

Deeks, J. and Perry, N. (eds.) 1992. *Controlling Interests: Business, the State and Society in New Zealand*. Auckland, New Zealand: Auckland University Press.

Deeks, J. and Rasmussen, E. 2002. *Employment Relations in New Zealand*. Auckland, New Zealand: Pearson.

Department of Labour. 1989. *Report of the Committee of Enquiry into Industrial Democracy. The Meaningful Participation of Workers in Decisions Affecting their Working Lives*. Wellington, New Zealand: Department of Labour.

Edwards, B. 2015. "Safety Legislation Already Watered Down." *Radio New Zealand*. Accessed April 3, 2017. http://www.radionz.co.nz/news/political/275352/safety-legislation-already-watered-down.

Firth, M., Keef, S. and Mear, R. 1987. "Some Preliminary Evidence on Employee Shareownership Schemes in New Zealand Listed Companies." *New Zealand Journal of Industrial Relations* 12 (1): 23–30.

Foster, B. and Farr, D. 2016. "Some Willingness to Engage: A Survey of Employment Relations Practices and Employee Voice Opportunities in SMEs in Regional New Zealand." *New Zealand Journal of Employment Relations* 41 (1): 41–64.

Foster, B., Rasmussen, E., Murrie, J. and Laird, I. 2011. "Supportive Legislation, Unsupportive Employers and Collective Bargaining in New Zealand." *Relations Industrielles/Industrial Relations* 66 (2): 192–212.

Foster, B., Rasmussen, E. and Coetzee, D. 2013. "Ideology Versus Reality: New Zealand Employer Attitudes to Legislative Change of Employment Relations." *New Zealand Journal of Employment Relations* 37 (3): 50–64.

Frick, K., Jensen, P. L., Quinlan, M. and Wilthagen, T. 2000. "Systematic Occupational Health and Safety Management – An Introduction to a New Strategy for Occupational Safety, Health and

Well-being." In *Systematic Occupational Health and Safety Management: Perspectives on an International Development*, ed. Frick, K., Jensen, P. L., Quinlan, M. and Wilthagen, T., 1–16. Oxford, United Kingdom: Elsevier Science.

Geare, A., Edgar, F. and McAndrew, I. 2006. "Employment Relations: Ideology and HRM Practice." *International Journal of Human Resource Management* 17 (7): 1190–1208.

Geare, A., Edgar, F. and McAndrew, I. 2009. "Workplace Values and Beliefs: An Empirical Study of Ideology, High Commitment and Unionisation." *International Journal of Human Resource Management* 20 (5): 1146–1171.

Gilson, C. H. J. and Wagar, T. H. 1997. "The Impact of the New Zealand Employment Contracts Act on Individual Contracting: Measuring Organisational Performance." *Californian Western International Law Journal* 28 (1): 221–234.

Gilson, C. H. J., Wagar, T. H. and Brown, M. 2002. "The Adoption and Retention of Joint Participation Programs. Preliminary Evidence from NZ." *New Zealand Journal of Industrial Relations* 27 (3): 269–281.

Harbridge, R. and McCaw, S. 1989. "The First Wage Round Under the Labour Relations Act 1987: Changing Relative Power." *New Zealand Journal of Industrial Relations* 14 (2): 149–167.

Harley, B., Hyman, J. and Thompson, P. 2005. "The Paradoxes of Participation." In *Participation and Democracy at Work: Essays in Honour of Harvie Ramsay*, ed. Harley, B., Hyman, J. and Thompson, P., 1–19. Hampshire, United Kingdom: Palgrave Macmillan.

Harris, P. 2004. "From Health and Safety to Employee Participation? The Impact of the New Zealand Health and Safety in Employment Amendment Act (2002)." *International Employment Relations Review* 10 (1): 1–12.

Harris, L-A. 2011. "Legislation for Participation: An Overview of New Zealand's Health and Safety Representative Employee Participation System." *New Zealand Journal of Employment Relations* 36 (2): 45–60.

Harvey, O. 1992. "The Unions and the Government: The Rise and Fall of the Compact." In *Controlling Interests: Business, the State and Society in New Zealand*, ed. Deeks, J. and Perry, N., 59–77. Auckland, New Zealand: Auckland University Press.

Haworth, N. 2012. "Commentary: Reflections on High Performance, Partnership and the HR Function in New Zealand." *New Zealand Journal of Employment Relations* 37 (3): 65–73.

Independent Taskforce on Workplace Health and Safety. 2013. "The Report of the Independent Taskforce on Workplace Health and Safety, Main Report." Accessed November 15, 2016. http://hstaskforce.govt.nz/.

Lamm, F. 1994. "Australian and New Zealand Occupational Health and Safety – A Comparative Analysis." *Asia Pacific Journal of Human Resources* 32 (2): 57–77.

Lamm, F. 2010. "Participative and Productive Employment Relations: The Role of Health and Safety Committees and Worker Representation." In *Employment Relationships: Workers, Unions and Employers in New Zealand*, ed. Rasmussen, E., 149–167. Auckland, New Zealand: Auckland University Press.

Lilley, R., Samaranayaka, A. and Weiss, H. 2013. *International Comparison of International Labour Organization Published Occupational Fatal Injury Rates: How does New Zealand Compare Internationally?* Commissioned report for the Independent Taskforce on Workplace Health and Safety. Accessed April 3, 2017. http://hstaskforce.govt.nz/working-papers.asp.

Marchington, M. 2005. "Employee Involvement: Patterns and Explanations." In *Participation and Democracy at Work: Essays in Honour of Harvie Ramsay*, ed. Harley, B., Hyman, J. and Thompson, P., 20–37. Hampshire, United Kingdom: Palgrave Macmillan.

Marglin, S. and Schor, J. (eds). 1990. *The Golden Age of Capitalism*. Oxford, United Kingdom: Clarendon.

Markey, R., Harris, C., Ravenswood, K., Simpkin, G. and Williamson, D. 2015. "Employee Participation and Quality of the Work Environment: Cases from New Zealand." *New Zealand Journal of Employment Relations* 40 (2): 47–66.

McAndrew, I. 1993. "The Process of Developing Employment Contracts: A Management Perspective." In *Employment Contracts: New Zealand Experiences*, ed. Harbridge, R., 165–184. Wellington, New Zealand: Victoria University Press.

McAndrew, I. 2006. "Employers, Unions and Workplace Partnership in New Zealand." *New Zealand Journal of Employment Relations* 31 (3): 51–65.

McLaughlin, C. 2000. "'Mutually Beneficial Agreements' in the Retail Sector." *New Zealand Journal of Industrial Relations* 25 (1): 1–17.

Mullen, E. 1990. "Voluntarism in Occupational Health and Safety: A New Zealand Response." *New Zealand Journal of Industrial Relations* 15 (2): 129–143.

New Zealand Employers Federation. 1990. *Response to the Report of the Committee of Enquiry into Industrial Democracy*. Wellington, New Zealand: New Zealand Employers Federation.

Parry, M., Davidson, C. and Hill, R. 1995. *Reform at Work*. Auckland, New Zealand: Longman Paul.

Pashorina-Nichols, V. 2016. "Occupational Health and Safety: Why and How Should Worker Participation be Enhanced in New Zealand?" *New Zealand Journal of Employment Relations* 41 (2): 71–86.

Ramsey, H. 1977. "Cycles of Control: Worker Participation in Sociological and Historical Perspective." *Sociology* 11 (3): 481–506.

Rasmussen, E. 1996. "Employee Awareness and Attitudes: A Pilot Survey." *Labour Market Bulletin* 2: 89–101.

Rasmussen, E. 1997. "Workplace Reform and Employee Participation in New Zealand." In *Innovation and Employee Participation Through Works Councils*, ed. Markey, R. and Monat, J., 389–410. Aldershot, United Kingdom: Avebury.

Rasmussen, E. 2009. *Employment Relations in New Zealand*. Auckland, New Zealand: Pearson.

Rasmussen, E., Foster, B. and Farr, D. 2016. "The Battle over Employer-determined Flexibility: Attitudes Amongst New Zealand Employers." *Employee Relations* 38 (6): 1–23.

Rasmussen, E. and Lind, J. 2003. "Productive Employment Relationships: European Experiences." *New Zealand Journal of Industrial Relations* 28 (2): 158–169.

Rasmussen, E. and Ross, C. 2004. "The Employment Relations Act Through the Eyes of the Media." In *Employment Relationships: New Zealand's Employment Relations Act*, ed. Rasmussen, E., 21–38. Auckland, New Zealand: Auckland University Press.

Royal Commission on the Pike River Coal Mine Tragedy. 2012. *Royal Commission on the Pike River Coal Mine Tragedy, Volume 1 + Overview*. Wellington, New Zealand. Accessed October 23, 2016. http://pikeriver.royalcommission.govt.nz/.

Ruck, K., Welch, M. and Menara, B. 2017. "Employee Voice: An Antecedent to Organisational Engagement." *Public Relations Review* (in press). Accessed June 5, 2017. http://dx.doi.org/10.1016/j.pubrev.2017.04.008.

Scoping a Partnership Resource. 2004. *A Report Prepared for the Department of Labour and the State Services Commission*. Wellington, New Zealand: Innovations and Systems Ltd.

Sissons, J. 2016. "A Bad Day at the Sausage Factory: The Health and Safety at Work Act 2015." *New Zealand Journal of Employment Relations* 41 (2): 58–70.

Small, V. 2015. "Small 'Low Risk' Workplaces Win Exemption in New Health and Safety Law." *Stuff*. Accessed April 3, 2017. http://www.stuff.co.nz/national/politics/70520997/Small-low-risk-workplaces-win-exemption-in-new-health-and-safety-law.

Smith, D. F. 1978. "A Critique of Worker Participation in New Zealand." *New Zealand Journal of Industrial Relations* 3 (2): 71–79.

Streeck, W. (ed). 1992. *Social Institutions and Economic Performance*. London, United Kingdom: Sage.

Tipples, R. 2015. "Commentary: The Dairy Workplace Action Plan, Kelly's 'Pledge Washing', and the Health and Safety at Work Act, 2015." *New Zealand Journal of Employment Relations* 40 (3): 103–107.

Townsend, K., Wilkinson, A. and Burgess, J. 2012. "Filling the Gaps: Patterns of Formal and Informal Participation." *Economic and Industrial Democracy* 34 (2): 337–354.

Waldegrave, T., Anderson, D. and Wong, K. 2003. *Evaluation of the Short Term Impacts of the Employment Relations Act 2000*. Wellington, New Zealand: Department of Labour.

Walters, D. and Frick, K. 2000. "Worker Participation and the Management of Occupational Health and Safety: Reinforcing or Conflicting Strategies?" In *Systematic Occupational Health and Safety Management: Perspectives on an International Development*, ed. Frick, K., Jensen, P. L., Quinlan, M. and Wilthagen, T., 43–66. Oxford, United Kingdom: Elsevier Science.

Wilkinson, A., Gollan, P., Marchington, M. and Lewin, D. (eds). 2010. *The Oxford Handbook of Participation in Organizations*. Oxford, United Kingdom: Oxford University Press.

Williamson, D. 2017. "In Search of Consensus: A History of Employment Relations in the New Zealand Hotel Sector – 1955 to 2000." PhD Thesis, Auckland University of Technology, Auckland, New Zealand.

Wilson, M. 2010. "A Struggle Between Competing Ideologies. In *Employment Relationships. Workers, Unions and Employers in New Zealand*, ed. Rasmussen, E., 9–23. Auckland, New Zealand: Auckland University Press.

Legal Transformation

Competing Visions and the Transformation of New Zealand Labour Law

Gordon Anderson

Introduction

The late Bruce Jesson stated that:[1]

> New Zealand was a state-created society in that the state did not emerge from some already existing social order, some civil society, but instead created it. The state was responsible for creating the infrastructure of the country – a social infrastructure, as well as an economic infrastructure.

The nature of the society created by the New Zealand state is highly contestable, reflecting the different ideologies and mythologies of those promoting them.[2] While the most popular mythology is that of a sense of nationhood developing in the cauldron of the First World War,[3] an alternative narrative might suggest that New Zealand had developed its own sense of nationhood, its own social and economic values, well before 1915 – indeed well before the end of the nineteenth century. That vision of society had its roots in the hopes and expectations of the early settlers and their wish for a society that did not recreate an antipodean version of the class-based English society from which they had sailed half a world to escape.[4] This vision was perhaps encapsulated by Bottomore, who postulated

---

1   Bruce Jesson *Only Their Purpose is Mad – The Money Men Take Over New Zealand* (Dunmore Press, Palmerston North, 1999) at 205.
2   Tony Simpson *A Vision Betrayed: The Decline of Democracy in New Zealand* (Hodder and Stoughton, Auckland, 1984) provides an excellent discussion on competing visions of New Zealand.
3   Helen Clark's 2005 comment that Gallipoli "stirred within our people a new sense of national identity" is typical of such sentiments <http://www.nzherald.co.nz/nz/news/article.cfm?c_id=1&objectid=10122323>.
4   I would like to acknowledge Peter Gray, formerly of the Federal Court of Australia, for planting the seed of this idea during his keynote address to the Australian Labour Law Associations 7th Biennial Conference, Sydney 2014, when he suggested that if soldiers had been asked why they were fighting it may have been for a shared vision of social justice.

a society where:[5]

> ... there should be a substantial degree of equality among men, both in the sense that all adult members of a society ought to have, as far as is possible, an equal influence upon those decisions which affect important aspects of the life of society, and in the sense that inequalities of wealth, of social rank, or of education and access to knowledge, should not be so considerable as to result in the permanent subordination of some groups to others in any of the various spheres of social life, or to create great inequalities in the exercise of political rights.

This vision of the right to participative voice and equality rather than subordination was manifested in the early introduction of political suffrage culminating in universal suffrage in 1893 and in the early foundations of the welfare state.[6] In labour relations it might be symbolically represented by Parnell's 1840 assertion of the eight-hour working day. In response to an employer's assertion that "in London the bell rang at six o'clock", Parnell responded "We're not in London". While Parnell's comment is regarded as inaugurating the campaign for the eight-hour day,[7] a broader interpretation neglected by historical amnesia,[8] may also be justified. This is that his comment was also a rejection of the draconian English law governing the relations between master and servants – a law where "Imprisonment and whipping and fines, rather than civil remedies, were deeply entrenched ..."[9] While whipping may have diminished by the nineteenth century,[10] any worker arriving in New Zealand until the late nineteenth century would have been well aware that any breach of an employment contract in Britain could, and in thousands of cases did, lead to imprisonment with hard labour.[11] The treadmill would have been personally familiar to many immigrants!

In Britain the early nineteenth century had seen a general intensification of anti-worker law in order "to impose a more rigorous system of work discipline upon the growing numbers of labourers and outworkers employed in manufacturing,

---

5   TB Bottomore *Elites and Society* (Pelican, London, 1964) at 129.
6   Michael Basset *The State in New Zealand, 1840–1984: Socialism without doctrines?* (Auckland University Press, Auckland, 1998) at 1-31.
7   Herbert Roth *Trade Unions in New Zealand Past and Present* (AH & AW Reed, Wellington, 1973) at 3.
8   Robert J Steinfeld *Coercion, Contract and Free Labour in the Nineteenth Century* (Cambridge University Press, Cambridge, 2001) at 5 notes how the memory of master and servant legislation was already fading by the late nineteenth century.
9   Douglas Hay "England, 1562–1875: The Law and Its Uses" in Douglas Hay and Paul Craven (eds) *Masters, Servants, and Magistrates in Britain and the Empire, 1562–1955* (University of North Carolina Press, Chapel Hill, 2004) at 61.
10 Steinfeld, above n 8, at 75 gives instances of whipping until 1866.
11 See generally Hay, above n 9; Christopher Frank *Master and Servant Law: Chartists, Trade Unions, Radical Lawyers and the Magistracy in England, 1840–1865* (Ashgate, Farnham, 2010); Steinfeld, above n 8.

as well as maintaining control of the agricultural labour market."[12] While the Master and Servant Act 1823 had strengthened the statutory regime of labour discipline, the common law courts were also active in strengthening the powers of masters at the expense of workers.[13] The increasing criminalisation of workers under master and servant legislation[14] was to continue until the repeal of the master and servant statutes in 1875,[15] a repeal that had nothing to do with any diminishing relevance of the statute[16] and which occurred "as the result of the efforts of organised labor . . ."[17]

It was this vision of the 'London' notion of labour relations that the New Zealand merchant and employer class attempted to enact in New Zealand through a domestic Master and Servant Bill in 1864–1865. Rather than social justice and equality, these employers would have preferred to enshrine in New Zealand law the system of class-based English law – "a model of employment based on the personal subordination of the worker to the employer, a model incorporating an open-ended duty of obedience",[18] where subordination was enforced through penal sanctions and that ". . . enabled masters to defeat the market and to hold on to skilled and experienced workers, undermined strikes and trade unions".[19]

The Parliamentary rejection of the Master and Servant Bill was a significant victory for labour. In the Empire New Zealand alone rejected this "ligament . . . that helped make the British Empire a thinkable whole".[20] The reasons for the Bill's rejection were complex. Henning points out that the perceived need for such a law was less obvious in New Zealand than other colonies, but he also stresses "a special ideological predisposition amongst the early New Zealand colonisers and colonists against forced servitude",[21] a disposition partly influenced by Wakefield's opposition to unfree labour in New Zealand.[22]

12 Simon Deakin and Frank Wilkinson *The Law of the Labour Market: Industrialization, Employment and Legal Evolution* (Oxford University Press, Oxford, 2005) at 62.
13 For example, *Spain v Arnott* (1816) 171 ER 638 (doctrine of the entire contract and the leading authority on the subordination of a servant), *Priestly v Fowler* (1837) 150 ER 1030 (doctrine of common employment)
14 On the extent of this criminalisation see Hay, above n 9.
15 At 105.
16 Imprisonment rates were at their highest in the years before its repeal: Steinfeld, above n 8, at 76.
17 At 5; and see Hay, above n 9, at 116.
18 Deakin and Wilkinson, above n 12, at 61.
19 John Henning "New Zealand: An Antipodean Exception to the Master and Servant Rules" (2007) 41 New Zealand Journal of History 62 at 67 partly quoting; Douglas Hay and Paul Craven *Masters, Servants, and Magistrates in Britain and the Empire, 1562–1955* (University of North Carolina Press, Chapel Hill, 2004).
20 Hay and Craven, above n 19, at 2.
21 Henning, above n 19, at 69.
22 At 75. In this context 'free' labour meant that workers could not be compelled by law to complete their contracts. Unfree labour included labour subject to penal sanctions for breach

The defeat of the Master and Servant Bill in 1865 may have been a set-back for many employers, but, legally at least, they were not particularly disadvantaged. While English labour law as it existed in 1840 applied in principle, it was not until the large-scale immigration from the 1870s that there were many workers to apply it to.[23] Employers remained free to dismiss workers and in the 1880s and 1890 were able to defeat strikes with relatively few problems without resort to the law.[24]

The Arbitral System

Simpson has suggested:[25]

> Our elites, pursuing their own preoccupations while they keep the gate of political power, have allowed, or been forced to grudgingly accept, a sharing of that power from time to time.

In terms of labour law the arbitration system, which dominated New Zealand's labour relations for almost a century, was the most important example of sharing of a power 'grudgingly accepted'. The Industrial Conciliation and Arbitration Act 1894 (IC&A Act) was the first comprehensive labour legislation introduced in New Zealand and once consolidated in the period before the First World War its basic structure remained largely unchanged until the final two decades of the twentieth century. The key principle of the Act was that the terms and conditions under which people worked should be jointly determined and regulated, under the mediation of the state, by employers and workers represented by their trade union. It was a principle totally at odds with the fundamental ethos of the common law – that workers were subordinate to their masters and that any form of combination or workers was unlawful – but it was one that fitted Bottomore's prescription.

As with most radical legislative reform, the IC&A Act was the result of a confluence of unusual social and political factors, which, in this case, came together at a propitious moment when labour law, being largely unformed, was open to innovative reform. The most important was the election of the reformist Liberal-Labour Government.[26] As Holt states, the Act "was passed by a

---

of contract but also forms such as indentured labour.
23 Noel Woods *Industrial Conciliation and Arbitration in New Zealand* (Government Printer, Wellington, 1963) at 17 comments that "Industrial relations problems did not assume any great importance in New Zealand until after 1870."
24 Although if challenged employers could have relied on their common law right to dismiss workers without reason.
25 Simpson, above n 2, at 11.
26 For a detailed account of the factors involved, see *James Holt Compulsory Arbitration in New Zealand: The First Forty Years* (Auckland University Press, Auckland, 1986) at ch 1; Roth, above n 7, at chs 1–2.

government seeking labour support with the approval of the unions and against the wishes of the organised employers".[27] The passage of the Bill was facilitated by a union movement devastated after 1891 and which saw arbitration as a viable alternative to industrial action, and the placation of the politically powerful farming lobby by the exclusion of farm workers from the system. Public opinion, shaped by the apprehension of drawn-out industrial conflict and by employer actions during the Maritime Strike and the Report of the Sweating Commission, also supported reform.

While this confluence of factors may have been relatively short-lived, it provided time for the system to become established, a process largely completed around 1908.[28] Holt argues that the system's success was because of its capacity to evolve over time while remaining sufficiently flexible to enjoy the support of parties with divergent economic interests – it delivered a balance of working conditions and industrial stability that were acceptable to both capital and labour.[29] Two important characteristics should be stressed.[30]

First, workers, through their trade unions, had an effective participative voice in the determination of terms and conditions and the award system ensured that the great majority of workers enjoyed at least some level of social justice through an acceptable level of remuneration and conditions of employment.[31]

Second, the system encouraged strong tripartite and bipartite relationships. The system relied on district or nationally organised industry/occupational-unions and industry/occupational employer associations. The effective settlement of disputes required that both parties had strong working relationships leading to mutual cooperation and joint regulation at both industry and, though job delegates, enterprise level.

The arbitration system was of course far from perfect, but its most serious problem was that the system was inherently unstable and had considerable difficulty in adjusting to rapidly changing economic circumstances.[32] Easton has argued that there had always been a potential instability in the arbitral system's wage settlement structure and "wages disruption was inevitable – an accident

27 Holt, above n 26, at 13.
28 Woods, above n 23, at 89.
29 Holt, above n 26, at 24.
30 For a description of the mature arbitration system, see Gordon Anderson *Reconstructing New Zealand's Labour Law: Consensus or Divergence?* (Victoria University Press, Wellington, 2011) at ch 2.
31 Public service workers were governed by a separate system: see Jane Bryson and Gordon Anderson "Reconstructing State Employment in New Zealand" in Marilyn Pittard and Phillipa Weeks (eds) *Public Sector Employment in the Twenty-First Century* (ANU e-Press, Canberra, 2007) at 253.
32 For a perspective on the forces that lead to the systems collapse see Peter Brosnan, David F Smith and Pat Walsh *The Dynamics of New Zealand Industrial Relations* (John Wiley, Auckland, NZ, 1990) at 32.

waiting to happen".[33] When that accident finally occurred with the 1968 nil-wage order[34] and the economic shocks of the 1970s, political and legal attention shifted to focus on the labour law structures needed to regulate labour relations in an environment increasingly characterised by collective bargaining and industrial stoppages. In retrospect, developments in labour law in the 1970s and 1980s can best be viewed as an attempt to translate the bipartite values inherent in the arbitration system into a reformed structure compatible with the new industrial relations realities – a task that ultimately proved impossible.

Two Decades of Turbulence: 1970–1990

An environment characterised by economic and political volatility is not the most propitious for the development of a coherent structure for labour law – and the two decades after the 1960s were some of the most turbulent in New Zealand's history, as governments sought to respond to increasing globalisation and severe external economic shocks.[35] Politically the later part of the period also saw a dramatic shift from the pluralist/tripartite philosophies that had characterised the post-war period in most developed economies, to the extreme neoliberal programme that gained increasing international traction from the late 1970s. The 1980s were to end with the Labour government's 'blitzkrieg'[36] of neoliberal economic deregulation.

From a distance of over three decades, the responses to industrial relations pressures between 1970 and 1990 seem very much a product of their time and place. The concerns of the time were largely short term and centred on the ubiquitous wage controls that dominated much of the period[37] and which inevitably generated industrial conflict.[38] Given political controversy, and the

---

33 Brian Easton *In Stormy Seas: The Post-War New Zealand Economy* (Otago University Press, Dunedin, 1997) at 95. A similar argument is made by Michael Barry and Nick Wailes "Contrasting Systems? 100 years of Arbitration in Australia and New Zealand" (2004) 46 NZJIR 430.
34 Compulsory arbitration had first been repealed during the depression of the 1930s.
35 These included Britain's entry into the EEC in 1973 and the 1973 and 1978, oil shocks. See, generally, Colin James *The Quiet Revolution* (Allen & Unwin/Port Nicholson Press, Wellington, 1986); Colin James *New Territory* (Bridget Williams Books, Wellington, 1992); Easton, above n 33; Paul Dalziel *The New Zealand Macroeconomy* (5th ed ed, Oxford University Press, Auckland, 2004).
36 Jane Kelsey *The New Zealand Experiment: A World Model for Structural Adjustment?* (Auckland University Press, Auckland, 1995) at 33 and see generally ch 2.
37 Jonathan Boston *Incomes Policy in New Zealand: 1968–1984* (Victoria University Press, Wellington, 1984) points out that from March 1971 until July 1984 there were only eight months of "what could legitimately be described as free wage bargaining".
38 Before 1965 the number of annual work stoppages rarely exceeded 100. In the following 20 years the number was rarely below and often over 300, peaking at over 400 in 1975–1976: Statistics New Zealand *New Zealand Official Year Book* (David Bateman, Auckland, 2010).

confrontational style of the Muldoon National government, any measured reform of the law was overshadowed by ad hoc legislation as a reaction to immediate events or to obtain short-term political advantage.[39]

Some significant structural reforms having a continuing impact were, however, effected during this period and in particular by the two major legislative reforms, the Industrial Relations Act 1973 (IRA) and the Labour Relations Act 1987 (LRA).

The Industrial Relations Act 1973

The IRA, a measure advanced and supported by both employers and unions, effected the most significant changes to the structure of labour law since 1894. While the Act became the victim of economic and political circumstance, it did introduce a number of innovations that continue to influence contemporary law.

The heart of the 1973 reforms was the introduction of a more sophisticated distinction between various forms of industrial dispute, which in turn allowed a more systematic approach to dispute settlement by enabling procedures and remedies to be tailored to the particular class of dispute. Disputes of interest settling the terms and conditions of employment were to be resolved through an industrial process. The 1973 Act also recognised, by repealing penalties for strikes and lockouts relating to disputes of interest, that work stoppages were a legitimate tactic during bargaining. The political debate thereafter focused on defining the subject matter of legitimate strikes[40] and the decriminalisation of strike law, the latter reform shifting the onus for initiating legal action against strikers on to the affected parties using civil remedies.

Disputes of rights, on the other hand, concerned matters typically resolved through an adjudicative process applying pre-determined legal rules to the factual situation identified by the court or tribunal. Once this conceptual distinction was formulated the framework existed to refine the law further by focusing on the most effective procedures for resolving particular types of dispute. The most important and far-reaching development was the establishment of the personal grievance process that allowed challenges to unjustified dismissals and other employer conduct. This reform established the principle that an employer was legally required to justify dismissals or other actions that disadvantaged an employee – a requirement that significantly constrained the common law's notion of unfettered management prerogative and which helped lay the foundation for the concept of good faith introduced in 2000.[41]

---

39 See Anderson, above n 30, at ch 3.
40 Particularly the Commerce Amendment Act 1976 Part VIA, which sought to restrict legitimate strikes to industrial matters, a provision that was the forerunner of the lawful/unlawful distinction introduced in 1987.
41 Gordon Anderson "Good Faith in the Individual Employment Relationship in New Zealand" (2011) 32 Comp Lab L & Pol'y J 685 at 692.

Labour's reforms 1984–1990

Although the Labour government's neoliberal economic programme fundamentally changed the country's economic landscape,[42] Labour, treading a fine line between a push for deregulation on the one hand and for re-regulation on the other,[43] made relatively limited reforms to labour law in spite of rapidly building pressure for deregulation led by the Business Roundtable.[44] Labour's reforms took place in two phases, the first being the abolition of compulsory arbitration,[45] and the second the more comprehensive reforms of the LRA. Labour's most long-reaching reform was the State Sector Act 1988, which repealed the separate state sector industrial relations system,[46] creating a single system of labour law for both the public and private sector.

Although little used since the late 1960s, compulsory arbitration retained significance as, without this option, employers became free to refuse to conclude an award and thus allow the existing award to expire, a tactic opening the door to non-award workplaces and enterprise-based agreements. Labour's reforms would almost certainly have resulted in significant changes to labour relations structures, but over a longer time period mediated by a number of transitional measures, in particular, union restructuring, which may have left unions better placed to deal with change. However, the reforms that survived the Employment Contracts Act 1991 (ECA) were few. Industrially the most important was the clear distinction made between lawful and unlawful industrial action, with lawful action being protected from common law legal constraints including tort-based actions.

The second was the restructuring of the (renamed) Labour Court to reinforce its judicial character and expand its jurisdiction. The role of lay members, who had been full members of the Court since 1894, was significantly reduced, thus largely eliminating its bipartite character, and the Court's jurisdiction was extended to include, in particular, actions in tort arising out of a strike or lockout. These reforms set the scene for the evolution of the modern Employment Court and, more importantly, the subsequent juridification of labour relations as lawyers came to dominate the Court's workload. This changed the role and culture of

42 See Easton, above n 33; James, above n 35; and also Brian Easton *The Making of Rogernomics* (Auckland University Press, Auckland, 1989).
43 Pat Walsh "A Family Fight? Industrial Relations Reform under the Fourth Labour Government" in Brian Easton (ed) *The Making of Rogernomics* (Auckland University Press, Auckland, 1989) at 149.
44 On the Business Roundtable's role and agenda see Paul Harris and Linda Twiname *First Knights: An Investigation of the New Zealand Business Roundtable* (Howling at the Moon Press, Auckland, 1998).
45 Industrial Relations Amendment Act 1984 s 13. This provision allowed reference of an unsettled dispute of interest to the Court only if both parties consented.
46 See Bryson and Anderson, above n 31.

the Court as industrial solutions gave way to legal solutions, which inevitably undermined bipartism and opened the door to common law unitarism.[47]

Unitarism Revived – the Employment Contracts Act 1991

As was suggested earlier, radical legal reform requires a 'perfect storm' where the forces pushing for reform are able to overwhelm those opposing it.[48] Such a confluence of events occurred in 1990–1991 although, unlike 1894, when the IC&A Act enjoyed wide support, the ECA was promoted by and for the benefit of one group only – employers. It may have taken over 120 years, but a twentieth-century version of the master and servant relationship advocated by New Zealand business in 1864 was finally to be realised.[49]

By 1991 the anti-worker/anti-union campaign pursued by the Business Roundtable and its ideological acolytes, including Treasury, had come to totally dominate political and economic discourse. Within that discourse workers were viewed as commodities and any voice they might seek was portrayed as an unwarranted interference with ownership rights.[50] In 1990–1991 there was little effective opposition to the Bill. The natural opposition, the Labour party, had been eviscerated of both its principles and much of its traditional support, as a result of 'Rogernomics'[51] and its deregulatory policies of 1984–1990 had laid the economic and political groundwork for the ECA. The Federation of Labour's failure to organise general industrial action to challenge the Bill further neutered effective worker opposition. Even if there had been coordinated and widespread opposition to the Bill it is unlikely that the government would have been deterred from implementing its policy objectives.

Moreover labour was deliberately excluded from any participation in the reform process prior to the Bill's introduction. The political process that led up to the introduction of the ECA has been dealt with elsewhere[52] and, as those

---

47 Susan Robson "Policy Operations and Outcomes in the New Zealand Employment Jurisdiction 1990–2008" (PhD, University of Otago, 2016).
48 However, unlike the ECA, which was introduced and enacted in six months, it took the IC&A Act several years to overcome resistance from the (unelected) Upper House.
49 For an Australian making this point in relation to its reforms, see Mary Gardiner "His Master's Voice? Work Choices as a Return to Master and Servant Concepts" (2009) 31 Sydney Law Review 53.
50 Ellen J Dannin *Working Free: The Origins and Impact of New Zealand's Employment Contracts Act* (Auckland University Press, Auckland, 1997) at ch 8.
51 Kelsey, above n 36, at 31 argues that when Douglas presented his policies to Labour's caucus and policy council "in effect he asked them to turn their back on what the party stood for."
52 Ellen J Dannin *Working Free: The Origins and Impact of New Zealand's Employment Contracts Act* (Auckland University Press, Auckland, 1997) at ch 6; Pat Walsh and Rose Ryan "The Making of the Employment Contracts Act" in Raymond Harbridge (ed) *Employment Contracts: New Zealand Experiences* (Victoria University Press, Wellington, 1993) at 13; and Robson, above n 47.

authors demonstrate, National made no secret of the general thrust of its proposed reforms. Even so, the abandonment of even a pretence of pluralism or consultation took many by surprise. The extent to which the unitary perspective had come to dominate policy development was illustrated by the stark differences between the legislative process in 1973 and 1987 and that of 1991. The draft of the IRA, the first comprehensive review of labour law since 1894, was primarily an agreed joint employer–union document that was taken to government, introduced by a National government and passed under a Labour government. The LRA was preceded by a lengthy consultative process including both a Green and a White Paper. In contrast, the initial drafting of the EC Bill was undertaken by a small coterie, led by a former Employers' Federation official, which limited its consultations to "key business leaders and others",[53] but the "NZ Council of Trade Unions and workers . . . have not been consulted".[54]

The government's view that employees need not be consulted over fundamental changes to their legal rights became even more apparent when, during the Act's second reading debate under urgency, its coverage was extended to all employees. Downey, rightly describes these changes, affecting close to half the private sector workforce, as "an act of political arrogance and of legal ignorance regarding the rights of citizens".[55]

The form of labour law as sought by the Business Roundtable and Treasury could, however, have been considerably more radical. The final form of the Bill was tempered by the Department of Labour's pragmatic approach prevailing over Treasury's simplistic neoliberal model of labour law.[56]

It would, however, be a mistake to regard these rejections of the neoliberal position as a defeat. The ECA's objectives were largely shared; what differed was the means by which they should be achieved. The pragmatists were prepared to limit the extent of the reforms, recognising some of the realities of labour relations but also to ensure the Act's success politically.[57] And the Act was devastatingly effective; within five years the labour landscape had fundamentally shifted from a pluralist system with strong worker voice to a unitary system anchored in the common law rules of master and servant, a perspective which harmonised closely with the neoliberal economic vision of employment.

In retrospect, the ECA is best seen as the culmination of the neoliberal

---

53 Walsh and Ryan, above n 52.
54 Memorandum from R Stockdill, Department of Labour, to the Minister of Labour, 3 December 1990.
55 Pat Downey "Work and Contract" (1991) May NZLJ 145. See also a letter by Dr R Harrison in a letter to the Minister of Labour reported in the *New Zealand Herald*, 6 May 1991, at 5.
56 Accounts of the internal political debate make it clear that such proposals were vigorously opposed by Treasury. For a full discussion of the political and drafting process, see the references in fn 52.
57 Robson, above n 47, at ch 2.

deregulatory reforms initiated by Labour. The Act transformed labour relations, creating a largely deregulated labour market characterised by individual employment, often precarious, on terms and conditions dictated by employers. Union density plummeted from about 52 per cent to 22 per cent over the decade and the coverage of collective agreements fell by over 50 per cent to 31 per cent.[58]

Outside the state sector, individualised employment contracts became the norm[59] and, as these contracts were largely dictated by employers, conditions that had been hard won over decades vanished in a few years: penal and overtime payments disappeared, hours of work became less constrained, rest breaks became discretionary, wage levels fell or remained static, and employer control and disciplinary powers were strengthened.[60]

These changes were achieved through three principal drivers which have continued, in a sometimes modified form, in the Employment Relations Act 2000 (ERA).

Support for negative freedom of association

By the late 1980s compulsory union membership and traditional union structures had been increasingly challenged, but the ECA's immediate abolition of compulsory membership prevented any transition. Instead, membership rapidly collapsed as did many previously large unions such as the Clerical Workers. Those that remained active[61] were left in financial and organisational disarray. Union capacity to recruit and defend workers, at a time it was most needed, was seriously compromised and it took some years for a weakened union movement to adapt to the new bargaining environment. Naturally, the absence of an effective, or any, union left employers free to dictate terms of employment.

Enterprise confinement and the containment of collective bargaining

While the default position of the ECA was the individual contract of employment, the right to bargain collectively and the right to strike were retained, but

---

58 'Update 1995/96' at 5 and 8, 'Update 1999/2000' at 13-15, *Employment Agreements: Bargaining Trends & Employment Law Updates*, Industrial Relations Centre, Victoria University of Wellington, and Robyn May, Pat Walsh, Glenn Thickett and Raymond Harbridge "Unions and Union Membership in New Zealand: Annual Review for 2000" (2000) 26 NZJIR at 317. Union density is reported as a percentage of wage and salary earners.
59 'Update 1999/2000', *Employment Agreements: Bargaining Trends & Employment Law Updates*, Industrial Relations Centre, Victoria University of Wellington, at 15, Table 4.
60 Bill Rosenberg "A Brief History of Labour's Share of Income in New Zealand 1939–2016" in this volume discusses the impact on income levels.
61 All registered unions at the time of the Act's commencement were automatically re-registered as incorporated societies under the Incorporated Societies Act 1908.

there was little legislative support for collective bargaining. Employers were not required to negotiate and even if negotiations occurred there were no significant constraints on bad faith behaviour. The Court of Appeal was to make it clear that the Act provided employers with considerable latitude to undermine bargaining,[62] confining bargaining to a single, employer-defined, enterprise.[63] It also compromised the ability of unions to negotiate, increased the cost of negotiations and made effective industrial action increasingly difficult. Perhaps the most egregious effect was that the ECA allowed employers to impose so-called collective bargaining on unorganised employers and to then use actual and partial lockouts to reduce conditions without stoppages of work.[64]

Ensuring the dominance of the contract of employment and the common law

With the collapse of union membership, the collectively determined award was rapidly displaced by "the indispensable figment of the legal mind known as the 'contract of employment'".[65] Such contracts typically became standard-form agreements prepared by solicitors drafting them to maximise the rights of the employer. Further embedding the influence of the common law was the increasing use of lawyers to resolve employment disputes.[66] Disputes became formulated and resolved in a manner increasingly shaped by the language and processes of the common law and more flexible and pragmatic industrial relations solutions gave way to the black and white approach of the law.[67]

Equally importantly, the discourse of employment obligations and disputes moved from a pluralistic, industrial perspective to a unitary common law mode that stressed the subordination of employees, the implied obligations of fidelity and obedience, and management prerogative. Case law, driven by the influence of a reactionary Court of Appeal,[68] became increasingly influenced by common law values, most notably in the approach to redundancies[69] and in the pro-

62 Gordon Anderson "Collective Bargaining and the Law: New Zealand's Employment Contracts Act Five Years On" (1996) 9 Australian Journal of Labour Law 103.
63 The definition of 'employer' in ECA s 2 was the legal entity employing the workers in question and was therefore easily able to be manipulated by corporate groups.
64 Anderson, above n 30, at 83.
65 Otto Kahn-Freund *Labour and the Law* (Stevens, London, 1972) at 8.
66 Margaret Wilson "The Employment Relations Act: A Framework for a Fairer Way" in Erling Rasmussen (ed) *Employment Relationships: New Zealand's Employment Relations Act* (Auckland University Press, Auckland, 2004) at 15.
67 Susan Robson "The Influence of the Legal Profession on Dispute Resolution after 1990" in this book.
68 Gordon Anderson "The Common Law and the Reconstruction of Employee Relationships in New Zealand" (2016) 32 IJCLL& IR 93.
69 See for example *Aoraki Corporation Ltd v McGavin* [1998] 1 ERNZ 601 (CA) at 618 where Court held that "to impose an absolute requirement [to consult on potential redundancies]

A New Approach? The Employment Relations Act 2000

In 2000 the Labour government opted to forgo radical reform, preferring a conservative approach that delivered only limited improvements for employees and posed little threat to the labour market reforms of the 1990s. Individualised employment and enterprise confinement continued to be the dominating characteristics of the law, although in the context of a more balanced framework regulating labour market interactions. Employers had little to fear from the reforms and, by 2008, when National returned to power, it appeared that a broad political consensus may have been reached on the overall architecture of labour law, if not its details.[71]

Margaret Wilson has, however, argued that sharpening ideological differences between political parties and the advent of MMP have meant that "the search for consensus becomes more difficult and often compromise is mistaken for consensus".[72] This may be so, but if compromise becomes necessary, stability in the law may be the result – at least for as long as a neoliberalist approach underpins the context within which reform takes place.

The ERA has now been in force for 17 years, a period roughly divided between Labour and National governments. Both have amended the Act, but the extent of these amendments has had limited impact on the overall architecture of labour law. The most important of Labour's amendments, those of 2004, reinforced aspects of the original Act where reforms, particularly good faith, had been undermined by the Court of Appeal.[73] National's reforms on the other hand have in part been concerned with reversing some of Labour's 2004 and later amendments, but have been principally directed at further weakening collective bargaining and worker voice generally.

---

would be inconsistent with the employer's prima facie right to organise and run its business operation as it sees fit. See Anderson, above n 41.

70   *W & H Newspapers Ltd v Oram* [2000] 2ERNZ 448 (CA).
71   Gordon Anderson "'The Sky Didn't Fall In' An Emerging Consensus on the Shape of New Zealand Labour Law ?" (2010) 23 AJLL 94.
72   Margaret Wilson "A Struggle Between Competing Ideologies" in Erling Rasmussen (ed) *Employment Relationships: Workers, Unions and Employers in New Zealand* (new ed, Auckland University Press, Auckland, 2010) at 20.
73   *Coutts Cars Ltd v Baguley* [2002] 2 NZLR 533 (CA) and *Auckland City Council v New Zealand Public Service Assoc* [2004] 2 NZLR 10 (CA).

Labour's act

Some years after 2000, Margaret Wilson, the then Minister of Labour, wrote that:[74]

> ... the approach of the Employment Relations Act is consistent with the values that underpinned the system of conciliation and arbitration. It is a model that attempts to manage conflict through negotiation, within a framework that recognises the responsibility of government to provide the institutional and procedural support for employers and employees and their representatives to resolve their differences in a peaceful, constructive manner. Conceptually, it is grounded on the notion that co-operative, inclusive regulatory frameworks produce better outcomes.

The two most important reforms mechanisms for achieving the Minister's vision were the statutory obligation of good faith and the promotion of collective bargaining as the primary mechanism for determining terms and conditions of employment. The ERA might legitimately be judged[75] on the success of these two objectives.

Good faith

The statutory obligation of good faith, now firmly embedded in the law,[76] is the reform that has had a lasting and positive impact on employment relations. The obligation recognises that not only are employees to be treated fairly but that they should have a meaningful voice in decisions affecting the security of their employment. The Chief Judge has stated:[77]

> [65] ... An employer who acts in breach of the statutory good faith obligations may find it difficult to justify a subsequent dismissal or disadvantage in employment because a fair and reasonable employer will not generally act towards an employee in contravention of the law.

Good faith now permeates all matters relating to employment relationships, often in a low key manner, but nevertheless in a way that continues to be accumulative over time.[78]

---

74 Wilson, above n 66, at 19.
75 It should be noted that Labour's initial ability to achieve reform in 2000, as the government did not have an overall parliamentary majority and was dependent on more conservative minor parties for support, was strengthened by a number of amendments to the ERA in 2004. These reforms particularly affected good faith and collective bargaining. On the politics of reforms see Wilson, above n 66, at 14.
76 Arguably, the broad concept of good faith had long been influential in New Zealand labour law: see Anderson, above n 68.
77 *Allen v Transpacific Industries Group Ltd (t/a "Medismart Ltd")* (2009) 6 NZELR 530 (EmpC).
78 A situation that has continued since 2008 as the National government elected that year has

While the duty impacts on the employment relationship as a whole, the most immediate impact of the duty, outside collective bargaining, has been in relation to matters under the general rubric of business restructuring. Under the ECA employees were not legally entitled to any voice in such decisions – an employer had only to communicate the decision by giving notice of dismissal.[79] The ERA has significantly improved that situation and now, if an employer proposes to make decisions that may adversely affect the continuation of its employees' employment, those employees must be provided with relevant information about the decision and given a meaningful opportunity to comment on that information before any decision is made.[80] The requirements of a consultative process are well established in New Zealand law[81] and, while the courts will not overturn a genuine redundancy, such decisions are now subject to much stronger scrutiny.[82]

Collective bargaining

While the good faith obligation can be seen as a successful reform, the same cannot be said of the objective of promoting collective bargaining, and unless there is bargaining it cannot be done in good faith. Under the ERA bargaining coverage and union density continued to decline and, when Labour lost power in 2008, union density was virtually unchanged since 1999,[83] but coverage of collective agreements had declined dramatically: from 30 per cent in 2000 to 17 per cent in 2009, a drop of almost 50 per cent.[84] If employees are to have any meaningful voice in the determination, improvement and operation of their employment relationships, collective bargaining is critical.

While the ERA abandoned the approach of spurious neutrality of the ECA by providing that collective bargaining could only take place between a union and an employer, and required employers to negotiate in good faith, the Act left ample opportunity for a determined employer to undermine bargaining to either avoid reaching an agreement or to minimise the impact of the bargaining. Facilitation at best provides a circuit breaker in some situations, but, in the absence of impasse arbitration, unions find it very difficult to successfully negotiate with

---

left the good faith obligation untouched although reducing worker protections in a number of other areas.
79 *Aoraki Corporation Ltd v McGavin*, above n 69.
80 ERA s 4(1A)(c).
81 Generally in *Wellington International Airport Ltd v Air NZ* [1993] 1 NZLR 671 (CA) and enumerated in an employment context in *Communication and Energy Workers Union Inc v Telecom New Zealand Ltd* [1993] 2 ERNZ 429 (EC).
82 *Grace Team Accounting v Brake* [2014] NZCA 541.
83 Department of Labour "Union Membership Return Report 2010" <http://www.societies.govt.nz/cms/registered-unions/annual-return-membership-reports/older-reports>.
84 The most dramatic drop in bargaining coverage was the result of the ERA's "join the union, join the agreement" approach, which saw coverage drop by around 100,000 employees.

a determined employer unless union membership is such that effective strike action is a realistic possibility – not the situation in most workplaces. The failure to legally constrain the anti-union activities of employers did little to ameliorate this situation.

National's reforms

The current National government has avoided dramatic reforms to the ERA, and has left its core provisions largely untouched. Instead, it has been prepared to play a long game, slowly reducing the collective legal rights of workers. The most dramatic manifestation of National's view that worker voice should be muted was illustrated when the Health and Safety at Work Bill was amended in its final stages to largely negate the right of workers to establish health and safety committees[85] – a move making it clear that voice is not to be regarded as a worker's right but rather a concession to be made by management.

Broadly speaking, National seems to have followed a three-part strategy. While it has made a number of reforms to ensure that minimum employment standards are more effectively enforced,[86] it has also made limited cuts to individual rights, most notably with 90-day trial periods. Most significantly, however, it has slowly introduced a range of measures intended to undermine collective bargaining or collective voice generally. Multi-employer bargaining has been made optional and good faith has been undermined by removing the requirement to conclude a collective agreement. The right to strike has been further constrained by more onerous notice provisions and amendments allowing employers to make a 10 per cent pay deduction for non-stoppage strikes.[87] In this last provision, which, given the extraordinary wide definition of a strike, penalises virtually any form of worker resistance to management powers or instructions – the spirit of the master and servant acts continues to thrive!

The Future

If one believes in the underlying values of democracy and social justice, those values must clearly apply to the workplace. Bottomore's vision of a society involving participative voice and reasonable equality is much more likely to be achieved through the joint regulation of employment where workers have a voice in the conditions under which they labour and in the distribution of the wealth generated by their labour. This vision was at least partially realised in the

---

85 HSW Act s 66(5) allows an employer to decline to establish a committee if "existing worker participation practices sufficiently meet the requirements of s 61".
86 National initiated a number of reforms to reinforce minimum employment rights, for example the ER Amendment Act 2016.
87 ERA ss 95A – 95E.

arbitration system, but destroyed in 1991. The common law alternative contains nothing of this vision. Workers are subordinate to capital and a commodity to be utilised by capital for capital's benefit. Worker voice has no place in this scheme. The rights of workers are defined by contract, a contract that is heavily weighted by common law and economic power, to heavily favour employers. The harshest effects of the common law are ameliorated by statute – minimum employment standards, personal grievance procedures and the duty of good faith – but these do not provide effective voice.

Effective worker voice requires both a political and industrial foundation.[88] The former has increased somewhat but remains weak, although there are signs that Labour is now prepared to advance somewhat bolder reforms[89] should they win office.[90]

It is suggested that at least four key reforms are required if labour law is to re-establish the principles of pluralism and effective worker voice for the 21st century. The reforms can be sub-divided into those promoting collective voice and those promoting and protecting the position of the individual.

The collective

If workers are to have an effective voice in their workplace they must have the right to effective representation though a representative trade union or through other mechanisms that allow the exercise of effective voice. While the ERA recognised independent trade unions as the preferred source of employee voice and restored them to their traditional role of collective bargaining, trade union membership has continued to decline. This may partly be due to the weak, but easily remediable, provisions protecting freedom of association, the high barriers to proving anti-union discrimination and the absence of any requirement for employer neutrality in relation to union membership. It is also attributable to negative attitudes to unions and to recruitment and organisational difficulties. While union involvement may be the most effective mechanism of voice, alternative mechanisms, such as mandatory elected workplace delegates and representative committees, also allow the expression of worker voice and provide a possible catalyst for union involvement. What must be enshrined into law, however, is that effective participative and representational structures within employing entities are a matter of right, a condition of employing labour, and not a matter of employer benevolence.

---

88 Gordon Anderson and Pam Nuttal "The Good-Faith Obligation: An Effective Model for Promoting Voice?" in Alan Bogg and Tonia Novitz (eds) *Voices at Work: Continuity and Change in the Common Law World* (Oxford University Press, Oxford, 2014) at 194.
89 See Labour's 2017 industrial relations policy.
90 This paper was written before the 2017 election.

The second requirement is to effectively enhance and promote collective bargaining. While the current provisions on good faith bargaining provide a solid foundation for collective bargaining, further key reforms should be enacted. In particular, the law needs to recognise the economic, rather than the legal character of employing entities, so that for the purposes of collective bargaining an 'employer' should be defined as any group of companies operating as a single economic unit. Multi-employer bargaining should be defined as bargaining with economically independent employers – effectively industry or occupational bargaining and possibly be dealt with by industry standard agreements setting the level of specified minimum terms in a defined industry or occupation. It is also clear that the current impasse processes need to be strengthened to encourage settlements including power for the Authority to make binding recommendations on at least some core terms.

The individual

First, the common law concept of employee must be replaced by that of a 'worker', broadly defined as any person employed on a contract requiring the personal performance of work. Such a definition is necessary to prevent the exploitation of workers by the increasing creation of non-employee work relationships. While workers should be free to enter non-employee work relationships (such as a contractor), which may have the effect of their not being covered by the ERA, there should be a strong presumption that any such relationship is based on the worker being genuinely in business on their own account and on terms and conditions that are substantially more beneficial to the worker than the minimum employment standards.

Matching this change needs to be an extension of 'employer' liability, possibly analogous to the 'person conducting a business or an undertaking' (PCBU) concept employed in the Health and Safety at Work Act, so that, for some matters at least, liability is imposed on parties able to control factors that impact negatively on workers. Obvious examples would be employing sub-contractors on terms that do not require or enable minimum employment standards to be complied with, at some point, in the contractual chain and the problem of 'dismissals' in triangular employment relationships.

The most important reform, however, is to negate the common law's view of employee subordination and the willingness of the courts to uphold increasingly intrusive controls of employees both within and outside work. It is suggested that, at a minimum, a new statutory 'key provision' should be enacted to make it clear that employment relationships must respect and protect the dignity of workers and recognise their right to personal and family life, including the right to participate in society as citizens. One such formulation (from the Bill of

Rights Act) might be that "an employee's personal rights and freedoms may be only subject only to such reasonable limits as can be demonstrably justified to be required by the employer for genuine and reasonable business reasons and which are consistent with the employee's rights and freedoms in a free and democratic society."

However, a simple but fundamental, reform is that the 'reasonable employer' test in the ERA should be replaced with that of the standard of a "fair and reasonable person, balancing the interests of both the employer and employee . . ." This test should be the basis of judging the validity of contractual clauses and employer policies and for evaluating personal grievance claims. It provides a clear signal that employees are not subordinate to the commercial interests of the employer but are to be independently evaluated against the interests of the employer.

Conclusion

Significant changes are required if labour law is to adequately tackle issues such as newly emerging modes of employment, including the increasing use of contractors, and mechanisms such as those used by Uber and the like, which do not fit comfortably into, and pose major challenges for, labour law structures. Additionally, the labour law structures of the mid- to late-twentieth century only partly reflect changing business structures as contractual chains replace organisational hierarchies and they fail to adequately reflect the drive by employers to minimise labour costs by avoiding the protections for workers that have developed over the last century and by increasingly shifting employment risk onto individual workers and the state.

However, most importantly, labour law also needs to be recast to reflect the principles of pluralism and promote effective worker voice for the 21st century. Economics should not trump democracy, human rights and societal values. It is time for labour law to be restructured to play its part in the type of society described by Bottomore, one in which all participants in the labour market have an adequate voice and influence.

The Influence of the Legal Profession on Dispute Resolution after 1990

Susan Robson

Introduction

The purpose of this chapter is to show how the replacement of a collectivist by an individualist advocacy culture contributed to changes to the significance of the personal grievance claim in labour relations, the means by which grievances were resolved (their timing, resolution location, advocacy and cost) and imposed additional cost on the public purse.

The 1990 General Election ushered in a National Government with policy to deregulate the labour market to ensure its future flexibility (by decollectivising the workforce and replacing awards with employment contracts) and to change the dispute resolution system by ending the union monopoly over personal grievances.[1]

Nine years later the incoming Labour-led Government sought to ameliorate the negative effects of labour market flexibility by incentivising collective bargaining and providing for more informal approaches to dispute resolution. However the radical changes introduced by the Employment Contracts Act 1991 (ECA) remained largely intact: substitution of stakeholder representatives in resolution roles by mediators and adjudicators; dominance by lawyers of the resolution system; exclusive reliance on employment contracts; and rising rates of dismissal and the domination of the resolution system by dismissal grievances.

Personal Grievance Resolution 1973–90

The personal grievance claim was introduced in the Industrial Relations Act 1973 to avert strike action concerning detriments suffered by individual employees in a workplace.[2] It was limited to union members who were unjustifiably dismissed

---

1   National Party *Policy on Industrial Relations* (8 May 1990).
2   Gordon Anderson "The Origins and Development of the Personal Grievance Procedure in

or disadvantaged. The founding provision[3] specified a process for raising a grievance, requiring that the claimant first attempt settlement by direct discussion with their immediate supervisor "rapidly and as near as possible to the point of origin".[4] Failure required the relevant union to discuss the grievance with the employer. Only when those two attempts to resolve the grievance in the workplace failed were outsiders called on. A written statement of the grievance was referred to a grievance committee composed of representatives of the union and the employer, with rights to refer it to the Industrial Court if the committee could not resolve it.

Additional grounds for grievances (discrimination, sexual harassment) were introduced in the Labour Relations Act 1987 (LRA), as were some process changes. The composition of grievance committees was formalised with the requirement for an independent chair (usually a mediator from the Department of Labour's Mediation Service) and a written decision.[5] This allowed more certainty of outcome than the previous practice of referring impasses to the Court.

Throughout the 1980s grievance committees were determining about 500 grievances annually, suggesting that significantly more than this were resolved informally.[6] The dominant resolution style of individual disputes was heavily influenced by the bargaining styles and relationships of parties to collective bargaining. Impasses were resolved in large part by assisted negotiation via the Mediation Service. Parties to bargaining were collectives – unions and employer associations – whose advocates were their salaried employees and whose major focus of attention was on the collective interests of their members.

Advocacy of individual problems was regarded as an incident of servicing the collective interests of their memberships, but not as an end in itself.[7] Individual casework was time consuming and, for union organisers, included consideration of the effects of the workplace problems on other members and the business enterprise itself. The interests of individual members could not compromise collective interests, particularly given that reinstatement was the primary remedy.[8] Individual advocacy was free of charge because it was an incident of membership fees. The grievance had to be taken in the name of the union to which the grievant belonged, so it was the union's (not the grievant's) decision

New Zealand" (1988) 13 NZJOIR 257.
3   Industrial Relations Act 1973, s 117.
4   Section 117(4)(b).
5   Labour Relations Act 1987, Schedule 7.
6   Joanna Cullinane and Dianne Donald *Personal Grievances in NZ* (University of Waikato, Waikato, 2000).
7   Dianne Donald "Unions and Personal Grievance Resolution: Managers of Discontent: The Role of Unions in Advancing or Impeding the Informal Resolution of Grievances in NZ" (Masters Dissertation University of Waikato, 1998).
8   Labour Relations Act, s 209(f).

whether to raise and advance a claim. This meant that only grievances with prospects of success were taken on.

Historically, part of the tension between union and employer interests in the labour jurisdiction concerned the means by which disputes were resolved, in particular the professionalisation of the institutions created for this purpose and the limits on direct action that were traded for formal rights of dispute resolution. Employers saw advantages for their interests in recourse to legal process, but unions regarded legal process as the means by which consideration of substantive issues was either ignored or subsumed. From the 1970s onwards the focus of union suspicion of the processes of the jurisdiction's institutions concerned growing backlogs of work, greater legalism and concentration on technical detail at the expense of substantive issues.[9]

The LRA also permitted the restructured specialist court, renamed the Labour Court, to deal with the interpretation of awards, grievances (reviews and appeals), and other actions regarded as 'legal matters'.[10] The effect of these changes of institution was seen as continuing and accelerating the trend of legalising labour issues.[11] The Labour Court, unlike its predecessors, was not a court of conciliation and arbitration. It was purely a court of record, with appeal, review and first-instance functions. It was also regarded as presiding over the waning use of employer and employee representatives in the resolution or disposition of labour disputes, generally operating on a Judge-alone basis except for demarcation disputes and personal grievance referrals or appeals.[12]

---

9   Rose Ryan and Pat Walsh "Common Law v Labour Law: the New Zealand Debate" (1993) 6 AJOLL 230.
10 Called 'disputes of rights' to distinguish them from 'disputes of interest' (wage and salary levels), the domain of the Arbitration Commission.
11 Department of Labour *Issues Raised by Unions and Employers in Recent Discussions* (undated memo, 1989): a record of discussions by the Department with unions and employers in the hotel, car assembly, meat and building industries in mid-1989, a major theme of which concerned the "increased formality or legalism [defined as sacrificing accepted practice to the letter rather than the spirit of the law] of the institutions under the new Act", although it was acknowledged that there were differences of perception about their effects. An employer representative viewed the change positively: "it assisted sanctity of agreement because there were more sanctions available for the employer." Union representatives reported that many more unions were hiring their own lawyers or using outside legal services much more frequently than they had in the past.
12 Ryan and Walsh, above n 10.

Policy for Employment Dispute Resolution

Employment Contracts Act 1991

The policy desire to decollectivise the workforce as part of the transition to a more flexible labour market uncovered sharp ideological divisions within the newly elected National Government Cabinet about how it would be achieved. Despite agreement that dispute resolution would come under the aegis of legal method, radical proponents of flexibility[13] wanted the High Court and the common law to form the basis of dispute settlement.[14] They perceived that high barriers to access to problem resolution would more quickly result in the power imbalances they regarded as necessary for flexibility. National Government moderates[15] had a different strategy. They recognised the Trojan horse potential of the personal grievance claim, then restricted to union members, as the means by which decollectivisation could occur if grievances were universally available,[16] and grievants free to rely on their advocate of choice.

The moderate strategy ultimately required the creation of a specialist employment jurisdiction, abolition of the Mediation Service and grievance committees, and the co-option of the personal grievance as the sole basis for claims concerning dismissal, disadvantage, discrimination or sexual harassment. The forum for claim was the subject of specific Select Committee consideration, to which four options were presented[17] (representing radical and moderate preferences and the status quo) and from which emerged the structure enacted, a low-level informal Employment Tribunal offering 'speedy fair and just' mediation and adjudication for all individual claims,[18] and the Employment Court for collective claims (strikes, lockouts, injunctions) and as appellate forum for individual claims.

---

13   The Business Roundtable was the chief lobbyist of the radical faction. Their advocate in Cabinet was the Minister of Finance, Ruth Richardson, who had the full support of officials from The Treasury.
14   The Treasury *Labour Contracts* (undated paper) faxed by A Sundakov to Department of Labour on 16 November 1990.
15   The moderates were led by the Minister of Labour, William Birch, who was supported by the State Services Commission, the Ministry of Justice and the Department of Labour.
16   Paul Bell for Minister of Labour "Minute" (16 November 1990); David Peetz "Individual contracts, bargaining and union membership" (2002) 28 ABOL 1.
17   Department of Labour *Options Paper for Institutional Arrangements* (undated, c February 1991).
18   Employment Contracts Act 1991, s 76(c).

Employment Relations Act 2000

The adoption of policy imperatives in 1999 based on the advantages of labour market flexibility – to trade and compete in a global economy – forced the incoming Labour-led Government into a policy position that sought to embrace both collectivism and individualism, diversity and flexibility, but that would also address labour market inequality.[19]

Both collective and individual rights would be enforced by the employment institutions, only more quickly and at less cost than under the ECA, by substituting its legalism for good faith, mutual trust and confidence and an emphasis on the human relational nature of employment. The Employment Relations Act 2000 (ERA) would focus on behaviours rather than contracts, on rebuilding cooperative workplace relationships for improved levels of productivity, buttressed by a new brand of mediation as the primary problem-solving process designed to be 'fair, flexible and free', neither institutionalised nor restricted to formal intervention, supported by a specialist decision-making body uninhibited by strict procedural requirements and reinforced by reinstatement as the primary remedy.[20] It was hoped that this approach would redress the decollectivisation of the workforce, increased casualisation, stagnant productivity gains, increased levels of income inequality and compliance costs and the decline of the workforce skill base.[21]

This policy ambition for institutional process – that it would influence the day-to-day behaviours and negotiations on which employment relationships depend, in the hope that increased productivity, innovation and skill development would result[22] – can be contrasted with the approach to the institutions under the ECA. In 1991 expectations of the institutions were limited to their role in 'order maintenance', in the workforce acceptance of a reduced need for unions by the creation of rights-based individual claims to redress.

Personal Grievance Resolution 1991–2008

Employment Contracts Act era

The Employment Tribunal was set up to offer both mediation and arbitration. From the outset, significantly more grievants chose adjudication over mediation.

---

19 Lorraine Skiffington "The Making of the Employment Relations Act – a Recipe for Success" [2001] ELB 37.
20 Ibid.
21 Hon Margaret Wilson, Minister of Labour "New Zealand's Path Forward" [2001] ELB 1.
22 David Mangan "Employment Tribunal Reforms to Boost the Economy" (2013) 42 ILJ 409 argues that recent reforms to employment tribunal procedures in Britain emphasise the use of law as a tool for economic stimulation rather than a source of rights protection, an apt description of this intention.

This led to a surging but haphazard rate of applications (mainly dismissal grievances) that resulted in problems of administration and delay. It ensured that a disproportionate use of Tribunal member time and effort was required for adjudicated than mediated outcomes, notwithstanding that mediation soon replaced adjudication as the dominant mode of resolution.

The trend noted above, of waning reliance on collective advocates by the newly established Labour Court in the late 1980s, accelerated under the ECA. Under the LRA around 60 per cent of parties were represented by union or employer association advocates and 36 per cent by lawyers in the Labour Court. Under the ECA this ratio "switched dramatically" to 70 per cent lawyers and 28 per cent advocates in the Employment Court and 60 per cent lawyers and 35 per cent advocates in the Employment Tribunal,[23] becoming cause for complaint: the Tribunal was accused of "operating too slowly, often as a result of the involvement of lawyers".[24] This led to legalistic processes that extended hearing times and delays from scheduling difficulties caused by lawyer unavailability.[25]

Initially held responsible was an influx of non-union white-collar grievants, regarded as a dominant influence on the grievance jurisdiction,[26] who had the financial resources to pursue appeals to the Employment Court, and whose approach to the procedure of dismissal became a consistent source of complaint from the Business Roundtable lobby throughout the term of the ECA.[27] This grievant class was associated with reliance on lawyers and adjudication[28] and thus locked into the outcome of exchanging jobs for compensation,[29] thereby establishing a norm capable of application to other classes of grievant, a phenomenon described as "courts must act when litigants call."[30]

23 Margaret Robbie *Representation, Procedure and Process in Mediation and Adjudication since the Employment Contracts Act* (Paper for Diploma in Industrial Relations, Victoria University of Wellington, 1993); This study did not include reference to grievance committees, the representatives before which were restricted to union or employer association officials: Labour Relations Act 1987, Sch 7.
24 Department of Labour *Notes of meeting between Minister of Labour and Rob Campbell* (Wheeler Campbell Labour Markets Ltd) (1992).
25 The Report of the Labour Committee *Inquiry into the effects of the Employment Contracts Act on the NZ Labour Market* (1993) at 46.
26 Ibid.
27 Colin Howard, Monograph, *Interpretation of the Employment Contracts Act 1991* (NZ Business Roundtable and NZ Employers Federation, Wellington, 1996); Hon Max Bradford "What Happens Now?" (paper presented to Labour-Management Government Relations Seminar, Industrial Relations Centre, Victoria University of Wellington, 20 March 1997).
28 The Report of the Labour Committee, above n 26.
29 This exchange essentially altered pre-1991 goals of grievance resolution, the retention of the job from which a grievant was dismissed.
30 Donald Horowitz *The Courts and Social Policy* (The Brookings Institution, Washington, 1977) at 38: This phrase refers to the absence of control or organisation over social policy issues that arise in the courts when individuals litigate. The ensuing decisions have precedent value for litigants who follow. The result is the unsequenced or haphazard development of

Measures to address delays included the gradual doubling of Tribunal members, opening new registries, and offering incentives to grievants to choose mediation, but complaints of delay dogged the Tribunal for all but the first few months of its existence.

Employment Relations Act era

The ERA established the Mediation Service as a first port of call. It dealt immediately and effectively with problems of delay, clearing 90 per cent of requests for assistance within three months. An inquisitorial adjudication service, the Employment Relations Authority, was established for those unable to resolve their differences via mediation with the right to challenge its determinations, de novo, at the Employment Court. While this institutional structure addressed the problem of delay it, like the Tribunal, was vulnerable to the imposition of the strictures of legal method, so that the informality required of it was never realised.

All institutions were dominated by dismissal grievances, but the primacy of reinstatement was never established and the exchange of job for compensation established during the ECA era was maintained and strengthened.

Advocacy in both eras

Although the dispute resolution institutions of each era were (slightly) different, the personnel that operated within them did not change. This helps to explain why policy for the earlier era continued to dominate the subsequent era.

Each statute provided for a range of representation for parties to proceedings.[31] The three major types, lawyers, self-employed advocates (with and without formal legal training) and union/employer association advocates, differed in their training and qualifications for the advocacy role and in their approaches to issues of process. They also differed in the business opportunity that representation offered, and in their approaches to remedy.

Union organisers regarded conciliation of employer and employee interests as the fundamental requirement of their task when confronted by conflict.[32] They regarded retention of the job for the employee as a major goal. Much of their effort, therefore, lay in the repair of damaged work relationships. This involved a heavy emphasis on negotiation, education and "keeping lines of communication

---

policy matters (like justification for dismissal) arising, not from the worst or most extreme examples of the behaviour at issue, but from litigants with the inclination and resources to litigate and the ability to provide a more favourable (to them), but incomplete view of the practices of which they complain.
31 Employment Contracts Act 1991, ss 59, 90.
32 Donald, above n 8.

open".[33] Unwinding a dismissal or a warning was therefore of greater importance to union representatives than pursing compensation.

Lawyers had a different focus. In part this arose from the imperative in legal training to identify the source of breach before determining remedy, generally associated with monetary compensation. The result was that the first task of the lawyer was allocation of responsibility for breach, which, in terms of the client relationship generally involved a search for fault by the other party. Of itself, this imperative lends itself more easily to position taking and confrontationalism, so that the search for breach rendered restoration of relationships much more difficult than assertion of remedy (compensation), even if restoration of the working relationship was the more desirable option for the client.[34]

A distinction, therefore, between collectivist and individualist advocacy for grievants lay in the pursuit of different outcomes, which in turn affected the means by which those outcomes were pursued. These differences can be considered in terms of timing, use of and effect on mode of resolution, grievant assumption of risk, and choice of representative.

Timing

Differences between collective and individual representative cultures were reflected in workplace resolution rates and institutional functioning. Unionised grievants and their employers had higher rates of disputing and resolving in-house (than their non-unionised counterparts) and employers accepted that union advocacy was a component of this effect. This meant there was less need for recourse to institutional dispute resolution. The opposite was established for those reliant on individual representatives. They experienced lower rates of in-house disputing and resolving, longer duration and more costly disputes and greater need for institutional intervention.[35]

These differences arise from the point at which assistance is sought. Unionised employees were better equipped to recognise problems in need of resolution than their non-unionised counterparts,[36] thus ensuring that attempts at de-escalation of conflict occurred before the need for disciplinary action arose.[37] This in turn was dependent upon the establishment of working relationships between union officials and management, which facilitated the dialogue necessary to negotiate problems in the workplace as they arose. Where no such relationships existed,

---

33 Donald, above n 8.
34 Carrie Menkel-Meadow "Towards Another View of Legal Negotiation: the structure of problem solving" (1984) 31 UOCLALR 754.
35 A C Nielson for Department of Labour, Research Report, *Survey of Employment Disputes and Disputes Resolution* (November 2000).
36 Ibid.
37 Donald, above n 8.

it was the role of union officials to determine with whom to negotiate problems in workplaces and to establish a working or negotiating dialogue likely to result in early or acceptable resolution.[38] By contrast, lawyers were less likely to be consulted until matters were seriously awry.[39] At this point the lawyer is less likely to have other sources of information about the dispute than the union advocate, who, in turn, is not required to advance a grievant's interests above those of others.[40]

Lawyers also have an obligation to a client to do the best they can for them, the tools available being the filing, or defending, of proceedings. Codes of ethics underline these obligations by endorsing zealous advocacy of clients' causes.[41]

This affected the point at which assessment of a grievant's prospects of success of achieving a remedy occurred. A union member with low prospects of success was unlikely to attract representative effort beyond the workplace.[42] Other grievants were less likely to obtain this assessment until they were at the Tribunal or Mediation Service. This difference of timing reduced the number of disputes resolved 'closer to the workplace' and increased the number of those requiring institutional assistance.[43]

Mode of resolution

While unions and employer associations expended much of their effort on avoiding the need for outside intervention,[44] lawyers were trained to regard courts and tribunals as their first port of call.[45] Negotiating skills were to collective advocates what litigation skills were to lawyers. This had the following effect on the Tribunal:[46]

---

38 Christine Evans and Adrian Parker *Inside Lawyers' Ethics* (Cambridge University Press, Cambridge; New York, 2007).
39 UMR for Department of Labour, Research Report, *The Process of Dispute Resolution: A qualitative study amongst employers and employees* (January 2002).
40 Donald, above n 8.
41 Robert Kagan *Adversarial Legalism, The American Way of Law* (Harvard University Press, Cambridge, 2001) at 55.
42 Donald, above n 8.
43 Department of Labour for Minister of Labour *The Employment Contracts Act – Institutions and Personal Grievances* (paper, 26 November 1993).
44 Donald, above n 8.
45 Evans and Parker, above n 39.
46 Ralph Gardiner "The Employment Tribunal: A Report from the Trenches" (paper presented to International Employment Relations Association Conference, University of Waikato, 1995); A study of 100,000 civil cases terminated in Taiwan from 2000 to 2006 showed settlement least likely when both parties were legally represented: Kuo-Chang Huang "How Legal Representation Affects Case Outcomes: An Empirical Perspective from Taiwan" (2008) 5 JOELS 309.

> At first, mediation was a bit of a mystery to some lawyers who argued their case across the table comfortably enough but then didn't seem to know how to negotiate and cut a deal. That, of course, had long been the very bread and butter of the union officials and their Employer Association counterparts ... Some representatives (c 1991 onwards) may as yet not fully appreciate a reality which those advocates and union officials with extensive service in the industrial trenches had long before identified – the job of the representative is to resolve a matter and the mediator is a tool of their trade.

These observations reflected the concerns of the Tribunal membership about the conduct of legal representatives at hearings, the quality of their advocacy, and their behaviour during the mediation process. The 'presence of legal counsel inexperienced in the mediation process' was regarded as frustrating the perceived advantages of an informal low-level specialist Tribunal, the use of lay advocates and the equity and good conscience jurisdiction.[47]

Lawyer reliance on adversarial posturing in non-judicial processes, arising from a tendency to view such processes through the optic of litigation, has been long understood.[48] For example:[49]

> These processes may be approached as if they were merely variants or extensions of the judicial, adversarial model which to so many lawyers is the paradigm of disputing.

The dominance of lawyers as representatives also affected the *style* of mediation as the result of its function (for them) as the forum that preceded adjudication. Likely adjudicated outcome, as predicted by the mediator, became the basis for settlement by parties who were legally represented. This in turn required mediators to sacrifice a facilitation role for assessment of litigation risk, turning them into 'deal makers', engineering agreements on 'exit packages' for often long-dead employment relationships.[50]

The ERA transfer of control over claim initiation and scheduling from advocates to the Mediation Service represented an attempt to alter that dynamic.

---

47 Department of Labour for Minister of Labour *The Employment Contracts Act – Institutions and Personal Grievances* (paper, 26 November 1993).
48 Menkel-Meadow above n 35; Justine Munro *Settling Treaty Claims: Litigation's contribution to adversarialism in Crown-Maori Negotiation* (New Zealand Centre for Conflict Resolution, Faculty of Law, Victoria University of Wellington, 1997): Munro argues that the Māori Fisheries negotiations were thwarted by the approach of the parties who locked themselves into litigation positions, maintained them as a point of principle and found as a result no basis for compromise.
49 John Murray, Allan Rau and Edward Sherman *Processes of Dispute Resolution: The Role of Lawyers* (Foundation Press, Westbury, 1989).
50 Ian McAndrew, Julie Morton and Alan Geare *The Employment Institutions* in Rasmussen (ed) *Employment Relationships: New Zealand's Employment Relations Act* (Auckland University Press, Auckland, 2004) at 99.

Its informality of process and active administrative control of these preliminaries limited the influence of representatives on timeliness of institutional response at the Tribunal. However, the attempt to introduce a different, less formal mediation style foundered in large part on opposition by lawyers to the incidents of facilitation. These included facilitation's need to elicit from disputants, directly, non-legalised cues about the dispute regarded as relevant to the means by which resolution occurs. Lawyers reacted to these attempts by denying mediators direct access to their clients, prompting the need to clarify and enhance mediator powers to direct and control mediations in the 2004 statutory amendments.[51] Lawyers also reacted negatively to the absence of any evaluation of the positions they had adopted in particular disputes. They sought to avoid facilitation by seeking mediators who relied on the evaluative model.[52]

Mediators were aware that reversion to litigation risk analysis was incompatible with the statutory focus on relationship problem solving. They were also critical of lawyer requirements of them to evaluate legal positions, noting that provision and evaluation of legal advice was a representative function, not a mediator one.[53] But there was no unanimity of response to the resulting lawyer insistence on choice of mediator. Some offices condoned the practice and others resisted it, but disparity of mediator workloads was the consequence, with ex-Tribunal mediators shouldering considerably heavier workloads than recent appointees.[54] Thus, the mediation style that met the requirements of lawyer representatives was imposed on the Mediation Service.

Lawyer effects on the Tribunal's adjudicative function were seen to be adversarial and controlling, and over time "they became more inventive with their arguments and challenges."[55] That the Tribunal should operate for the convenience of legal representatives was underlined shortly after it began when it was asked to depart from its practice of starting at 9 a.m. in favour of traditional Court hearing times.[56] This struggle for control over the resolution process intensified under the ERA.

51 This raises the issue of control – who controls a mediation – identified as a problem for commercial mediation: Tony Willis "Overlawyering of ADR a major issue" (2014) 853 Law Talk at 27; "As the gatekeepers [lawyers] don't just want control but they have control at a very early stage. And once they get involved in the process, they are very reluctant to let go . . .".
52 Julie Morton "Reducing Legalism: The Impact of the Employment Relations Act 2000" (Masters Dissertation, University of Otago, 2003).
53 Morton, above n 53 at 78, citing a mediator interviewee: "In reality the person responsible for providing employment law advice to party isn't really us, it's them. It's actually a failing on the lawyers, because they arrive here saying they really want you to reality check this person. The answer is why haven't you done it? I'm not their adviser, they should be doing this."
54 Morton, above n 53.
55 Morton, above n 53.
56 Penny Swarbrick to Auckland Employment Tribunal, letter 7 May 1992.

Authority members embraced the investigative function for the width of powers it conferred on them to utilise a range of resolution strategies and control the pace and time required for investigations. As a result investigation meetings took up less time (overall) than Tribunal hearings.[57] But lawyers were concerned that the Authority act 'judicially'. If the conclusions of the Employment Court about the natural justice implications of refusing representatives 'rights' to cross-examine are indicative, then acting judicially appeared to be regarded as synonymous with adversarial modes of adjudication.[58] The Court's decisions in *David v Tilley*[59] and *David v Employment Relations Authority*[60] represented an attempt to impose upon the Authority the adversarial mode of adjudication legislatively discarded in favour of the investigative mode. The Law Society, granted intervener status for the Full Court hearing of *David v Employment Relations Authority*, supported the Court's position. It remains unclear whether the Court of Appeal would have upheld this position, because the legislative amendments confirming cross-examination's discretionary status were passed before it could hear and determine the Crown appeal.[61]

It is possible that the speed (or predictability) of the legislative reaction deterred other attempts to have the Authority revert to the adversarial status quo via the Employment Court. Resistance to informality took other forms and was, as a result, more successful. Thus in the drafting of statements of problem and reply and in the briefs of evidence required for investigations, lawyers felt able to revert to the language of litigation. This caused Authority members to associate it with negatively influenced party expectations of and participation in the problem resolution process.[62] Lawyer insistence on the provision of written submissions following the conclusion of investigations increased the time devoted to individual problems and deferred the formulation and dissemination of determinations – the time period that attracted complaints of delay. Increased proportions of ancillary over substantive but relatively stable numbers of determinations issued annually suggest that fewer problems required adjudicative resolution as time passed, but required greater institutional input. This reflected a similar trend at the Tribunal.[63]

Over time, costs awards increased but compensation awards did not.

---

57 Kathryn Beck and Ian McAndrew "Decisions and Damages: An Analysis of Adjudication Outcomes in the Employment Tribunal and the Employment Relations Authority" (paper presented to NZ Law Society Employment Law Conference, October 2002).
58 *David v Employment Relations Authority* [2001] ELB 99.
59 *David v AE Tilley* [2001] ERNZ 93.
60 *David v Employment Relations Authority* [2001] ERNZ 354.
61 Employment Relations Act, s 179(5) was inserted on 1 December 2004 by Employment Relations Amendment Act (No2) 2004, s 60.
62 McAndrew, Morton and Geare, above n 51.
63 Robson, above n 1.

Risk

The cost of representation by counsel, particularly for adjudication, was payable regardless of outcome. Analysis of adjudicated outcomes revealed that almost half of the grievances litigated yielded no remedy for the grievant. Of those who did obtain a remedy, over half were awarded less than $5,000 in compensation. Ninety-three per cent of successful grievants were awarded less than $12,000. Costs awards never met the full cost of representation.[64]

By contrast the cost of union membership was seen as akin to an insurance premium that offered representation for individual problems at no extra charge. If advocacy was required, it carried with it exemption from indemnification of the other party if unsuccessful, the full benefit of any compensation award, and vigorous attempts to resolve the problem in the workplace (that is, before matters escalated to dismissal).[65]

The consequences for grievants of choice of representative therefore differed in terms of risk. Union/employer association members took the risk, when litigating, that their organisation would refuse to represent them if their prospects of success were too low. Those relying on lawyers or self-employed advocates had little or no risk of a refusal to assist but they undertook all the risk associated with their prospects of success. They risked paying a costs award to the other party if they were unsuccessful and even if successful they took the risk that the cost of representation would match or exceed any compensation awarded.

Choice

One explanation for the persistent dominance of lawyers as representatives in this jurisdiction is that lawyers are more likely to be associated with getting 'the best deal' at the other party's expense, notwithstanding that this assumption is not generally supported by research.[66] A related, but opposing idea, "that negotiation on financial matters through lawyers will do little to increase independent communication between the parties" does appear to have some validity.[67]

Lawyers were, however, available to all-comers, took their fees from remedies, were associated with the vindication of individual rights and redress, won (and publicised) lottery-like compensation awards, and so ensured that

---

64 Gardiner, above n 47.
65 Ibid.
66 PSC Lewis, Monograph, *Assumptions about Lawyers in Policy Statements: A Survey of Relevant Research* (Lord Chancellors Department, United Kingdom, 2000); Marc Galanter "Law Abounding: Legalisation Around the North Atlantic" (1992) 55 MLR 9 at 22 observes that "support for the law can survive large doses of realism and that common law populations combine realistic cynicism about how law works with a strong commitment to law as an institution".
67 At 22.

rights of grievance were perceived to be superior to or an adequate substitute for membership of unions and employer associations.[68]

Workforce understanding of dispute resolution practices

A factor affecting choice of representation is the availability of information about problem solving in the workplace. Research from the start of the ERA era suggested a lack of common understanding of remedy systems in workplaces, with differences between unionised and non-unionised employees: 61 per cent of all employees who had experienced a problem were aware of written guidelines in the workplace for their resolution; 79 per cent of union members were aware. This is consistent with other data indicating that written procedures were more likely to be available in more unionised sectors, and that unionised employees were more likely to be aware of them.[69] Employees had a low, and employers (by the act of having to produce or revise employment agreements) a high awareness of the new Act, the Employment Relations Service and changed employer obligations; employees found it difficult to visualise dispute resolution as a process but larger employers maintained a process-driven approach influenced by the ECA; employers viewed these processes as fair to both parties with a few perceiving it as biased in favour of employees, while high levels of frustration were articulated by employees about the lack of clear resolution of disputes, delaying tactics and the difficulty of remaining in employment after raising a dispute.[70] This may explain why employees were dissatisfied generally with dispute outcomes and employers believed the majority of disputes were settled amicably.

For employees, third parties in disputes had support or advisory roles, but for employers they had a very specific role of providing expertise on the new legislation. Introducing them to resolve a dispute was regarded as escalating the problem. While most employers wanted to avoid formal mediation, most unions chose it as their first port of call.[71]

Choice of problem-solving process was dependent on its desired outcome. If

---

68 Kagan, above n 42, argues that the basic causes of adversarial legalism – popular demands for fair treatment, recompense, and protection combined with mistrust of government and fragmentation of political and economic power – remain unchanged and unchangeable in the United States.

69 AC Nielsen Ltd for Department of Labour *Survey of Employment Disputes and Disputes Resolution* (November 2000); UMR Research Ltd for Employment Relations Service *The Process of Dispute Resolution – A qualitative study amongst employees and employers* (January 2002); Tony Waldegrave, Diane Anderson and Karen Wong *Evaluation of the Short-Term Impacts of the Employment Relations Act 2000* (Department of Labour, Wellington, 2003).

70 Comparison of employee satisfaction rates between the UMR 2002 survey and the Waldegrave (ERS) 2003 survey: UMR 57 per cent dissatisfied with process and 49 per cent dissatisfied with outcome; ERS 65 per cent dissatisfied with actions taken by employer to resolve dispute.

71 UMR Research Ltd, above n 40.

employers wanted a workplace relationship to continue, private interventions (for example, private mediation) were preferred, but if they sought to end it, a confidential settlement or resort to the Mediation Service were the accepted options.[72]

Unionised employees had higher levels of satisfaction with dispute resolution processes than their non-union peers and employers of unionised employees (large employers) had a more positive view of union involvement in disputes than non-unionised business employers. There were clear differences in formality of process between large (80+ employees) and small employers. The latter were more reluctant to air a dispute outside the workplace and more suspicious of the Mediation Service ("as a pseudo court process with the employer on 'trial' for alleged breaches").[73] Employers with experience of the Service were more positive about it than those with none.

Although there were no common views about the outcomes of disciplinary disputes (except that reinstatement following dismissal was rare), there was a consistent acceptance that the outcome of an employee complaint was either withdrawal or resignation.

Timing and Location

The absence of statutory guidance about resolution of dismissal grievances[74] and the disappearance of stakeholder involvement in their consideration shifted their focus away from the workplace into the courtroom. This meant that, while the right to claim a grievance was based in statute, the resolution of such claims became more obviously rooted in the common law than prior to the ECA. This was a function of individual claiming unmediated by context that resulted from the transfer of responsibility for claiming from collective to individual interests.

Because this process demanded an exclusive focus on the circumstances of the individuals engaged by the grievance, it invited further (similar but apparently different) claims and more refinement, but was the means by which practices that affected collective interests could be ignored, thus establishing judicial

---

72 Ibid.; Employer preferences for private mediation were higher in the early years of the Mediation Service than later years. They reported that their early reservations about the quality of Mediation Service mediators was subsequently addressed: Martin Risak and Ian McAndrew "Who Mediates Employment Relationship Problems" (paper presented to Labour, Employment and Work in New Zealand Conference, Industrial Relations Centre, Victoria University of Wellington, 2010).
73 UMR Research Ltd, above n 40, at 77.
74 The Employment Contracts Act 1991, Part III Personal Grievances (ss 26-42) defines unjustifiable dismissal as one of five types of personal grievance in s 27(1)(a) but is thereafter silent about the basis for such a claim. By contrast grievances based on discrimination (s 28), sexual harassment (ss 29, 35, 36) and duress (s 30) attract detailed statutory grounds for claims.

consideration of the principles of justification as an element in the shift from collectivist to individualist approaches to labour disputes.

It furthermore changed the purpose of mediation, becoming triage by Tribunal administrators, and as a preliminary process of adjudication for individual representatives. Effective pre-claim litigation risk analysis in the labour jurisdiction (on which administrators had previously relied for management, budgeting and planning purposes) atrophied with the transfer of representative function from collective to individual advocates. For those represented by the latter groups, mediation became the first occasion on which their positions on the grievance were subject to the litigation risk analyses conducted by collective advocates *before* claims were made.

The administration's recognition of this effect drove its decision to persuade those choosing adjudication under the ECA to first attempt mediation. By promoting mediation as earlier available and settlement as more desirable for litigants it was able to significantly reduce the proportions of those awaiting an adjudication function over which it had much less influence or control. Greater reliance on mediation arising from the consistency of time required for this function promised efficiencies in management, budgeting and planning. The time required to achieve finality in each adjudication was incapable of accurate prediction. While it was possible to assume approximate hearing times, it was not possible to make similar assumptions about scheduling hearings, withdrawals, interlocutory and costs applications, and decision writing times. The uncertainties that arose from these incidents of the adjudicative function dominated the problem of time management for the administration, such that they were never overcome. Its success in reducing the proportions of applications that required adjudication never translated into the efficiencies of administration (reducing delays) that it anticipated with each increase of resource, because fewer substantive adjudications resulted in more applications per adjudication.

This helps to explain the quasi-compulsion to first attempt mediation in the ERA.

Cost

When the Department of Labour was required to establish for the Treasury[75] why it wished to increase its Tribunal mediation settlement rate, rather than offer more adjudication, it revealed that the 3,150 mediations it held in 1996 each cost $416–588 (depending on whether they occurred at a city base or on circuit) and the 225 one-day adjudications each cost $2,480–3,000, rising to $7,230–8,250 for the 40 longer ones. These are the costs to the state. Given that 56 per cent

---

75 Department of Labour to Treasury *Cost of mode of resolution* (memo, 6 March 1997).

of compensation awards were $5,000 or lower, these costs show that for many successful claims, the cost of the professionals – Tribunal and representatives – was higher than the remedy at stake.

The comparative costs of the institutions were calculated at the end of 2004 to reveal that the Mediation Service cost $134 per settlement (or partial settlement), the Authority $493 per determination and the Court $2,579 per judgment.[76] However these calculations were based on costs to the Department, so the cost of the mediation workforce was included but Authority member and judicial salaries excluded. Inclusion of member salaries raised the Authority cost to $9,221 per determination.[77]

A utility analysis, whereby expenditure and economic benefit of the institution at issue were calculated, indicated a benefit of $58.9m from the Mediation Service but $3.2m from the Authority and a negative result from the Court of -$527,107.[78]

The major cost incurred by each institution was in salaries, set by the Remuneration Commission for Authority members and by the Department for mediators. Authority members received higher salaries than mediators, thus institutionalising differences of status between the two groups. But for their use of different resolution functions (and the need for written determinations) there was no difference in the types of problem the Service and the Authority were required to resolve, or in the remedies that resulted, the most common of which involved payments of compensation and costs. The remedy of reinstatement was insufficiently agreed or awarded to warrant publication of its incidence. Greater certainty of result (predictability) was available from the Authority, given that its determinations were public, mediated settlements were not and there were proportionally fewer adjudicated outcomes than at the Tribunal, but this had no effect on applications to the Authority, the basis on which its membership requirements were measured.

There was a major difference in the number of outcomes each institution produced. The Authority's membership constituted 40–50 per cent of the number of mediators but it investigated between 9 and 15 per cent of the annual number of problems mediated by the Service.[79]

The cost per case of problems investigated by the Authority was higher than the majority of its awards of compensation. This calculation excludes the cost of the mediation to which almost all Authority cases were referred, and is further

---

76 Dr Geoff Plimmer and Chris Cassels for Department of Labour *Greater strategic positioning of service delivery to achieve outcomes* (undated report, c November 2004).
77 Department of Labour *Average cost per Authority case 2007/08 year* (undated paper, c 2009).
78 Plimmer and Cassels, above n 76.
79 Department of Labour *Key Messages: Employment Relations, The Employment Relations Act is working* (undated, c late 2005): These figures are based on number of applications resolved, rather than on number of determinations issued.

complicated by those cases that require more than one determination. Cost of obtaining aggregate results can be calculated by reference to the Authority's costs and compensation tables. In 2007, 182 compensation orders were made (from 861 determinations, 14 of which concerned collective issues). On the basis that individual awards were made at the upper limit of their individual categories, the maximum total amount awarded was $1.383m. Similarly 148 costs orders amounted to $453,000. The cost to the public purse of achieving these money transfers totalled $6.03m.

A survey of the cost of employment disputes showed that for employers the direct cash cost of disputes arose from legal and advisory fees (31 per cent of total cash costs), the payment of compensation (40 per cent) and the cost of temporary or replacement staff (29 per cent). In-house resolution took the least amount of time (one–two months) and incurred the lowest direct cash cost ($300–3,000), followed by use of external parties ($5,000–13,000), the Mediation Service ($7,000–13,600), private mediation ($3,200–6,800), the Authority ($13–14,000) and the Employment Court ($75,000).[80]

Satisfaction rates were highest for in-house processes (79 per cent) and lowest for reliance on third parties (40 per cent). Large employers (more than 100 employees) were the most satisfied with resolution systems and medium employers (10–19 employees) the least satisfied.[81]

Facilitation and frustration of policy about dispute resolution

Labour market flexibility shifted workplace balances of power between workers and management, conferring on the latter increased autonomy in setting terms and conditions of employment. The corresponding reduction of union influence resulted in a greater role for the Tribunal and the Court in matters concerning discipline and employment security, while simultaneously feeding the perception among the business community that these institutions prioritised the interests of employees.[82]

This was not, however, the reality. For grievances resolved under the ECA there were reasonably consistent outcomes for employers and employees. In 1994 54 per cent of employers were ordered to remedy the problem raised by the grievance, meaning 46 per cent of grievants failed to obtain any remedy.[83] Later analysis focused on outcomes rather than remedy, but grievant success

---

80   Department of Labour, Workplace Strategic Policy Research and Evaluation (McDermott Miller), *Social and Economic Costs and Benefits of Employment Disputes* (12 July 2007).
81   Department of Labour for Cabinet Economic Development Committee *Review of the Employment Problem Resolution System,* (9 October 2007) (EDC (07) 185), Appendix 1.
82   Erling Rasmussen and John Deeks "Assessing the Impacts of the Employment Contracts Act" (1997) 28 CWILJ 275.
83   Gardiner, above n 47.

rates were fixed at 52 per cent. This mirrored the results from the Authority for a similar period.[84]

Business Roundtable complaints[85] that the ECA institutions had made it "impossible to dismiss employees"[86] had a corollary. They, along with media reports of large compensation payments (and the lower prominence accorded unsuccessful claims)[87] suggested a dispute resolution system accessible and responsive to individual employees.

Thus, if an orderly transition from collectivist to individualist bargaining was regarded as dependent on a dispute resolution system acceptable to individuals (who would otherwise be either collectivised with expectation of remedies or not, with no expectation of redress), the moderate ECA policy goal (of acceptable outcomes for employers in greater flexibility of wages and conditions on offer while offering employees the reassurance of a responsive system of grievance redress) was achieved.

Its continuation, under the ERA, has established frustration of the Labour Government's goals of a rise in mended over ended employment relationships and a more informal approach to dispute resolution. A more streamlined dispute resolution system became even more accessible and responsive to individual grievants, thus embedding the National Government's moderate strategy of exchanging collectivism for grievance rights of redress.

Conclusions

Legal capture of the dispute resolution process was an important tool for the imposition of flexible labour markets via the replacement of a pluralist with a unitarist approach to labour relations.[88] Common law and legal method were vital elements of this power transition by their focus on the recurring problems

---

84 McAndrew, Morton and Geare, above n 51.
85 Roger Kerr "The New Zealand Employment Contracts Act: Its Enactment, Performance and Implications" (1997) 28 CWILJ 89 argued that changes to the Court, the law of personal grievances, including opting-out, were necessary as redress.
86 Erling Rasmussen and Felicity Lamm "From collectivism to individualism in New Zealand employment relations" (paper presented to AIRAANZ Conference, Auckland, October 2005).
87 Ibid.
88 Alan Geare "Ideology in Industrial Relations" (1994) 19 NZJOIR 117 defines the unitarist ideological position as an acceptance of managerial authority and prerogatives which views conflict as pathological and the pluralist position as accepting the existence of different sectoral groups with objectives that sometimes coincide and sometimes clash so that conflict is accepted as inevitable; Gordon Anderson "The Capability Approach and the Legal Regulation of Employment: A Comment on Deakin" (2009) 34 NZJOER 27 at 31 describes the Employment Contracts Act as abolishing "the pre-existing pluralistic industrial relations system that provided for a high degree of joint regulation of working conditions and replaced it with one of employer dominated, individualised, regulation of the employment relationship."

of individual dismissals as the means of ignoring the collective detriments of a dominant non-union sector based on the principle of cost-minimisation that experienced higher levels of turn-over and injury rates, greater use of casualised labour and compulsory redundancy and a dismissal rate twice that of the unionised sector:[89]

> NZ has been through a period of social Darwinism wherein the strong have got stronger, the weak, weaker, the rich richer and the poor poorer, the advantaged have become more so and so have the disadvantaged. Almost any schism in society that existed has widened and become more overt.

The result, higher proportions of employees who could be dismissed, effectively at will so long as there remained the promise of money as the means of exchange, was crucial to widespread employee acceptance of this particular bargain.

---

89 Kevin Hince and Raymond Harbridge "The Employment Contracts Act: An Interim Assessment" (1994) 19 NZJOIR 237.

ACC and Workers' Health: Compensation, Compromises and Consequences

Dawn Duncan

Introduction

The Accident Compensation Corporation (ACC) scheme performs the primary workers' compensation function in New Zealand. Introduced in 1972, New Zealand's ACC scheme was unique in the world, and can be argued to have had a significant positive, but also negative, impact on workers' health in the decades that followed. Replacing the prior workers' compensation regime, the ACC scheme extended cover beyond those harms "arising out of, or in the course of, employment", to a range of accidents unrelated to work.[1] This extension of cover was a considerable gain to working people who were injured in the home, on the sports field or at school, with few options to obtain compensation. Reformers at the time envisioned a comprehensive social insurance scheme that would provide for "all the hazards of modern living".[2] However, to ensure the political viability of the proposal, a significant compromise was made and the boundary line for cover was drawn around 'accident'. This original compromise created an inherent rationing problem that, particularly when combined with the political climate of the 1980s and 1990s, has resulted in a pattern of ad hoc amendment, patchy and inconsistent coverage and incomplete data. This chapter outlines the key compromise of the ACC scheme and the consequences for working people in the decades that followed. It then suggests key areas of reform needed to ensure the ACC scheme can meet the needs of New Zealand working people in future.

---

1   Workers' Compensation Act 1956, s3.
2   Royal Commission of Inquiry into Compensation for Personal Injury in New Zealand *Compensation for Personal Injury in New Zealand: Report of the Royal Commission of Inquiry* (Government Printer, Wellington, 1967) (The Woodhouse Report) at 34.

Origins of ACC: Workers' Compensation and the Woodhouse Report

The ACC scheme arose out of the 1967 *Report of the Royal Commission of Inquiry in to Compensation for Personal Injury in New Zealand*, chaired by the then Justice Woodhouse (Woodhouse Report).[3] The Royal Commission was set up with the original brief to survey and report on "the law relating to compensation and claims for damages for incapacity or death arising out of accidents (including diseases) suffered by persons in employment".[4] Concerns had been raised about the costs and operation of the existing workers' compensation regime.[5] The Royal Commission, however, went much further than its original brief to improve workers' compensation, and proposed a radically different approach. The report advocated the expansion of compensation beyond those harms resulting from work, and asserted that accidental harms from whatever source were equally deserving of a community level response.[6] The Woodhouse Report formulated the problem as:[7]

> One hundred thousand workers are injured in industrial accidents every year ... This is not all. The same workforce must face the grave risks of the road and elsewhere during the rest of every 24 hours ... The toll of personal injury is one of the disastrous incidents of social progress, and the statistically inevitable victims are entitled to receive a coordinated response from the nation as a whole.

Work-related injuries were seen as no different to those suffered in a vehicle collision, while playing sports, or at home. What made harm compensable in this analysis was not the circumstances of the cause, nor the breach of a legal duty, but rather the harm and resulting incapacity itself. As the report stated, "[i]njury, not cause, is the issue".[8]

Woodhouse had grand visions for a scheme of universal coverage for all the "hazards of modern living",[9] including all diseases.[10] However, to ensure the success of the proposal at the time, a boundary line for cover was drawn around 'accidents', and the wider ambitions of the scheme were left to be realised at a later date. The Labour Party opposition at the time supported the Bill, but expressed an intention to amend the legislation, expanding it to "introduce not only the

---

3   Woodhouse Report, above n 2.
4   At 30.
5   Brian Easton "The Historical Context of the Woodhouse Commission" [2003] 34 VUW Law Rv 293; Murdo MacMillan "Accident Compensation in New Zealand: A Study of Change 1979–1982" (Victoria University Thesis Repository, 1983).
6   Woodhouse Report, above n 2.
7   At 19.
8   At 20.
9   At 34.
10 At 144.

letter of the Woodhouse [R]eport but also the concept behind it".[11] In 1989 an attempt was made to extend ACC cover to all sickness and disease, following an Officials Committee Report[12] and a Law Commission Report (headed by Sir Owen Woodhouse).[13] However, these proposals were scrapped by the incoming National Government in 1990,[14] which favoured a shift towards a private insurance model.[15] No attempts to substantially widen ACC cover were made by the 1999-2008 Labour Government, or the current National Government.

Workers' Compensation or Social Insurance?

From 1900 New Zealand had a workers' compensation regime, originally based on the English legislation, and similar in scope to that in Australia and Canada.[16] The Woodhouse Report advocated a radical shift to a social insurance model. The difference between the schemes was more than just scope. Workers' compensation schemes and social insurance schemes have very different assumptions, objectives and understandings of the cause and nature of the harm being compensated and, as a result, who ought to be made responsible for it.

Workers' compensation schemes, such as those operating in Australia, seek to compensate workers for the negative health consequences of work, whether accidental physical injury or work-related disease. The schemes are designed for 'workers', as defined, and for those conditions that have a sufficient causal connection to work. Workers' compensation schemes emerged from the "human carnage" of the industrial revolution.[17] While the law at the time recognised the legal duty of master to servant, it offered little practical assistance to injured

---

11 Arthur Faulkner, MP for Mt Roskill, *Hansard: Second Reading of the Accident Compensation Bill* (3 October 1972).
12 New Zealand Officials Committee *Review of the Officials Committee of the Accident Compensation Scheme* (NZ Government, Wellington, 1986).
13 Three reports occurred in the period leading up to the Labour Government introduction of proposed reforms. New Zealand Law Commission *Accident Compensation Scheme: Interim Report on Aspects of Funding* (New Zealand Law Commission, Wellington, 1987) and New Zealand Law Commission *Personal Injury Prevention and Recovery: Report on the Accident Compensation Scheme* (Law Commission, Wellington, 1988). There was also New Zealand Royal Commission on Social Policy *April Report: Report of the Royal Commission on Social Policy* (Government Printer, Wellington, 1988).
14 William Birch *Accident Compensation: A Fairer Scheme* (Government Printer, Wellington, 1991).
15 See discussion of these reforms in Hazel Armstrong *Blood on the Coal: The Origins and Future of New Zealand's Accident Compensation Scheme* (Trade Union History Project, Wellington, 2008).
16 The New Zealand Workers' Compensation for Accidents Act 1900, like the early legislation in Australia, was based on the English Workmen's Compensation Act 1897.
17 Kevin Purse and Robert Guthrie "Workers Compensation Policy in Australia: New Challenges for a New Government" (2008) JOALAP 99. See also Armstrong, above n 15, and Gregory Guyton "A brief history of workers' compensation" 19 IOJ 106.

workers, with few cases able to get past the "unholy trinity of defences" even if the money to bring a case could be raised.[18] The original workers' compensation schemes were set up and operated by trade unions and friendly societies. Workers' compensation formed part of the bargain over the terms and conditions of work and "established that, regardless of fault, employers had to accept some part of the losses their workers suffered from injuries and accidents in their workplaces".[19]

Comprehensive social insurance schemes, such as envisioned by Woodhouse, arose in a different context and rest on a different set of principles. Rather than emerging from an industrial relations context, concerned with the conditions of work, the social insurance model traces its intellectual origins to the early public health reformers. Social insurance sought not only to cover those health conditions directly connected to the performance of work, but also the wider category of 'workers' diseases'. The term workers' diseases, coined in the 1880s, refers to the "maladies which occurred more frequently in one class or stratum of society, irrespective of specific categorisation or cause".[20] Workers' diseases were linked with the so-called "social question":[21]

> This social question ... can be regarded as the costs of capitalist industrial development, and includes the conflict with regard to pay, working hours, working conditions in the factories, poverty, pauperisation, particularly in the cities, the question of lodgings for the workers, and the lack of social security for the old and infirm. Added to this ... problems like cholera, public health and infant mortality.

The social insurance model sought to spread the costs of the negative health effects of capitalist modes of production among society as a whole. The goals of social insurance were improved public health and welfare in society. It formed part of a 'social contract' between citizen and state, and sat alongside calls for

---

18   The unholy trinity of defences were contributory negligence, the fellow servant rule, which operated to defeat claims where the individual or any other worker was in any way responsible for the injury and the assumption of risk which excluded claims where workers had agreed to the risk in some way, such as signing their employment contracts. See Chapter 2 of Richard Johnstone, Elizabeth Bluff and Alan Clayton *Work Health and Safety Law and Policy* (3rd ed, Thompson Reuters, New South Wales, 2009), for discussion of the early development of the law regulating work-related injury, disease and death.
19   Melanie Nolan "Inequality of luck: Accident Compensation in New Zealand and Australia" (2013) 104 Labour History 189.
20   Muir Popper *Lehrbuch der Arbeiterkrankheitan und Gewerbehygiene* (Stuttgart, 1882) in Dietrich Milles "From Workers' Diseases to Occupational Diseases: The Impact of Experts' Concepts on Workers Attitudes" in Paul Weindling (ed) *The Social History of Occupational Health* (Croom Helm, Kent, 1985) at 61.
21   Dietrich Milles "From Workers' Diseases to Occupational Diseases: The Impact of Experts' Concepts on Workers Attitudes" in Paul Weindling (ed) *The Social History of Occupational Health* (Croom Helm, Kent, 1985) at 58.

the provision of pensions, unemployment benefits and a national health service. By the time of the 1967 Royal Commission, conditions were ripe for advocating such an approach, with the idea also put forward during the 1973 Whitlam Government in Australia.[22] The growing post-war trend toward state provision[23] coincided with a peak in the rates of industrial and road accidents,[24] increasing critiques of the compensation available at common law,[25] and a number of major studies and reports, including the Meredith Report in Canada and the Beveridge Report in the United Kingdom.[26]

What, Then, Was the ACC Scheme?

The New Zealand ACC scheme was, however, not the comprehensive social insurance provision imagined by Woodhouse and his fellow reformers. It was a compromise, a partially enacted social insurance scheme, which was to apply, at least initially, only to 'accidents'. While this compromise ensured the success of the proposal and the considerable expansion in cover, drawing the boundary lines of cover around the concept of 'accident' left the scheme with an inherent tension. Social insurance schemes are an 'all or nothing' deal. The underlying rationale of a social insurance scheme is that all people suffering from harm deserve to be cared for equally. This type of reasoning does not easily lend itself to drawing lines between different claims. A scheme with coverage only for accidents leads to an inevitable question of definition. An accident, in plain meaning, is "an unexpected event with negative consequences"[27] or something "happening by chance or accident; not planned [or] unexpected".[28] If the scheme cannot (or there is no political will to) compensate all such consequences, then a

---

22 The Whitlam Government appointed a *Committee of Inquiry into Compensation and Rehabilitation in Australia* chaired by Justice Owen Woodhouse; National Rehabilitation and Compensation Scheme Committee of Inquiry *Report of the Committee of Inquiry into Compensation and Rehabilitation in Australia* (Government Printer, Canberra, 1976). The National Compensation Bill, which would have seen an Australian-wide ACC equivalent, became a casualty of the fall of the Whitlam government in 1975. See also discussion by Nolan, above n 19.

23 Nolan, above n 19 at 109, and Purse and Guthrie, above at n 17.

24 Nolan, above n 19 at 109.

25 Lord Parker of Waddington "Compensation for Accidents on the Road: An Address" in Current Legal Problems 18 (1965); Terence Ison *The Forensic Lottery: A Critique on Tort Liability as a System of Personal Injury Compensation* (Staples Press, London, 1967).

26 William Meredith *Final Report on the Liability of Employers to make Compensation to their Employees for Injuries Received in the Course of their Employment which are in Force in other Countries, and as to How Far Such Laws are found to Work Satisfactorily* (Government Printer, Toronto, 1913) (The Meredith Report). William Beveridge *Social Insurance and Allied Services Report by Sir William Beveridge* (MNSO, London, 1942) (The Beveridge Report).

27 Merriam Webster Dictionary Online (Feb 2017).

28 Dictionary.com (Feb 2017).

question as to which accidents should be compensated naturally arises. Compare this with a workers' compensation scheme. To ration cover, a line can be drawn between work-related harms and those unrelated to work, and the extent of the required causal relationship between work and harm can be adjusted back and forward along the spectrum of causal connection to meet budgetary constraints. The underlying rationale of workers' compensation, 'to compensate workers harmed at work', can remain, but the causal tests, the margins of cover, and the interaction of the provisions with the rest of the legal system can shift with the ideological tides.

In an 'accident' compensation scheme there is no basis in principle for what should be included or excluded from cover. If the starting assumption is, as in the Woodhouse Report, that all incapacities are equally deserving, regardless of cause, and notions of fault are inappropriate, to ration cover the legislation must draw lines between different medical conditions, and the entitlement question begins to focus on exactly where and how in the body harm comes to be. The body-focused basis of the scheme can, for example, be seen in the current definition of 'accident'. An accident requires the application of external force to the body,[29] or the inhalation or oral ingestion of any solid, liquid, gas or foreign object "on a specific occasion" but not the inhalation of a virus, bacterium, protozoan or fungus, although the oral ingestion of a fungus would meet the definition.[30] Likewise, absorption of chemicals through the skin would be covered, so long as this doesn't continue for more than one month, in which case there would be no 'accident'.[31] As early as 1977 Geoffrey Palmer commented that a "cut and fill approach to legislative reform has now become so ingrained with the accident compensation legislation that the pattern will be difficult to alter".[32] That cut and fill approach also made it easier to nibble away cover during the many ACC reforms of the 1980s and 1990s.

Occupational Disease: An Uneasy Exception

The accident focus of the scheme posed a particular problem for work-related harm. Occupational diseases, which had been covered under the Workers' Compensation Act 1956, did not fit within the new boundary lines of the scheme. They could not be excluded, however, as to do so would deprive workers of an existing entitlement and result in enormous resistance to the proposal by

---

29 Section 25(1)(a).
30 Sections 25(1)(b) and (ba). Note there may be cover where inhalation occurs as a result of criminal activity or, if work-related, and within section 30 as discussed below.
31 Section 25 (1)(d). Note certain conditions exceeding one month, if work-related, may fall within s 30 or the Occupational Diseases Schedule.
32 Geoffrey Palmer "Accident Compensation in New Zealand: The First Two Years" (1977) 25 AJCL 1 at 8.

organised labour, which had not been in favour of the scheme.[33] The original Accident Compensation Act 1972 imported the occupational diseases provisions, as they stood, from the workers compensation legislation, and described them as an "extension of cover", making their status as an exception to the accident focus of the legislation clear.[34] The occupational disease provisions were an interim measure until all diseases could be covered.[35] The ACC legislation has been re-enacted and amended many times since, but significant problems in the coverage of work-related health conditions remain.[36]

The current legislation makes provision for 'occupational diseases' in two ways: the Occupational Diseases Schedule, and a test for "gradual processes, diseases or infection" in section 30. The Occupational Diseases Schedule provides a list of certain occupational diseases, such as lead or arsenic poisoning, silicosis, a limited range of zoonosis diseases (from animals and carcasses) and a few diseases from inhaling toxic substance containing dusts or fumes. In 2005 a Ministerial Advisory Panel reported concerns that the schedule was too restrictive and, based on a 2004 NOSHAC Technical Report,[37] the then Minister for ACC commissioned a further review with the resulting report recommending a new schedule.[38] The recommended schedule was not adopted but some new diseases were added in 2008.

Section 30 contains a complex four-part legal test for those conditions not included on the Schedule.[39] It is designed to limit cover (and as a result costs) to a narrow range of conditions. 'Occupational disease' is itself a narrower concept than 'work-related disease', which the legal tests in modern workers' compensation schemes are formulated to cover. Work-related diseases are any diseases that can be shown to have a sufficient causal connection to a worker's work. Occupational diseases, on the other hand, are those conditions where the medical profession has accepted there is a strong statistical relationship between

---

33 See record of the trade union response at the time in Murdo MacMillan "Accident Compensation in New Zealand: A Study of Change 1979–1982" (VUW Thesis Repository, 1983).
34 Sections 65 and 67 of the Accident Compensation Act 1972.
35 Woodhouse Report, above at n 2 at 144.
36 Compare reformulation in Accident Compensation Act 1982, s 28 "disease due to nature of employment." The Accident Compensation, Rehabilitation and Insurance Act 1992 further amended and reformulated the test for "personal injury caused by gradual process, disease or infection arising out of or in the course of employment" in s 7. Section 30 was most recently amended by the Accident Compensation Amendment Act 2010.
37 Neil Pearce and others *NOSHAC Report: The Burden of Occupational Disease and Injury in New Zealand* (NOSHAC, Wellington, 2004).
38 Tim Driscoll and others *Review of Schedule 2 of the Injury Prevention Rehabilitation and Compensation Act 2001* (NOHSAC, Wellington, 2005).
39 See *Christian v ACC and Nelson Pine Industries Ltd* [2006] NZACC 133 (30 May 2006); *Wakenshaw v ACC* [2003] NZAR 590 (19 June 2003); *Knox v ARCIC* [2000] NZHC 1215.

the rates of disease in a given industry compared with the general population. The difference between occupational and work-related disease is more than just terminology, it reflects a significant difference in the underlying rationale of the legislation and matters a great deal at the margins of cover. The drafting of the current provisions to cover occupational diseases reflects the body-focused nature of the accident compensation scheme, the focus being on the categorisation of the particular condition, rather than the factual connection to work. The current drafting results in less cover for many workers in newer or less researched forms of work, such as that in many female-dominated industries.[40] It also limits the ability of the scheme to adapt to changes in the nature of work or medical thinking, in some cases effectively codifying specific diagnoses.

These problems can be seen in the coverage of work-related mental health problems and stress-related illnesses. Section 30 expressly excludes "mental injuries" from "gradual processes, diseases or infection". In 2008 a new s 21B was inserted to extend cover to one category of work-related mental harm, that resulting from single incident trauma (for example, a train driver whose train hits a suicidal person and develops post-traumatic stress disorder). However, the ACC scheme continues to exclude other work-related mental health problems, such as a police officer who develops post-traumatic stress disorder due to multiple traumatic exposures,[41] pain syndromes as a result of repetitive work (which ACC treats as mental),[42] stress-related mental illnesses such as depression or anxiety,[43] or any stress-related physical illnesses.

The current coverage of heart attack and stroke illustrate the problem of drafting for specific diseases based on the medical understandings of a given time.[44] There is cover for "a cardiovascular or cerebrovascular episode" (a heart attack or stroke) suffered by a worker if "the episode is caused by physical effort or physical strain, in performing his or her employment that is abnormal in application or excessive in intensity for the person".[45] Essentially, cover is only

---

40 *Christian v ACC and Nelson Pine Industries Ltd* [2006] NZACC 133 (30 May 2006) and *Purdie v ACC* [2010] NZACC 13 (1 February 2010).
41 *KB v ACC* [2013] NZACC 44 (22 February 2013) and *OCS Ltd v TW* [2013] NZACC 177 (21 June 2013); See earlier cases of *ETN v ACC* [1998] NZACC 227 (27 Oct 1998) and *Gable v ACC* [2003] NZACC 212 (27 Aug 2003) for pre-2008 law. Note the recent case of *MC v ACC* [2016] NZACC 264 (20 September 2016) may result in a shift to previous interpretations.
42 *Meikle v ACC* [2008] NZACC 158 (11 July 2008); *Teen v ACC and Telecom Ltd* [2002] NZACC 244 (3 Sept 2002).
43 *Nilson-Reid v AG (In respect of Dir. Dept. of Conservation)* [2005] 1 ERNZ 951 (EC); *Rosenburg v Air New Zealand Ltd* (unrep. ERA, AA 311/09, 1 Sept 2009); *Davis v Portage Licensing Trust* [2006] ERNZ 286.
44 Mervyn Gotsman and Stephen Adler "Under what circumstances can an acute myocardial infarction be regarded as a work-related accident? Multi-causal diseases at work-related accidents" (2009) 1 IJSSAWC 1.
45 Section 28(3).

available where the heart attack or stroke is 'caused by' some unusual physical exertion on the part of a worker and not from particularly stressful work.[46] In *MacFarlane v Accident Compensation Corporation*[47] it was confirmed that "a stroke cannot be a work related gradual process injury" and will only have cover if it is caused by physical effort or strain. There has been a significant shift in the understanding of heart attacks and stroke since the original inclusion of the section.[48] In the early workers' compensation schemes heart attacks were considered by many to be caused by physical strain; essentially, the heart, like any other muscle, simply gave out through overexertion.[49] Now heart attacks and stroke are viewed as acute events caused by a blockage in blood vessels to the heart or brain in cases of cardiovascular or cerebrovascular disease.[50] It would be rare for a worker to have a heart attack in the circumstances set out in s 28(3) without pre-existing heart disease or a pre-existing structural defect. The physical exertion would at best, be considered to operate as a trigger to an inevitable event, and would not likely, on review of the medical evidence, be considered "the cause".[51]

The ACC scheme provides cover for work-related health problems in ss 21B, 25, 28, 29, 30 and the Occupational Diseases Schedule. There are more than six different legal tests for the cover of work-related health problems, and, reflecting the cut and fill approach identified by Palmer, they are all different in their approach, operation and scope.[52] For example, what is the difference between catching a disease from handling sheep carcasses and catching a disease from handling chicken carcasses? Yet the eligibility test for cover is different. Why should contracting a disease at work "via an arthropod as vector" (for example, a mosquito carrying infected blood) be treated differently to contracting the same disease via infected bodily fluids directly? Why should it be easier to obtain compensation for lung cancer caused by asbestos exposure than laryngeal or ovarian cancer caused by asbestos exposure? Why should an ambulance officer who develops PTSD after witnessing a single traumatic event be entitled to cover, when an ambulance officer who develops depression after witnessing 500 such events over the course of a career is not? Why is the heart attack of an office

---

46 See *A-G v Gilbert* [2002] 2 NZLR 342; *Cross v ARCIC* (1995) 1 BACR 146; DC Whangarei 145/95, 20 December 1995 and *O'Flaherty v ARCIC* [1994] NZAR 499.
47 *McFarlane v Accident Compensation Corporation* [2014] NZACC 141.
48 See discussion on changing thinking in the time in Mel Bartley "Coronary Heart Disease – A Disease of Affluence or A Disease of Industry?" in Paul Weindling (ed) *The Social History of Occupational Health* (Croom Helm, Kent, 1985).
49 At 137–141.
50 See discussion in Commonwealth of Australia *Work-Related Cardiovascular Disease Australia* (April 2006).
51 Gotsman and Adler, above n 44, and Commonwealth of Australia, above n 50 at 1–4.
52 Palmer, above n 32.

worker engaged in unusual physical exertion covered, when a heart attack as a result of years of mental stress at work is not?[53] These inconsistencies are the logical consequences of the inherent boundary line tensions at the heart of the ACC legislation.

The "plight of hundreds of thousands of injured New Zealanders denied ACC support" has recently been highlighted in a series of Law Foundation backed reports.[54] The most recent report, issued in May 2017, called for changes in the way causation is dealt with. It concluded, "ACC's narrow, legalistic application of the causation test, which determines coverage, is shutting out many legitimate claimants and shifting costs to other institutions like Worksafe, the Coroner and the criminal courts."[55]

The Rise of Personal Grievances to Fill the Gaps

The gaps in the ACC scheme's coverage of work-related health problems have had an impact on employment relations. New Zealand employment lawyers have filled the gaps in ACC cover with a creative combination of personal grievance, breach of statutory duty and breach of contract claims, especially after the decision in *AG v Gilbert*.[56] If an employee suffers from an excluded condition caused by their employment, they can sue their employer to obtain compensation. This, however, requires the employee to prove the employer was at fault by failing to provide healthy or safe work. The New Zealand Court of Appeal has described this requirement as posing "formidable obstacles".[57] Even if successful, an employee's remedies are usually limited and rarely provide for treatment, ongoing income support for incapacity, or rehabilitation.[58]

Workers with excluded health conditions are at a considerable disadvantage. Even for those workers with private insurance, many find their policies contain blanket exclusions for mental-health conditions. In the absence of insurance cover or a successful legal case, affected workers are left with whatever support

---

53   Originally set out in Dawn Duncan "Regulating work that kills us slowly: The challenge of chronic work-related health problems" (2016) 41 NZJER 2.
54   Law Foundation "Seeking justice for ACC claimants" <www.lawfoundation.org.nz>. Warren Forester, Tom Barraclough and Tiho Mijaov *Solving the Problem: Causation, Transparency and Access to Justice in New Zealand's Personal Injury System* (22 May 2017) <www.lawfoundation.org.nz>.
55   At 1-2.
56   *Attorney-General v Gilbert* [2002] 2 NZLR 342.
57   At [87].
58   The remedies of reimbursement of lost wages are generally capped at 12 weeks' ordinary time and compensation for "humiliation, loss of dignity, and injury to the feelings" under s 123(1)(c)(i) of the Employment Relations Act 2000 is intended to be an award for the intangible harms of the employer's unjustifiable conduct rather than allowing for medical treatment or support.

may be available to them through the benefit system. In 2013 research was conducted on the socioeconomic impact of the difference in financial support from the ACC scheme versus that provided through WINZ. The study involved a group of people of a similar age and level of functional impairment and concluded that those not covered by ACC had "considerably poorer socio-economic outcomes", did not return to work as early, and were the "most vulnerable for decline into poverty and ill health".[59] The gaps in ACC cover also impact on employers, exposed to civil liability for an employee's work-related mental harm or chronic health problem in a way they are not with accidental physical harm. The lack of ACC cover impacts on the cost and management of sick leave, employee absence, rehabilitation and return-to-work planning.

The Relationship between ACC and Health and Safety

The ACC scheme is an important part of New Zealand's occupational health and safety regime. Its primary function under statute is to "reduce the incidence and severity of personal injury" and to provide "a framework for the collection, coordination, and analysis of injury related information".[60] Work-related health statistics come almost exclusively from ACC administrative data in New Zealand. This means that where there is a gap in the ACC cover, there is a gap in the available data. The lack of data has a flow-on effect for health and safety, limiting research and the development of policy and enforcement activity. The *Report of the Royal Commission on the Pike River Coal Mine Tragedy* and *The Report of Independent Taskforce on Workplace Health and Safety*[61] highlighted the lack of available occupational health information, stating they were "left with a profound unease about the quality of data in New Zealand".[62] The Taskforce concluded that:[63]

> While New Zealand's acute harm and workplace safety statistics are woeful and rightly attract considerable attention, the much more damaging occupational health impacts of the workplace go almost completely under the radar.

The lack of reliable data was a key reason for occupational diseases being left out of the current *Working Safer* national targets.[64] Worksafe has recently

---

59 Sue McAllister and others "Do different types of financial support after illness or injury affect socio-economic outcomes? A natural experiment in New Zealand" (2013) 85 SSAM 93.
60 Accident Compensation Act 2001, s 3.
61 Independent Taskforce on Workplace Health and Safety *The Report of Independent Taskforce on Workplace Health and Safety: He Korowai Whakaruruhau* (April 2013). Royal Commission on the Pike River Coal Mine Tragedy *Report of the Royal Commission on the Pike River Coal Mine Tragedy* (Wellington, October 2012).
62 Independent Taskforce on Workplace Health and Safety, above n 61.
63 At 16.
64 Ministry of Business, Innovation and Employment *Working Safer: Reducing Work-Related*

issued *Healthy Work: A Strategic Plan for Work-Related Health 2016–2026*. This document acknowledges New Zealand's failure "to adequately address work-related health risks and the harm associated with them", which they recognise are having an "even greater impact on our country . . . than acute work-related injuries".[65] The report also acknowledges that one of the major challenges for Worksafe to be able to meet its goals is the lack of data. Worksafe estimates that work-related health problems result in an additional 600–900 deaths and affect about 30,000 more workers each year.[66]

The Changing Nature of Work and Changing Health Impacts

The need to address the gaps in ACC cover has particular urgency given the rapidly changing nature of work performed in New Zealand. Work has changed a great deal since the late 1960s when the Woodhouse Report was written, as other chapters in this book set out. When work changes, the types of hazards that workers are exposed to also change, and so do the resulting health problems. Fewer New Zealand workers are performing work with hazards associated with a high risk of accidental physical injury, and greater numbers of workers are performing work with hazards associated with the development of chronic musculoskeletal problems and stress-related illnesses.

Stress-related illnesses are a particularly significant excluded category. Although there are no reliable New Zealand statistics on these conditions, in 2009 the Department of Labour commissioned a study, *Understanding Stress and Bullying in New Zealand Workplaces*.[67] This report provided a snapshot of the extent to which stress and bullying were a problem in given industries. The survey and interview results indicated "the prevalence was relatively high compared to international findings".[68] Australian research suggests that "mental illness is now the leading cause of sickness absence and long-term work incapacity in most developed countries",[69] costing businesses in absenteeism, reduced work performance, increased turnover rates and compensation claims.[70]

Fatalities and Serious Injury by 2020: Progress Toward the Target (2015) at 20.
65 WorkSafe New Zealand *Healthy Work: A Strategic Plan for Work-Related Health 2016–2026* (Worksafe, August 2016) at 6.
66 Latest estimate in the *Healthy Work: A Strategic Plan for Work-Related Health 2016–2026*, above n 65.
67 Tim Bentley and others *Understanding Stress and Bullying in New Zealand Workplaces: Final Report to the OH&S Steering Committee* (December 2009).
68 At i.
69 Samuel Harvey and others *Developing a mentally healthy workplace: A review of the literature* A report for the National Mental Health Commission and Mentally Healthy Workplace Alliance (November 2014).
70 National Occupational Health and Safety Commission *National Occupational Health and Safety Commission Annual Report 2002–2003* (NOSHC, Canberra, 2003). A LaMontagne, K

In Australia the highest number of mental injury claims was for "work pressure related illness", then harassment and bullying and then "exposure to workplace violence".[71] Claims increased with worker age, with men aged 55–59 and women aged 50–54 making the most claims.[72] Younger workers were more likely to be exposed to occupational violence and women were more likely to be sexually harassed. Health care and social assistance, and public administration each made up 21 per cent of claims, with education and training a further 14 per cent.[73] It was also found that:[74]

> The types of occupations of workers receiving compensation for a work-related mental disorder tend to be those who work in occupations which involve high levels of interaction with other people, often rendering a service to the public and often doing their job in difficult and challenging circumstances.

The Australian statistics reflect many of the industry trends identified in the New Zealand research, which highlights the prevalence of bullying and stress-related health problems particularly in the health and education sectors.[75]

A Gender Divide in Cover

The current ACC cover provisions exclude many workers performing work with hazards associated with the development of chronic health problems. This has a particular impact on workers in female-dominated occupations. The New Zealand labour market remains highly segregated by gender.[76] Different gendered patterns of work result in different patterns of hazard exposure, and different patterns of resulting health problems. Jobs in female-dominated industries tend to have risk profiles associated with the development of chronic health problems and in particular stress-related illnesses.[77] Looking to Australia, when analysed per hour worked, "women were three times more likely than men to have a claim caused by work-related harassment and/or workplace bullying" (15 claims per 100 million hours worked compared with five) and were twice as likely to have a

---

Sanderson and F Cocker "Estimating the Economic Benefits of Eliminating Job Strain as a Risk Factor for Depression" (2011) OAEM 68 at 3.

71 SafeWork Australia *The Incidence of Accepted Workers' Compensation Claims for Mental Stress in Australia* (SafeWork Australia, April 2013) at 8.
72 At 10.
73 SafeWork Australia *Work-Related Mental Disorders Profile 2015* (SafeWork Australia, 2016) at 6.
74 SafeWork Australia "International Women's Day: Reflecting on women's health and safety in the workplace" (2016) <http://www.safeworkaustralia.gov.au/sites/swa/news/pages/tn09072016>.
75 Bentley Report, above n 67 at i.
76 Statistics New Zealand *Women at Work: 1991–2013* (Statistics New Zealand, October 2015).
77 SafeWork Australia *Work-Related Mental Disorders Profile 2015*, above n 73.

claim caused by "exposure to workplace or occupational violence".[78]

There is currently no ACC cover for workers affected by harassment or bullying, whether sexual or otherwise, the psychological effects of occupational violence or any work pressure related illnesses. The health conditions most likely to affect workers in female-dominated industries are the least likely to receive ACC cover, leaving these workers without support and assistance. The lack of cover also results in a lack of data on the health effects of work in female-dominated industries. This creates a vicious cycle, with the lack of data leading to a lack of research focus and action. NOSHAC Technical Report 13 concluded that:[79]

> Very little is known about women's OHS. The lack of research in exposures and health effects associated with women's jobs have enforced the widespread belief that women's jobs are safe, thus perpetuating the lack of knowledge and action on women's occupational ill health.

The lower rates of female injuries and illnesses appearing in the ACC statistics create a perception that women's work is safer and less of a priority for research, monitoring or intervention.

Meeting the Needs of New Zealand Workers in Future

The most prominent theme in the labour law research over the past two decades has been the need to respond to the changed nature of work and the mechanisms by which people are engaged to perform it.[80] There is a growing international literature tracing the shifts towards 'flexible' work,[81] the 'gig economy'[82] and the growing 'precariat'.[83] The impact of these trends was also recently highlighted in New Zealand.[84] The pace of change looks set to continue, if not increase, with many commentators heralding a "fourth industrial revolution"[85] changing the

---

78   At 12.
79   NOSHAC *Women's Occupational Health and Safety in New Zealand NOSHAC Technical Report 13* (NOSHAC, Wellington, 2009) at iv.
80   See for example the essays in Guy Davidov and Brian Langille *Boundaries and Frontiers of Labour Law* (Hart Publishing, Oregon, 2006); and the more recent Guy Davidov and Brian Langille *The Idea of Labour Law* (OUP, Oxford, 2011).
81   Deirdre McCann *Regulating Flexible Work* (OUP, Oxford, 2008).
82   Gerald Friedman "Workers without employers: Shadow corporations and the rise of the gig economy" (2014) Review of Keynesian Economics at 171, and Juliet Webster "Micro workers and the Gig Economy: Separate and Precarious (2016) 23 NLF 56.
83   Guy Standing *The Precariat: The Rise of the New Dangerous Class* (Bloomsbury, London, 2011).
84   New Zealand Council for Trade Unions *Under Pressure: A Detailed Report in to Insecure Work in New Zealand* (NZCTU, October 2013).
85   See commentary by Klaus Schwab, Chairman of World Economic Forum "The Fourth Industrial Revolution: What it means, how to respond" (14 January 2016) first published in *Foreign Affairs* and available on the World Economic Forum Website <https://www.weforum.org/agenda/2016/01/the-fourth-industrial-revolution-what-it-means-and-how-

nature of work and the hazards inherent in the performance of that work:[86]

> The possibilities of billions of people connected by mobile devices, with unprecedented processing power, storage capacity, and access to knowledge, are unlimited. And these possibilities will be multiplied by emerging technology breakthroughs in fields such as artificial intelligence, robotics, the Internet of Things, autonomous vehicles, 3-D printing, nanotechnology, biotechnology, materials science, energy storage, and quantum computing.

The current drafting of the ACC cover provisions will struggle to respond to these changes. The potential for rapid and destabilising change has led to calls to review the wider regulation of work and the provision of welfare to New Zealanders. If reformed, the dual workers' compensation and social insurance functions of the ACC scheme could form a core component of future provision, allowing for the changing needs of health and safety to be met alongside the universality of provision advocated in the Woodhouse Report and made more relevant by projected rates of job loss.[87]

Moving from Accident to Distinguished Social Insurance Scheme

The accident focus of the current scheme arose, not because accidents represent some identifiable or particularly deserving category of circumstances, harms or recipients, but as a pragmatic decision on political palatability at the time. Accident is difficult to define, of limited value to occupational disease, and conceptually inconsistent with workplace health and safety objectives.[88] Removing 'accident' as the central pillar of the scheme would allow for a more consistent and principled set of cover provisions to be developed and assist the scheme to better adapt to changing circumstances. It is possible to reimagine ACC as a "distinguished social insurance" scheme, performing two different functions, but offering the administrative and cost-saving advantages of delivery through a single scheme. The key division within a distinguished scheme would

---

to-respond/>.
86 Schwab, above n 85.
87 World Bank *Digital Dividends: World Development Report 2016* (World Bank Group, 2016), United Nations Conference on Trade and Development (UNCTRAD) Report No 50 Robots and Industrialisation in Developing Countries (October 2016) and The Economist "Special Report: Artificial Intelligence: The Impact on Jobs" (June 25, 2016).
88 The critique of 'accident' in workplace health and safety can be seen in Theo Nichols *The Sociology of Industrial Injury* (Mansell Publishing, London, 1997) at 2-3; Philip Bohle "Work Psychology and the Management of Occupational Health and Safety: An Overview" in Michael Quinlan (ed) *Work and Health: The Origins, Management and Regulation of Occupational Illness* (Macmillan, Melbourne, 1993); William Breen Creighton, William Ford and Richard Mitchell *Labour Law: Text and Materials* (2nd ed, Law Book Co, Sydney, 1993) at 1340; Harry Glasbeek "Occupational Health and Safety Law: Criminal Law as a Political Tool" (1998) 11 AJLL 95 at 99.

be between work-related and non-work-related harms. The scheme would continue to cover all the existing non-work-related health problems (and allow for further expansion), but work-related conditions would be 'distinguished' on the basis that work-related health problems operate in a different context, and the ends of work health and safety require a different approach to prevention than other types of harm.

Moving from a 'partially enacted' to a 'distinguished' social insurance scheme would allow the workers' compensation provisions in the current ACC legislation to be redrafted with that purpose, to perform that role, rather than as a begrudging exception. The scattered ad hoc provisions for work-related health problems could be replaced with a single new test based on establishing a causal relationship between work and health, similar to that in the Australian workers' compensation legislation. A workers' compensation test would allow for all health problems sufficiently related to work to receive cover, whether accidental injury, or mental or physical disease. A single relationship-to-work test would allow the legislation to respond to new health conditions, changing medical understandings and new forms of work, without frequent amendment. As a result, this would allow for more of the conditions affecting workers in female-dominated industries to be included. It would also allow for the work-related health provisions to be aligned with the goals of work health and safety and result in better data on which to develop policy and interventions. Such a test could operate either in the current Act or in the context of an expanded but still distinguished social insurance system.

Moving to a distinguished social insurance scheme may better allow for the incremental reform of the remaining social insurance functions in the direction of the Woodhouse vision. Once the notion of accident is removed from the centre of the scheme, additional categories of non-work harm can be added without having to appear 'accident-like'. If future governments wanted to add a category of non-accident cover, for example cancer or mental health, they could do so without undermining the structure of the scheme. There have been many calls over the decades to fully enact the wider social insurance scheme imagined by Woodhouse and fellow reformers, and there is a strong case to be made for doing so. However, in a comprehensive social insurance scheme, distinguishing the workers' compensation functions would be still desirable. As Woodhouse himself was aware, a social insurance scheme provides no guarantee of improving workplace health and safety and may, if poorly implemented, undermine it.[89] Recognising that an individual's incapacity deserves to be treated equally well by their community, does not require the law to ignore the different dynamics or context of workplace health and safety.

---

89 Woodhouse Report, above n 2 at Part 7.

Conclusion

The creation of the ACC scheme in the 1970s extended cover beyond that provided in the former workers' compensation regime. This extension was a real gain to the working people of New Zealand who were harmed in accidents unrelated to work. However, the original compromise needed to achieve this expansion has meant that this gain came at the expense of non-accidental work-related health problems in the decades that followed. The leftover and compromised nature of the workers' compensation provisions in the ACC legislation were less able to adapt to the changing health effects of work, and left a significant gap in the cover of, and data on, chronic work-related health problems. This, in combination with changes to the industrial relations and welfare system made during the 1980s and 1990s, meant worker health became "the poor cousin"[90] to accidental physical injury. While the need to address these failures is being recognised by Worksafe, the goals of improving worker health in New Zealand will not be achieved without reforms to the work-related cover provisions of the ACC scheme. The Woodhouse Report called for the equal treatment of all citizens regardless of the particular circumstances of their misfortune. This call has as much resonance as it did in 1967. Reconceiving of the ACC scheme as a distinguished social insurance scheme could allow for both the universal care advocated by Woodhouse and the specific needs of workplace health and safety to be met, contributing to the future health of New Zealand working people at work and outside of it.

---

90 Department of Labour *Occupational Health Action Plan to 2013: Workplace Health and Safety Strategy for New Zealand to 2015* (Originally issued December 2011 but revised) at 5.

Conclusion: Industrial Relations in 40 Years
The Editors

Nearly 40 years ago, Donald Cullen, recognised as one of the leading theorists of his day, wrote a paper predicting the future of American industrial relations. He concluded the paper (Cullen 1985, 319) with the observation:

> The knowledgeable reader will treat these predictions, of course, with the disrespect they deserve. It is well established that American specialists in industrial relations have a record of predicting that future that easily matches that of economists, political scientists, and generals.

This begs the obvious question: should our predictions about industrial relations in 40 years also be treated with disrespect? While we are confident that they will be disrespected in the present by editorial commentaries, we can assure the reader that in 40 years' time it will be universally acknowledged, by the occasional readers of this volume, that our predictions were uncannily accurate, far surpassing any of Nostradamus' quatrains.

One prediction is that 'Industrial Relations' as a *label* or a term will be unfamiliar to almost everyone. Indeed, the label has been fast losing significance over the past twenty years. However, the *concept* of industrial relations will still be totally relevant in 40 years. Whether it will be called 'Workplace Relations', 'Employment Relations' or perhaps, once again, 'Labour Relations' remains to be seen.

The epigram *"Plus ça change, plus c'est la même chose"*[1] will seem most apposite when comparing industrial relations in 40 years to what it is today or, indeed, what it was in 1976. There will be major changes in the world of work, but many of the core basics will remain the same. A higher percentage of employees may be given opportunities to work from home or vary their hours of work (that is, be a 20th-century university academic). However, in 40 years it will be simply a dream that all employees will select their hours and place of work. Many will be working at home because they are required to and because advances in electronic monitoring and management by algorithm will allow employers to exercise at

---

1 "The more things change, the more they stay the same."

least the same control they exercise today, but probably more, and over a much wider range of workers. Whatever else may change, it is unlikely that labour's subordination to capital will have changed significantly.

On the subject of dreams, Ed McCurdy's song "The Strangest Dream" will *not* have come to pass with respect to war – or even with respect to conflict in the workplace. Conflict will always exist between managers and the managed, owners and employees, and the state and all other parties. It will always exist because parties have different objectives, or place different weight on the same objective, or have different priorities. Conflict in the workplace today – and in 40 years' time – can be settled in many different ways.

We might further predict that within industrial relations over the next 40 years we will not see steady progressions but rather waves or cycles, or waxing and waning. Even Kondratieff long cycles, referred to by Ernesto Screpanti (1987) which are "Waves in the growth rate of industrial output, consisting of a long phase of rapid growth, lasting 20–30 years followed by an equally long phase of stagnation" (99) are short enough to show waxing and waning over 40 years.

The state, the most powerful party in industrial relations, may be more or less *prominent* in 40 years but no less influential. On the basis that in New Zealand the state has very much been becoming more overtly powerful in the workplace over the last 20–30 years, it may be that the State will make a tactical retreat and will *appear* much less significant in 40 years. However, both withdrawal and advance are tactical decisions – decisions as to how the state will exercise control of the labour market – withdrawal usually equates to allowing self-regulation, the 'self' of course being the employer. Indeed the story of the 1990s was in part at least a move to self-regulation, after having ensured that only one party retained the power to dictate the regulation.

It would, however, be churlish to deny future readers the opportunity scoff at at least some predictions. One prediction that might be made with relative safety is that the course of workplace relations over the next 40 years will be largely determined by the balance of political forces and the perceived dominant interests of the electorate. Advances for workers have historically occurred following the achievement of universal suffrage and the ability to direct the resulting political power though a political party, most usually a Labour party. While there are signs that labour issues may again be a growing concern, for example in the recent United Kingdom and United States elections, it is still a large step for such half-articulated discontent to be channelled into a coherent political programme let alone an electoral victory. Such a programme is unlikely in the absence of some form of collective organisation, and in practical terms this means the revival of the trade union movement in either its traditional or some new form and in a way that attracts, retains and utilises the leadership and vigour of younger workers and voters.

It seems that we might also safely predict that New Zealand and the world are entering a period of considerable uncertainty that may, or may not, result in beneficial changes. The neoliberal programme appears to be slowly losing credibility, although, as that programme was always political rather than economic, any reversals that affect the balance of power in workplace relations will be hard fought. Political parties, including the New Zealand Labour Party, are slowly developing industrial relations policies that include strengthening worker rights including collective rights. The need for such policies is becoming increasingly apparent – the developing gig economy, and increasing levels of inequality and poverty even among the employed are examples of issues that need to be addressed but where articulated solutions seem to be lacking. What is less apparent is whether they will capture the public imagination.

Against this, however, is the possibility that during the next 40 years there will be a clear backlash against the moves we are seeing at present towards less discrimination against groups in society and greater tolerance and inclusiveness. There is a nasty side to human nature and unfortunately the majority like to be better than some sections of society. The problems caused by the neoliberal agenda including much increased levels of inequality and poverty do not seem yet to have been countered by strong societal pressures for change. If anything, the coercive and punitive character of the contemporary welfare system, the blame-the-victim approach, seems to have a strong resonance with a significant proportion of the electorate. However much we will have in our society in 40 years, there will be those who will consider themselves 'have nots' and will be resentful. There will always be owners, managers and leaders who wish to reap the benefits of other people's efforts without making similar efforts themselves. By nature many, if not most, will wish to 'comfortise' at work rather than 'maximise'. *"Plus ça change, plus c'est la même chose"*.

More than that we would not venture. In the September of the year the *Journal* was first published Mao died. The editors of this collection certainly did not then predict the consequences of this event for both China and the world. We are certainly not planning to predict the next 40 years in the year that Donald Trump became President of the United States and Britain gave notice of its intention to leave the European Union.

But, to end on a more positive note, there will always be a place somewhere in the workplace for those interested in the study of industrial relations!

References

Cullen, D. E. 1985. "Recent Trends in Collective Bargaining in the United States." *International Labour Review* 124 (3): 299–322.
Screpanti, E. 1987. "Long Cycles in Strike Activity: An Empirical Investigation." *British Journal of Industrial Relations* 25 (1): 99–124.

Index

90-day trial, 39, 41, 57, 206

accident, definition of, 235
Accident Compensation Act 1972, 236
Accident Compensation Corporation (ACC) scheme, 230–246
  and changing nature of work, 241–242
  compromises in, 19, 230, 234–239, 246
  coverage, 230–232, 234–243, 246
  data and statistics, 240–241, 243, 246
  definition of 'accident,' 235
  and female-dominated occupations, 237, 242–243, 245
  future needs, 243–245
  and government, 232
  'gradual processes, diseases or infection,' 236
  and health and safety, 137, 139, 239–241, 245–246
  heart attack and stroke, 237–238
  historical context for, 232–234
  impacts on employers, 240
  introduction of, 230
  Labour Party support for, 231–232
  MacFarlane v Accident Compensation Corporation, 238
  mental health, 237, 239–243
  occupational disease, 235–239
  Occupational Diseases Schedule, 236, 238
  and personal grievance, 239–240
  reports and inquiries, 231–232, 234–236, 239–241, 243
  as social insurance model, 232–234, 244–246
  stress and bullying, 237, 241–243
  WINZ benefit socio-economic comparisons, 240
  Woodhouse Report, 231–232, 234–235, 241
  workers' compensation scheme comparison, 232–233, 235–238
  work-related health problems, tests for, 238–239
Accident Rehabilitation and Compensation Insurance Act 1992, 135
administration sector, 121
Advisory Council on Occupational Safety and Health (ACOSH), 133–134, 144–145
agriculture sector
  exports, 24
  health and safety, 147, 173, 183
  income, 85–86, 90–92, 94, 98
  subsidies, removal of, 97–98
Alliance Party, 55
AMECO database, 103
annual leave, 41, 122–123
anti-worker law (UK), 192–193
appointment process, 39
Arbitration Court, *see also* Employment Court; also Labour Court, 27, 30–31, 48–49, 86, 91, 93, 155
'Arbitration Era,' 25–30, 44–45
arbitration system, *see* industrial conciliation and arbitration system (IC&A)
armed forces, pay to, 89–90
artificial intelligence, 15, 59
Asian Financial Crisis, 102
Association to Advance Collegiate Schools of Business (AACSB), 64
Attorney-General v Gilbert, 239
Australia
  comparison with, 84, 103, 108
  EEO policies, 165
  health and safety, 129, 138, 145, 148, 172, 182
  human resource management, 66, 68
  as trading partner, 24
  work practices, 178
  worker compensation in, 232, 234,

241–242, 245
Australian Model Health and Safety Act 2011, 138, 143, 148
awards, 27, 32, 49, 51, 53–54, 60–61, 81, 86, 91, 99, 109, 111, 121, 124, 155, 174, 195

back pay, 30
bargaining, direct, 91, 111
bargaining coverage, *see also* collective bargaining
   and bargaining structure, 32, 119, *120*
   decline in, 20, 35, 107–115, 124, 201, 205
   definition, 109
   disparity in, 115
   extension of coverage to new employees, 116–117
   international comparisons, *108*
   non-union collectives, 116
   statistics, 110–112, *110*, *112*, *114*, 205
   trends, 16
bargaining flexibility, 53
bargaining process agreement (BPA), 119
bargaining structures, 117–121, *120*, 208
Bartlett v TerraNova, 40, 163, 167
benchmarking processes, 61, 70
benefits, social welfare, 24
bereavement leave, 123
Beveridge Report (UK), 234
Bill of Rights Act, 209
bipartite relationships, 195–196, 199
'Black Budget,' 91
'blitzkrieg,' 24, 196
Bowley's law, 79
Bradford, Max, 15, 44
Brexit phenomenon, 24
bullying, workplace, 241–243
Business NZ, 35, 40
Business Roundtable, *see* New Zealand Business Roundtable (NZBR)
business structures, changes in, 209
business success, perceptions of, 16

Canada, 182, 232, 234
Capital in the Twenty-first Century, 79–80
capital income share, 16, 79–105
   analyses, discrepancies in, 96
   foreign transfer of, 83, 95–96
   and income inequality, 79, 102
   locally owned corporates, 95
   and power relationships, 79–80
   'profit squeeze' claims, 83
   and publicly-owned market sector, 100
   and redundancies, 84
casualised labour, 19, 122, 214, 229
Caucus Labour Committee, review by, 134
Census of Women's Participation (2012), 165
Centre for Labour Employment and Work (CLEW), 16, 107, 115, *176*
change, drivers of, 15
Chief Judge's statement, 204
child care, access to, 14, 17, 160–161, 165, 167
China, 23, 24, 249
civil liberties suppression, 90
Clark, Helen Elizabeth (Prime Minister), 100, 158
Clarke, John, 149
class-based system, English, 191–193
Clerical Workers Case (1986), 155
Clerical Workers Union, 201
climate change, 23
Coalition for Equal Value Equal Pay, 155
Code of Employment Practice, 159
Code of Practice for Health and Safety Representatives and Health and Safety Committees, 182
collective bargaining, *see also* bargaining coverage
   'composite agreements,' 117
   contracts and agreements, 16–17, 27, 56, 107–108, *110*
   decentralisation of, 108, 124, 174
   definition, 107
   development, 48
   Employment Institutions Project database, 107
   erosion of, 15, 33, 35–36, 38, 41, 54, 57–58, 63, 99–100, 102, 170, 202–203
   influence on labour markets, 108
   and mediators, 31
   opposition to, 38, 44, 177
   promotion of, 204–206, 208
   trends, 16, 47, 49, 54–59, 94–95, 100, 124–125
'Collective Bargaining Era,' 31–33
collective employment agreements (CEAs), *see also* multi-employer collective agreements (MECAs); also single employer collective agreements (SECAs)
   decline in, 35, 63, 110–112, *110*, 115
   expiry provisions, 117, 119
   terms and conditions of, 16–17, 121–124
   work not covered by, 117
collective representative culture, 216–219
collectivism, 24, 30, 170, 175, 177–178, 181, 184

Index

Combined State Service Organisations, *see* Combined State Unions
Combined State Unions, 29
Committee of Enquiry into Industrial Democracy, 172, 174–175, 177–178
commodity price boom, 98
commodity prices, 90, 92, 95, 98
commodity-based export economy, 91
common law ethos, 194, 197, 200, 202–203, 207–208, 228–229
Companies Empowering Act 1924, 172
Compensation of Employees (COE), 85, *87*
'composite agreements,' 117
compulsory arbitration, removal of, 30
conciliated agreements, 117–118, 121
'Conciliation and Arbitration Era,' *see* 'Arbitration Era'
conciliation and arbitration system, *see* industrial conciliation and arbitration system (IC&A)
conciliation process, 27
conflict, industrial, *see* industrial conflict
consensus, 203
Conservatives (UK), 36
consultants, use of, 16, 63
consumer price index (CPI), 84, 89–90, 93, 95–97
contractors, employee designation as, 57, 59
contracts, *see also* collective employment agreements (CEAs)
    individual, 53–56, 202–203, 207
    non-standard, 40
    zero-hours, 40
corporate income share, *see* capital income share
corporate sector operating surplus, 96
corporatisation, 30, 33
cost-minimisation principles, 19
Council of Trade Unions (CTU), 177, 200
Court of Appeal, 34, 202–203, 221, 239
Crown Entities Act, 161
Cullen, David, 247
current account deficit, 91

dairy exports, 24, 91, 97
dangerous work, 135
David v Employment Relations Authority, 221
David v Tilley, 221
Deeks, John, 13, 45–46, 52–53
Denmark, 103, 104, 105
Department of Labour, *see also* Ministry of Business, Innovation and Employment, 134–135, 141–142, 161, 180–184, 200, 211, 225–226, 241
dependent contractors, 57, 59
devaluation (NZ dollar), 93
direct bargaining, 91, 111
discrimination, 14, 17, 161, 167, 207, 211, 213, 249
dismissals and disadvantage
    in 19th-century, 194
    90-day trial, 39, 41, 57
    collective employment agreements (CEAs), 122
    common law, 27
    procedures, 47
    Employment Contracts (EC) Act 1991, 54, 213, 228
    justification of dismissal, 202–205
    non-union sector, 19, 229
    personal grievance provisions and processes, 20, 197, 210, 215–216
dispute resolution provisions and processes, 18–20, 38, 49, 52, 69, 163, 197, 202, 210
disputes, government intervention in, 97
disputes of interest, 49, 197
disputes of rights, 49, 54, 197
Diversity Works, *see* EEO Trust
domestic leave, 123
domestic violence rates, 166
Douglas, Sir Roger Owen (Minister of Finance), 31, 97
Dunlop, John, 25
Dunlop's model of industrial relations, 14–15, 25
duties of PCBUs, 143–144, 146–148, 182–183

E tū, 175
Economic Management, 50
Economic Stabilisation Regulations, 91, 94–95
economics, neoclassical, 79, 81
economy, global, 47
economy, New Zealand
    challenges to, 49–50, 52–53, 58, 196
    commodity-based export, 91
    devaluation of NZ dollar, 93
    economic growth, 81, 83
    floating of NZ dollar, 97
    market-focused, 51, 56
    protection of, 24
    recessions, 90–91, 93–96, 102, 114–115
    restructuring, 30–33, 60, 62, 69, 82, 92, 97, 103, 105, 198–199

education and training sector, 16, 116, 119, 121
EEO Trust, 70, 156
eight-hour day, 192
employee engagement, 66, 68, 70–71, 73, 177–179
employee participation, 169–185
  collective bargaining weaknesses, 174
  collectively negotiated forms, 171
  consultative committees, 176–177, 179
  'cycles' concept, 170–171, 184
  employee interest in, 179–180
  employee share ownership plans (ESOPs), 172
  employer attitudes to, 169–171, 173, 175, 177, 179, 181–184
  fluctuations in, 170–173
  government attitudes to, 177–178, 180
  health and safety, 17–18, 130–132, 144–145, 148, 170–173, 175, 181–184, 206
  international influences, 169, 175, 178
  legally-based forms, 171, 175, 181–182, 184–185
  legislative effectiveness, 182–184
  managerially implemented forms, 171
  models, 44–45
  non-union forms, 170
  research needs, 183–184
  significant events, 172–173
  union attitudes to, 169–171, 173–175, 177, 179, 181
  'waves' concept, 170–171, 184
  workplace employee participation system, 182
  workplace partnership, 173–175, 180–181
  workplace reform, 173–175, 178–180
employees
  and ACC scheme, 19
  bargaining power of, 15, 31, 33–35, 41, 54–55, 80, 201
  designation as contractors, 57, 59, 69, 208
  dismissal of, 19–20, 39, 41, 54, 57, 194
  health and safety role of, 132, 135–137, 142, 144–148
  impacts of change on, 19–20, 53, 61–62, 99, 201
  industrial and political voice of, 13, 17–18, 20, 73, 131, 169–170, 195, 199, 203, 205–209
  isolation of, 20, 63, 113
  leave entitlements, 41, 86, 122–123, 153–155, 158–159, 162, 165
  loyalty and engagement, 66, 68, 70–71, 73, 177–179
  need for redefinition of, 208
  objectives, 25
  personal rights and freedoms, 70–71, 73, 208–209
  protections and entitlements, 39–42, 45–46, 52, 54–55, 57, 68–69, 86, 98–99, 121–124, 135, 153–155, 194, 201
  representation of, 113, 113
  rest breaks, 41, 57, 201
  rights and duties, 121
  and social media, 70–71
  surveillance of, 70, 73
  turn-over and injury rates, 19, 229, 241
  understanding of dispute resolution practices, 223–224
  vulnerability to retaliation, 20, 123
  working hours, 17, 122, 153, 192, 201, 223
employer brand, 61, 70–72
employers
  and ACC coverage gaps, 240
  attitudes of, 123, 134, 169–171, 173, 175, 177, 179, 181–184, 193, 227
  behaviour norms, 41
  benefits of legislation for, 48–49, 199
  communication focus of, 175, 177
  direct bargaining by, 91
  domination by, 13, 33–35, 38, 55–56, 205–206
  and employee participation, 169–171, 173, 175, 177, 179, 181–184
  groups, 29, 34, 36, 39, 48, 54, 195, 198–199, 215, 222–223
  health and safety role, 142–144, 148, 182–183
  liability of, 208
  multi-employer collective agreements (MECAs), 99–100, 102, 108, 117–121, 124–125, 206, 208
  need for redefinition of, 208
  objectives, 25, 62
  and personal grievance claims, 211, 215–217, 227
  rights and duties, 121
  risk management, 15, 60–61, 67–69, 136, 141, 209
  surveillance by, 70, 73
  understanding of dispute resolution practices, 223–224
  union collaborations, 169, 178–180, 217–218
Employers' Federation, 29, 93, 200

Index

Employment Contracts (EC) Act 1991
  bargaining coverage, 109–112, 114–116
  bargaining structure, 118–119, 121
  consultation in drafting, 200
  drivers of change, 201–203
  employee participation, 174, 184
  as 'employer revenge,' 103, 105
  Employment Institutions Project database, 107
  health and safety, 135
  human resource management, 62–63
  impacts of, 13, 16, 38–41, 45–46, 124, 198
  judicial views of, 34–35
  labour income share, 82–84, 99
  neoliberalism, 18, 32–36, 53–55
  personal grievance claims, 69, 210, 213–216, 225, 227–228
  women's equity, 156–158
Employment Court, *see also* Arbitration Court; also Labour Court, 34, 38, 54, 198–199, 213, 215–216, 221, 226–228
employment disputes, *see* dispute resolution provisions and processes
Employment Equity Act 1990, 155–157, 162
Employment Equity Commission, 155
employment growth, 112, 114
Employment Institutions (IE) Project database, 107
employment law, *see individual Acts*
employment lawyers, 34, 38, 54, 198–199, 202, 210, 215–223, 228, 239–240
employment modes, newly emerging, 209
Employment Relations Amendment (ER Am) Act 2004, 36, 38–39, 100, 102, 105, 203, 220
Employment Relations Amendment (ER Am) Act 2010, 39, 105
Employment Relations Amendment (ER Am) Act 2014, 117, 162
Employment Relations Authority (ERA), 38, 124–125, 166–167, 216, 226–228
Employment Relations (ER) Act 2000
  bargaining coverage, 107, 111–112, 114–117, 119, 124
  bargaining structure, 121
  collectivism, 175, 180
  dispute resolution, 38–39, 228
  employee participation, 177–178, 182
  future reforms to, 206–209
  'good faith' ideology, 35–36, 69
  health and safety, 137, 145
  labour income share, 82, 100, 105
  labour market reforms, 203–206

non-employee relationships, 208
  personal grievance claims, 27, 216, 219–220, 225
  political ideologies, 46, 55–58
  women's equity, 158, 163
Employment Relations (Flexible Working Arrangements) Amendment Act 2007, 57, 159–160
employment relations, industrial relations becomes, 13, 60, 62–63
Employment Relations (Rest Breaks, Infant Feeding and Other Matters) Amendment Act 2008, 57, 159
Employment Relations Service, 223
employment rights, 41, 68
employment security, 20, 57, 68, 73, 122, 209, 227
employment standards, minimum code of, 57–58, 125, 206–208
Employment Tribunal, 34, 38, 54, 213–216, 218–221, 225–228
Engineers Union, 51–52
English, Simon William (Bill) (Prime Minister), 102
English class-based system, 191–193
enterprise bargaining, 16, 32–33, 51, 53, 108, 118, 124, 184, 198, 202–203
Equal Employment Opportunities Commissioner, 57, 161
Equal Employment Opportunities (EEO) plans and practices, 155, 161, 164–165, 167–168
equal pay, *see* pay equity
Equal Pay Act 1972, 14, 92, 94, 123–124, 151–152, 155, 163
equality, vision of, 191–193, 206–207
ethnic makeup (New Zealand), 14
European Commission, 103
European Economic Community (EEC), 24, 49
European Union (EU), 249
exploitive behaviour, 34
exports, agricultural, 24

facilitation, lawyer opposition to, 220
factor prices, 85
Factories Amendment Act 1972, 151
'factors of production,' *see* labour income share, capital income share
Factory and Commercial Premises Act 1981, 133
Fair Pay Agreements, 125

Farmer, James, 45
farming, *see* agriculture sector
farming lobby, 195
Federation of Labour, 28–29, 50, 93, 199
female-dominated occupations, 152, 162, 167, 237, 242–243, 245
film production industry, removal of worker entitlements, 41
final offer arbitration provision, 52
financial markets, 30, 80
financialisation, increase in, 80
Finland, 182
First World War, 191, 194
fishing sector, 98
fixed capital consumption, 95
flexibility
   bargaining, 53, 59
   functional, 69–70
   labour market, 19, 53, 63, 66–70, 72, 210, 213, 227–228
   temporal and geographic, 70, 159–160, 162, 165, 247
   workplace, 17, 32, 40, 51, 53–54, 57, 62–63, 122, 243
food retail industry, 116
France, 122, 182
free labour, 193
future industrial relations, 247–249
Future of Work Forum, 40

GDP Deflator, 84, 94, 96
gender equity, 17, 149–150, 155, 159, 164–165
gender pay gap, *see also* pay equity, 14, 17–18, 40, 86, 92, 94, 149–152, 157, 163–165, 168
general wage adjustments, 95
general wage orders (GWOs), 27–28, 49, 81, 86, 89–91, 93, 95–97
Germany, 122, 153
gig economy, 14, 243, 249
global changes, 23–24
Global Financial Crisis, 102, 113–115, 181
globalisation, 15, 23–24, 46, 59, 80, 105, 118, 196
'good faith' behaviour, 35–36, 55–56, 69, 100, 124–125, 163, 177–178, 197, 203–208
government, role of, 15, 17–18, 25, 27, 29, 31, 40–42, 44–48, 51, 53–54, 57–58, 248
government administration and security services sector, 16, 116
Government Policy Statement on Labour Relations, 51

Government Service Equal Pay Act 1960, 14, 92, 151
government spending, 80
Great Britain, *see* United Kingdom (UK)
Great Depression, 99
Green Paper (1985), 51
grievance procedure, *see* personal grievance provisions and processes
Gross Domestic Income (GDI), 85, 103, *104*
Gross Domestic Product (GDP), 85–86, *88*, 91–92, 96, 99, *101*

Hardie Boys, Justice, 33
hazard-control procedures, 135
Health & Safety in Employment Act, 57
health and safety, 129–148
   and ACC scheme, 19, 139, 239–241, 245–246
   Act components, 136
   Amendment components, 137
   committees, 18, 145–148, 170–172, 175, 182–183, 206
   development of, 133–134
   duties, 143–144, 146–148, 182–183
   employee participation systems, 181–184
   employee role, 132, 135–137, 142, 144–148
   employer role, 142–144
   failings, 17, 39–40, 70, 129–131, 133, 167, 182, 229
   'high risk list,' 183
   inspectors, 139–142
   joint participation in, 17–18, 130–132, 135–138, 181–184
   and PCBUs, 143–144, 146–148
   penalties, 137, 140
   principle objectives, 131
   reforms, 17, 71, 129–148
   regulatory frameworks, 129–148
   reports and inquiries, 17, 40, 57, 71, 129–134, 138, 181, 240–241
   representatives, 145–148, 172–173, 182–183
   research needs, 183–184
   self-regulation in, 132, 134–135, 142
   and small businesses, 147–148
   state role, 139–142
   statistics, 40, 130, 240–241
   tools, 139–140
   tripartism in, 133–135
   violations, 20
   work-related deaths, 130
Health and Safety at Work Bill, 206
Health and Safety at Work (HSW) Act

Index

2015, 17, 129, 138, 140–144, 146–148, 173, 182–183, 208
Health and Safety Commission (proposed), 134
Health and Safety in Employment Amendment Act 2002, 136–138, 140, 142, 144–145, 170, 173, 182–183
Health and Safety in Employment (HSE) Act 1992, 129–130, 134–137, 139–140, 142–145, 147, 182
health and social services sector, 16, 116, 119, 121
Healthy Work: A Strategic Plan for Work-Related Health 2016–2026, 241
Holidays Act, 57–58
Holland, Eric, 172
Holland, Sir Sidney George (Prime Minister), 90
Holmes, Sir Frank, 44–45
Holyoake, Sir Keith Jacka (Prime Minister), 91
home ownership, imputed rents of, 83, 96
housing construction boom, 96
Human Resource Institute of New Zealand (HRINZ), 64
human resource management, 60–74
　changing scope of, 60–61, 66–69
　courses in, 64
　'crisis of trust in,' 68
　culture change and organisation development role, 66–69
　devolution of functional activities in, 67
　diffusion of practices, 65–66
　employee advocacy by, 73
　employee engagement, 66, 68, 73
　external HR service providers, 65
　and functional flexibility, 69
　future role, 72–74
　grievance processes role, 69
　increased use of, 34, 38, 56–57
　internal credibility of, 65
　international practices, influence of, 16, 61, 63–64, 66, 74
　and marketing, 70–71
　metrics and monitoring, 68–70
　neo-pluralist approach, 73
　nomenclature changes, 68, 72
　number of practitioners, 64–65
　performance management, 67, 70
　policy and compliance role, 66–67
　priorities, 61–63
　professionalisation and feminisation of, 15–16, 60, 64–66
　in public sector, 67
　recruitment and selection practices, 70–71
　risk management by, 67–69
　role of legislation, 60
　and social media, 70–71
　staff education levels in, 64
　strategic role, 63, 66–68
　surveys of HRM practice, 66–67
　transformation of personnel management to, 15, 61–63
　unitarist behaviour by, 70–73
　Workplace Relations Advisor role, 64
Human Rights Amendment Act 2001, 57, 161
Human Rights Commission, 162, 166–167
Human Rights Commission Act 1977, 14, 124, 151, 156–157
Human Rights Review Tribunal, 166–167

ideologies, *see also* pluralism; *also* unitary model, 15, 41, 44–47, 50, 52–53, 60, 62, 124, 156, 158, 182, 191–193, 203, 213
image, organisational, 15
IMB 'Best places to work' in New Zealand, 70
immigration (1870s), 194
import controls, 97
Income Distribution in New Zealand, 83
income inequality, measure of, 79, 100
Income Tax Act 1976, 172
independent contractors, 57, 59
Independent Taskforce on Workplace Health and Safety (2013), 129–130, 182, 183
individual employment contracts and agreements, 53, 61–62, 69, 72, 99, 108, 111, 113, 117, 124, 184, 201–202
individual representative culture, 216–219
individual rights, 49, 53, 57, 59, 68, 206
individualist advocacy culture, 18–19, 108
industrial action, *see* industrial conflict
Industrial Conciliation and Arbitration Act 1894, 18, 26, 49, 109, 194, 199
Industrial Conciliation and Arbitration Act 1954, 94, 121
industrial conciliation and arbitration system (IC&A)
　bargaining structure, 117, 204
　and employee participation, 174
　end of, 94, 109, 124, 156–157
　and first Labour Government, 86
　historical significance of, 47–49, 194–196, 207
　and ideology, 18, 44–45, 52–54
　and labour income share, 81, 91, 94, 103

Industrial Conciliation Service, 31
industrial conflict, 13, 28–29, 31, 45, 50, 57, 81–82, 86, 89–91, 89, 93–96, 98, 119, 124–125, 174, 179, 194–199, 202, 206
Industrial Court, 211
industrial democracy, *see also* Committee of Enquiry into Industrial Democracy, 169, 172
Industrial Mediation Service, 27, 31
industrial relations
    becomes employment relations, 15–16, 60, 62–63
    definition and objectives of, 25
    Dunlop's model of, 14–15, 25
Industrial Relations Act 1973
    bargaining structure, 26, 49–50, 107, 109, 117–118, 123
    and collective bargaining, 109
    and labour income share, 96
    and personal grievance claims, 20, 210–211
    and political ideologies, 46
    terms and conditions of, 121–122, 197, 200
Industrial Relations Amendment Act 1984, 30
Industrial Relations Centre, *see* Centre for Labour Employment and Work (CLEW)
Industrial Relations Council, 172
industrial welfare tradition, lack of, 71
industry agreements, 51
industry segments, union density figures for (2013), 38
industry standard agreements, need for, 208
Industry Training Act 1992, 135
industry training system, 105
inequality, 14, 73, 79–80, 125, 192, 249
inflation, 28, 30, 84, 90–91, 93, 95–97, 174
Injury Prevention, Rehabilitation and Compensation Act 2001, 137
in-plant agreements, 122
Inquiry into Hazardous Substances in the Workplace, 57
Institute of Personnel Management (IPMNZ), 64
International Labour Organisation (ILO), 55–56, 80, 107, 138, 157
International Labour Organisation (ILO) Convention on Equal Remuneration, 154
international terrorism concerns, 23
internet, 23–24
Iran, revolution in, 97
Ireland, 73–74

Japan, 109, 122, 178–179
job descriptions, 69
job growth, *see* employment growth
job losses, in SOEs, 62–63
job security, *see* employment security
job segregation, 152
joint participation programmes, 175
Joint Working Group on Pay Equity, 125, 163, 167

Key, Sir John Phillip (Prime Minister), 102, 162, 166
Kirk, Norman Eric (Prime Minister), 94, 105
Kondratieff long cycles, 248
Korean War, 81, 90, 92

Labour Court, *see also* Arbitration Court; also Employment Court, 31, 34, 198, 212, 215
Labour Department survey (on collective agreements), 56
Labour Disputes Investigation Act 1913, 48
labour force
    growth in, 38, 111–112
    survey results, 161
Labour Government
    first (1935–1949), 49, 86
    second (1957–1960), 91–92
    third (1972–1975), 94–97, 105, 172
    fourth (1984–1990), 24, 30–31, 51, 53, 97, 99, 105, 118, 134, 154–155, 168, 172, 196, 198–199, 201
    fifth (1999–2008), 35–36, 41, 46–47, 55, 100, 136–137, 158, 161, 173, 180, 182, 203, 210, 228, 232
labour income share, 79–105, *82, 87*
    adjusted, 83–86, 90, 98, 102, *104*
    after-tax level of, 84
    and employment law, 80, 82–84
    and external events, 80, 102
    gap, 83
    and government, 80
    and imputed rents, 83, 96
    and income inequality, 20, 79, 100
    and industrial disputes, 80
    and labour market, 79
    manufacturing sector, 99
    methodology, 85–86, 96
    OECD decrease in, 79–80, *104*
    and private market sector, 100, *101*
    and productivity, 79–84, 86, 91, 94
    'profit squeeze' claims, 83

Index   259

and publicly owned market sector, 84, 100, *101*
and rural Māori, 89, 92
Second World War, 86, 89–90
and self-employed, 82–83, 85–86, *87*, 90–92, 93, 94–98, 102
summary of changes, 16
and technology, 79–80
labour market
    and collective bargaining, 15, 108
    competition in, 79
    complexity, 143
    flexibility, 19, 53, 63, 66–70, 72, 210, 213, 227–228
    functioning of, 159
    gender segregation in, 242
    manufacturing sector share, 115
    reforms, 59, 84, 109, 118, 123, 203, 227–228
    shortages, 91
Labour Opposition, 35
Labour Party, 31, 39–41, 46, 51, 55, 125, 178, 199, 207, 231–232, 248–249
labour productivity, *see* productivity
"Labour Relations - A Takeover by the State?," 45
Labour Relations (LR) Act 1987
    bargaining structure, 31–32, 109, 118, 121
    personal grievance provisions and processes, 211–212
    political ideologies, 46, 51–53, 198
    sexual harassment provisions, 155
    union impacts, 98
labour relations procedures, 52
'*Laissez-faire* Era,' 31, 33–35, 38
Lange, David Russell (Prime Minister), 31, 97
Law Commission Report (on ACC), 232
Law Foundation, 239
Law Society, 221
legislation, *see individual Acts*
liability, need for, 208
Liberal-Labour Government, 194–195
lockouts, *see* industrial conflict
long-service leave, 123

MacFarlane v Accident Compensation Corporation, 238
management influences, 16, 74
Management of Health and Safety in Employment, 134
managerial model, private sector, 52
manufacturing sector, 92, 99, 115, 179

Māori, rural, 89, 92
Māori and Pasifika women in workforce, 153, 161–162, 165
Maritime Strike (1890), 26, 195
marketing, overlap with HRM, 70–71
Master and Servant Act 1823 (UK), 193
Master and Servant Bill (NZ), 193–194
master and servant values, 18, 191–193, 199–200, 206
maternity leave, *see* parental leave
Maternity Leave and Employment Protection Act 1981, 153
meat exports, 24, 94–95, 97
Meat Workers Union, 31
media coverage, 40, 42, 69, 228
Mediation Service, *see also* Resolution Services, 38, 211, 213, 216, 218–220, 224, 226–227
mediators, role of, 27, 38, 56, 210–211, 219–220
mental health, 237, 239–243
Meredith Report (Canada), 234
migrant labour, 14
minimum employment standards statutory code, 57–58, 206–207
minimum wage, 54, 57, 80, 86, 91, 94, 98, 100, 102, 159
Minimum Wage Act 1982, 154
mining industry, 121
Ministerial Inquiry into Tranz Rail Occupational Safety & Health 2000, 57
Ministry of Business, Innovation and Employment, *see also* Department of Labour, 38–39, 140
Ministry of Women's Affairs, 154
MMP electoral system, 55, 203
mobilisation, effects of, 89–90
Muldoon, Sir Robert David (Prime Minister), 93, 96
Muldoon administration, *see* also National Government, third (1975–1984), 50, 154, 196–197
multi-employer collective agreements (MECAs), 99–100, 102, 108, 117–121, 124–125, 206, 208
181–184, 208

Nash, Sir Walter (Prime Minister), 91
National Accounts, 85–86
national award system, *see* awards
National Business Review, 33

National Domestic Income, 92, 94–96
National Government
　first (1949–1957), 90
　second (1960–1972), 91, 105
　third (1975–1984), 50, 96–97, 105, 151–154, 172, 196–197
　fourth (1990–1999), 33, 46–47, 52, 97, 99, 105, 134, 156–157, 182, 210, 213, 228, 232
　fifth (2008–Present), 39, 57, 102, 116, 162, 164, 168, 173, 203, 232
national income, history of, 16
National Party, 33, 39, 41, 46, 50
'national security tax,' 89
National Working Party on Equity in Employment, 156
neoclassical economics, 79
neoliberal agenda, 60, 62, 249
neoliberalism, 15, 18, 19–20, 46–47, 50–59, 82, 84, 97–102, 196, 198–201, 203, 249
neo-pluralist approach, 73
Net Domestic Income (NDI), 85–86, 87
'New Labour' (UK), 36
New Public Management, 180
'New Right,' 32–33, 35
New Zealand Business Roundtable (NZBR), 32–33, 198–200, 215, 228
New Zealand Educational Institute (NZEI), 29
New Zealand Employers Federation (NZEF), 32–33, 35
New Zealand Journal of Employment Relations (NZJER), 14–15, 17–18, 20, 150, 162, 166–167, 184
New Zealand Journal of Industrial Relations (NZJIR), 13–15, 17–18, 20, 35, 44, 123, 150, 162, 169, 178, 184, 249
New Zealand Manufacturers Association, 35
New Zealand Official Yearbooks, 91
New Zealand Productivity Commission, 83–84
Nil Order (1968), 28, 49, 93–94, 105, 123, 196
'Nissan Way,' 179
non-employee work relationships, 208
non-standard contracts, 14, 40, 63, 69–70, 122, 229
non-union sector dominance, 19, 228–229
Norway, 182
NOSHAC technical reports, 236, 243
NZ Institute of Management, 64
NZI Sustainable Business Network awards, 70

occupational health and safety, *see* health and safety
Occupational Safety and Health Bill 1990, 134–135, 182
Occupational Safety and Health Reform, 133–134
Occupational Safety and Health Service (OSH), 136, 139, 141–142
OECD, *see* Organisation for Economic Co-operation and Development (OECD)
Officials Committee Report (on ACC), 232
Ohinemuri Mines and Batteries Employees' IUW v Registrar of Industiral Unions (1917), 28
oil shocks, 23, 94–95, 97, 103, 105
operating surplus, 85, 96
Organisation for Economic Co-operation and Development (OECD), 79, 100, 103, *104*, 122, 130, 149–150, 169–170, 178, 181–183
organisational goals, 62, 66–67, 72
organisational image, 15, 60, 68, 70–72
Organization of the Petroleum Exporting Countries (OPEC), 94
output per capita, 98
overtime, 28, 69, 86, 90, 122–123, 151, 201

Paid Parental Leave and Employment Act 2004, 57
Palmer, Sir Geoffrey Winston Russell, 133, 235, 238
parental leave, 14, 41, 123, 153–155, 158–159, 162, 165
Parental Leave and Employment Act 1987, 154–155, 158
Parental Leave and Employment Protection Amendments Act 2002, 158
Partnership for Quality arrangements, 57
Partnership Resource Centre, 173, 180
Pasifika and Māori women in workforce, 153, 161–162, 165
Pay and Employment Equity Plan of Action, 161–162
Pay and Employment Equity Unit, 161–162
pay equity, *see also* gender pay gap, 17, 40, 57, 73, 125, 155, 161–163, 167
pay security, 122
penalties (for public servants), 29–30
Penn World Tables, 85
People working in HR related occupations, 65
person conducting a business or undertaking (PCBU), 143–144, 146–148, 208

Index

personal grievance provisions and processes, 210–229
  90-day trial introduction, 41, 57
  1973-1990 period, 27, 197, 210–212
  1991-2008 period, 34, 214–228
  and ACC coverage gaps, 239–240
  adjudicated outcomes analysis, 222
  administrative efficiency issues, 225
  assessment of prospects, 218
  choice of representation, 222–224
  and collective interests, 211–212
  collective representative culture, 216–219
  control issues, 220
  costs and compensation awards, 221–222
  costs of, 217, 225–227
  delays in, 215–216, 225
  determinations, 221
  duration of, 217
  Employment Contracts (EC) Act 1991, 54, 213–216
  Employment Relations (ER) Act 2000, 214, 216, 219–220
  evaluative model in, 220
  and flexible working relationships, 160
  individual representative culture, 216–220, 224–225, 228
  institutional dispute resolution, 217–220
  and legal process, 212, 215–220, 228
  modes of resolution, 218–221
  policy, 213–214
  promotion of mediation before adjudication, 225
  in public sector, 52
  remedies and outcomes, 227–228
  resistence to informality in, 220–221, 228
  risk management, 69, 222, 225
  summary of changes, 18–20
  timing influences, 217–218, 225
  Tribunal adjudicative function, 220–221
  Tribunal investigative function, 221
  types of advocacy, 215–217
  types of outcomes pursued, 216–217
  white-collar grievant class, 215
  and worker voice, 207, 209
  workplace awareness of, 223–224
  workplace resolution, 217–218
personnel management, *see* also human resource management, 15, 61–63, 66, 71
personnel procedures, removal of constraints to, 52
Pike River Coal Mine disaster, *see* also Royal Commission on the Pike River Coal Mine Tragedy (2012), 141–142, 167, 182
Piketty, Thomas, 79–80
Plan of Action on Pay and Employment Equity, 161
pluralism, *see* also ideologies; also unitary model, 18–19, 46–47, 52–53, 60, 62, 72–74, 196, 200, 202, 207, 209, 228
population demographics (New Zealand), 24
population increases, 23–24
post-war economic prosperity, 169
power distribution
  employer dominance, 13, 33–36, 38, 205–207
  and labour income share, 102, 105
  and labour market flexibility, 213, 227–229
  redressing imbalance, 55–56, 73, 194, 209, 248–249
  State role, 25, 48–49
  and women workers, 157
precarious work, *see* also security of employment, 19–20, 159, 161, 168, 201, 243
price controls, 84, 89–90, 96–97
price index, *see* consumer price index (CPI)
principles and values, 15, 18, 47, 59, 80
Private Members Bill 1974, regarding worker participation, 18, 169, 172
private sector system
  bargaining coverage, 63, 109–116, *110*, *112*, *114*
  bargaining structure, 25–29, 32, 52, 58, 119, 121
  employee representation in, 113, *113*
  Equal Employment Opportunities (EEO) plans and practices, 156, 164
  leave entitlements, 123
privatisation, 30, 33, 62, 80, 97–100
productivity, 16, 63, 79–84, *81*, *82*, 86, 91, 94, 103, 105, 165
'profit squeeze,' 83
property sector, 121
Public Advisory Group on Restructuring and Redundancy 2007, 57
public interest approach, 59
public sector system
  bargaining coverage, 16, 58, 108–116, 110, 112, 114
  bargaining structure, 25, 29–30, 52, 119, 121
  commercialisation and privatisation of, 97–100, 105
  employee representation in, 113, 113
  Equal Employment Opportunities (EEO)

plans and practices, 155, 161, 164, 168
leave entitlements, 123
human resource management in, 62–63
women's employment in, 92, 151
worker voice, 20, 29–30
Public Service Association (PSA), 29, 175, 180
Public Service Commission, 151
Public Service Regulations 1964, 151
public services, 24, 30

Race Relations Act 1971, 14
racial discrimination, 14
Reagan, Ronald, 169
real consumption wage, 84, 86, *88*, 89–91, 94–99, 102
real product wage, 81–84, *81*, 86, *88*, 89–91, 94–99, 102–103
recessions, 90–91, 93–96, 98, 102, 114–115
recruitment and selection practices, 70–71
redundancies, 19, 24, 31–32, 53, 84, 122–123, 202–203, 205, 229
reforms, *see also* Employment Contracts Act (1991); also Industrial Relations Act 1973; also Labour Relations (LR) Act 1987
    (1984–1987), 51–53, 198–199, 201
    (1991), 18–20, 199–201, 203
    19th century, 194–195
    fifth Labour Government, 203–205
    fifth National Government, 203, 206
    needed in future, 206–209
    state sector, 51–53, 60, 62–63, 97–100, 180
    workplace, 173–175, 178–180
regulatory frameworks, 15, 44–59
Remuneration Commission, 226
rent controls, 96–97
Report of the Independent Taskforce on Workplace Health and Safety (2013), 17, 71–72, 240
Report of the Royal Commission of Inquiry in to Compensation for Personal Injury in New Zealand (Woodhouse Report) 1967, 231–232, 234–235, 241, 244–246
Report of the United Kingdom Committee on Safety and Health at Work (Robens' Report), *see also* Robens' model, 131–133, 144, 147–148, 181–182
Resolution Services, *see* also Mediation Service, 38–39
resolution system, *see* dispute resolution provisions and processes
rest breaks, 41, 57, 201
retail sector, 16

Ricardian hypothesis, 102–103
Ricardo, David, 79
rights, collective and individual, 49, 53, 55–56, 59
risk management, 15, 60–61, 67–69, 141, 209
Robens, Lord, 131, 181
Robens' model, *see* also *Report of the United Kingdom Committee on Safety and Health at Work* (Robens' Report), 130–134, 138–139, 144, 147–148
Robertson, Grant (MP), 40
Rodger, Stanley Joseph (Stan) (Minister of Labour), 30, 51
'Rogernomics,' 154, 199
Royal Commission on the Pike River Coal Mine Tragedy (2012), 17, 71, 129, 131, 138, 182, 240
ruling rate agreements, 49, 59

science and technology sector, 121
Screpanti, Ernesto, 248
Second World War, 81, 86, 89–90, 102
sector interest approach, 59
security of employment, 20, 57, 68, 73, 122, 209, 227
self-employment, 82–83, 85–86, 87, 90–92, 93, 94–98, 102
services, employment in, 92
settlement procedures, *see* bargaining structures
settlement ranges, influences on, 27
settler society, 18, 191
sexual harassment, 14, 155, 166–167, 211, 213, 242–243
share market crash
1987, 32, 174
1997, 98
shift leave, 123
single employer collective agreements (SECAs), 118–121
skill margins, 92
skilled occupations, union effectiveness of, 38
Skinner, Sir Thomas 'Tom' Edward (FOL President), 93
small and medium-sized enterprises (SMEs), 67, 72, 147–148, 181
social contract, 16, 68, 73–74, 223
social insurance, 232–234, 244–246
social justice, 80, 193, 195, 206–207
social legitimacy, 61, 70
social media, 70–71
'social question,' 233

Index

social values, 191–193
social welfare benefits, 24, 99, 105
social well-being, 72
societal change, 14–15, 23–25, 30, 33, 49, 62, 80, 191–193, 209, 243–244, 247
solo parents, 161
Soviet Union, 23
Spain, 182
Stabilisation of Remuneration Act 1971, 50, 94
staff numbers, statistics for, 67
staff surveys, 70
state ownership, 24
State role of, *see* government, role of
State Sector Act 1988, 31, 32, 52, 62, 155, 198
state sector system, *see* public sector system
State Services Commission, 40
State Services Conditions of Employment (SSCE) Act 1977, 29–30
State Services (SS) Act 1962, 29–30
State-Owned Enterprises Act 1986, 52
state-owned enterprises (SOEs), 62–63
Statistics New Zealand
   Household Labour Force Survey (2011), 98
   National Census (2006), 65
   National Census (2013), 64–65, 65, 67
   Serious Injury Outcome Indicators, 130
statutory employment rights, 41
statutory frameworks, *see* regulatory frameworks
statutory protections, 122, 135
stock market crash, *see* share market crash
strategic enterprises, 24
stress, workplace, 237, 241–243
strikes, *see* industrial conflict
subsidies, removal of, 97
'subsistence wage rate,' 103
suffrage, universal, 192
supermarkets, collective employment agreements in, 116
superpowers, 23
Sutton, Roger, 166
Sweating Commission (1890), 144, 195
Sweden, 182

tariffs, 30, 97, 99
taxation, 24
taxes, indirect, 85
technologies
   challenges of, 52–53, 59
   and employee surveillance, 70, 73
   information and communication, 15, 23–24, 60–61, 66, 69–71
   and labour income share, 79–80
   new, 14, 15, 70–71
terms of trade, 86, 88, 91, 93–95, 97–98, 102
TerraNova Homes and Care Ltd v Service and Food Workers Union Nga Ringa Tota Inc (2014), 40, 163, 167
Thatcher, Margaret, 169
Timberworkers Union, 51–52
'Towards Employment Equity,' 155
'Toyotaism,' 179
trade barriers, removal of, 118
trade unions, *see* unions
trading partners, 24
training investment, 64, 66–67
treadmill, 192
Treasury, 199–200
tripartism, 46, 48, 133–135, 138, 148, 174, 195–196
Tripartite Pay and Employment Equity Taskforce, 161
Tripartite Steering Group, 161
Trump, Donald, 249

Uber employment mechanisms, 209
'under employment,' 24
Understanding Stress and Bullying in New Zealand Workplaces, 241
unemployment, 24, 31–32, 81, 83, 90–91, 99, 102, 174
unfree labour, 193
unions
   alternative mechanisms to, 207–208
   attitudes of, 18, 45, 50, 169–171, 173–175, 177, 181
   Clerical Workers Union, 201
   compulsory membership of, 28, 31–33, 35, 49, 86, 97–98, 201
   density, 13, 20, 37, 38, 56, 61, 63, 109, 115, 170, 178, 182, 201, 205
   deunionisation, 98, 111, 124, 135
   direct bargaining by, 91
   dissention within, 48
   and employee participation, 169–171, 173–175, 177, 179, 181, 184
   employer collaborations, 169, 178–180, 217–218
   Engineers Union, 51–52, 174
   and enterprise bargaining, 32, 53, 123
   extension of coverage to new employees, 116–117
   future role, 58–59, 207, 248
   health and safety role, 133–135, 137, 145

industrial conflict, 13, 28–29, 31, 45, 50, 57, 81–82, 86, 89–91, *89*, 93–96, 98, 119, 124–125, 174, 179, 194–196, 199, 202, 206
   legislative support for, 28, 31, 33–36, 45–46, 48, 55–56, 86, 98, 115, 194–195
   members not covered by CEA, 117
   membership, 32, *37*, 38, 52–54, 56–58, 86, *89*, 94, 99–100, 111, 113, 116–117, 174–175, *176*, 179, 201–202, 207, 222–223
   opposition to, 31, 38, 50, 64, 123, 199, 206–207
   'paper' unions, 36
   and pay equity, 125
   and personal grievance claims, 210–211, 213, 215–219, 222–224
   political lobbying by, 54, 59
   power of, 29, 33–34, 38–39, 41–42, 45–46, 48–49, 57–59, 63, 69, 80, 92, 109, 124, 195, 201–202, 205–206, 227
   as preferred agent, 119
   private sector, 56, 63, 94, 110–111, 115, 123
   public sector, 29, 52, 56, 61, 63, 98, 110–111, 115
   public view of, 26
   registration of, 26, 31, 98, 113, 116
   single-site, enterprise-based, 116
   state influence on, 48, 97
   strategies of, 58, 116, 174
   success of, 16, 38, 115–116
   Timberworkers Union, 51–52
   waterside workers dispute, 90, 98
   and women workers, 152–154, 163, 168
unitarist approach, 16, 18, 71, 73–74, 177, 184, 199, 199–201, 202–203, 228
unitary model, *see* also ideologies; also pluralism, 18–19, 46–47, 52, 53, 60, 62, 66, 72
United Kingdom (UK)
   comparison with, 48, 71, 108–109, 153, 175
   EEC entry, 49
   employment rights in, 41, 184
   exit from EU, 249
   health and safety model, 129–133, 145, 172, 181–182
   labour concerns, 248
   as trading partner, 24
   worker compensation in, 232, 234
United Nations, 72
United Nations Convention on the Elimination of all Forms of Discrimination against Women (CEDAW 2003), 151, 159

United States (US), 23–24, 62–63, 66, 74, 109, 178, 248–249
universal suffrage, 192
university international (US) accreditation agencies, 64
unpaid work, even distribution of, 17

values and principles, 15, 18, 47, 59, 80
violence, workplace, 242–243
voluntary agreements, 26–27, 117–118, 121
Voluntary Settlement Collective Agreements, 49

Wage Adjustment Regulations 1982, 50
wage fixing systems, 30, 47, 49, 54, 93, 156, 195–196
wage freezes, 28, 81, 84, 97–98
wage policies and controls, 28, 44, 47, 50, 89, 96–97, 196–197
Walker Report (1981), 133
waterside workers' dispute, 90, 98
wealth distribution, 207
welfare state, 24, 192
well-being at work, 72–73
Whitlam Government (Australia), 234
Wilson, Margaret, 145, 156, 203–204
wine exports, 24
WINZ benefits, socio-economic comparisons with ACC, 240
women, participation in workforce, 149–168
   bargaining position, 157
   child care, access to, 14, 17, 160–161, 165, 167
   employment rate, 149–150
   employment restrictions, 151
   Equal Employment Opportunities (EEO) plans and practices, 155–156
   equality in workplace, 17, 149–151
   female-dominated occupations, 152, 162, 167
   gender pay gap, 14, 17–18, 40, 86, 92, 94, 149–152, 157, 164, 168
   job segregation, 152
   labour market statistics, 150–152
   legislative support, 151, 153–158
   Māori and Pasifika women, 153, 161–162, 165
   parental leave provisions, 153–155, 158–159, 162, 165
   pay equity, 155, 161, 163, 167
   second world war employment, 89
   in senior positions, 17, 150, 162, 164–165, 167
   sexual harassment, 155, 166–167
   and unions, 152–154
   women as dependents, 151

Index

work-family balance mechanisms, 153, 158–161, 165–167
Woodhouse, Michael (Minister of Workplace Relations and Safety), 40
Woodhouse, Sir Arthur Owen (Justice), 19, 231–234, 245–246
Woodhouse Report, *see Report of the Royal Commission of Inquiry in to Compensation for Personal Injury in New Zealand* (Woodhouse Report) 1967
Woods, Noel (Secretary of Labour), 48
wool exports, 24, 81, 90–91, 93–95, 97
work stoppages, *see* industrial conflict
worker, new definition of, 208
worker participation, *see* employee participation
workers, *see* employees
Workers' Compensation Act 1956, 235–236
workers' compensation schemes, 232–233, 235–238
'workers' diseases,' 233
work-family balance mechanisms, *see also* work-life balance, 17, 153, 158–161, 165–167
workforce participation, ethnic differences in, 153
Working for Families scheme, 161
working hours, 17, 122, 153, 192, 201, 223
Working Safer national targets, 240
work-life balance, *see also* work-family balance mechanisms, 17, 41, 57, 70, 122, 158, 165, 209
workloads, 122
workplace climate surveys, 177
workplace democracy, 206–207
workplace employee participation system, 182
workplace flexibility, 17, 32, 40, 51, 53–54, 57, 62–63, 66–70, 122, 243, 247
workplace partnership, 173–175, 180–181
workplace reform, 173–175, 178–180
Workplace Reform Conference 1992, 173, 179
Workplace Reform New Zealand, 178–180
WorkSafe New Zealand, 17, 19, 40, 71, 129, 140–141, 148, 239–241, 246
world changes, 23–24
work stoppages, *see* industrial action

Yom Kippur War (Middle East), 94

zero-hours contracts, 40, 47, 122
zero-investment threshold rate of return, 103